NEW TOWNS
and the
SUBURBAN DREAM

Kennikat Press
National University Publications
Interdisciplinary Urban Series

General Editor
Raymond A. Mohl
Florida Atlantic University

NEW TOWNS
and the
SUBURBAN DREAM

IDEOLOGY and UTOPIA in PLANNING and DEVELOPMENT

Edited by

IRVING LEWIS ALLEN

National University Publications
KENNIKAT PRESS   //   1977
Port Washington, N. Y.   //   London

Manufactured in the United States of America

Published by
Kennikat Press Corp.
Port Washington, N. Y./London

Library of Congress Cataloging in Publication Data
Main entry under title:

New towns and the suburban dream.

(Kennikat Press national university publications)
Bibliography: p.
Includes index.
1. New towns—United States—Addresses, essays, lectures. 2. Suburbs—United States—Addresses, essays, lectures. 3. Sociology, Urban—Addresses, essays, lectures.
I. Allen, Irving L., 1931-
HT167.N427   301.36'2'0973   76-41728
ISBN 0-8046-9161-4

CONTENTS

ACKNOWLEDGEMENTS

I wish to thank the authors who gave their generous permission to reprint their work and who therefore made this anthology possible.

My study of the sociology of new towns that gave rise to the idea for this anthology was greatly assisted by the University of Connecticut's support of my sabbatic leave in 1969-70 and by a grant in 1970-72 from the University of Connecticut Research Foundation. The Research Foundation, in addition, has more recently supported the project to facilitate publication of this volume.

The Editor

NEW TOWNS
and the
SUBURBAN DREAM

PART ONE
INTRODUCTION

IRVING LEWIS ALLEN

NEW TOWNS AND THE SUBURBAN DREAM

It is now the wisdom among most planners and urbanists in applied practice and in academia, and I believe also, that "new towns," smaller "new communities," or even smaller "cluster developments" are the preferable ways to guide further suburban growth in America. These plans efficiently use space within residential communities, provide essential facilities, and conceivably can conserve open space in metropolitan areas. New towns could, therefore, offer an alternative to some of the problems resulting from low-grade, low-density sprawl that has characterized so much suburban growth in the past three decades. Few observers, however, believe that enough new towns will be built to contain a significant amount of future suburban growth, short of truly massive and currently unlikely federal support. But new towns could offer a feasible alternative for some of the 100 millions who will be living in suburbs and beyond in the outer suburban fringes in a decade or two.

The new town idea has been around for three quarters of a century and has long been embraced by every developed region in Europe. But it is only within the last decade that the idea has found acceptance in this country in nearly every quarter, from visionary to pragmatist, though there have been earnest planner-advocates for half a century. Politicians from the local to the federal level have applauded new town proposals. The 1968 and 1970 Federal Housing Acts, through the Department of Housing and Urban Development, extended financial backing though much of this support was withdrawn in 1975.* The mass media report a high level of public interest in new town proposals. But the fanfare that surrounded the introduction of the idea to the mass of Americans in the 1960s has now quieted to the proselytizing by commercial developers of an ever-widening public. The public is now familiar with several completed new towns such as Columbia and Reston, and it knows of others being built or on the drawing boards. Assuming that the many economic problems, which generally came to trouble the housing

*In late 1976, most of the thirteen HUD-backed, privately developed new towns were in severe financial difficulty and several were imminently to be taken over by HUD.

industry in the mid-1970s, pass in time, it is likely that the national interest in new towns will remain great.

The impetus of federal loan guarantees attracted some developers in the early 1970s, but many other developers went it alone. New towns are, for the most part, large-scale plans by private enterprise. Increasingly these are corporations with large investment capital and some with interests in the construction industries. Many suburban development schemes that would have been large tract developments in the 1950s—Levittowns at best—have been improved by a different land-use plan, the promise of varied facilities, and are equipped with an ideologically-inspired sales appeal. The commercial developers, while reflecting immediate wants and needs of the marketplace, have also selectively borrowed ideas from the visionary planners of new towns. They have not only planned land use and services, but have gone on, as visionaries are wont to do, to suggest that the physical plans will somehow foster a new form of community, a new way of life for residents of such new towns, offering an alternative to the social and moral ills of the metropolitan community. Haar (1970:3) quips that

the ballyhoo surrounding "New Communities" . . . implies that American technology has accomplished the unprecedented feat of locating the Garden of Eden within one-hour commuting time of Sodom and Gomorrah.

It is pertinent to ask why some advocates and developers have chosen to promote *new towns* as a *new way of life* and why the concept has so fired the imagination of intellectuals and the public. The new town concept, it is evident, has touched some responsive chord in the American mind and appeals to what Americans have always sought in their cities and suburbs but have never found—or have lost—or believe they have lost.

The new town idea has won wide acceptance at a time of confluence of several trends, events, and national moods. The idea rose to national prominence in the 1960s on the eve of the suburban population in the early 1970s becoming numerically dominant over central cities, which made even firmer the long standing suburban power dominance. Urban Renewal and the War on Poverty had failed. Racial troubles in the cities quickened the white out-migration, and middle-class America is now irreversibly committed to the suburbs. But the suburbs have not proved to be the escape that many believed. Indeed, suburbanites are increasingly faced with the whole array of urban social problems that were supposedly left behind and, in addition, a variety of new ones that hinge on the problems of low density, dependence on the automobile, and a lack of certain facilities (Sobin, 1971:79-92). It is not surprising that suburbanites are interested in solutions, and the new town planners and developers are providing ready-made ones.

The community planning profession, particularly the architectural wing, was criticized in the 1960s for an underlying anti-urbanism in its redevelopment of the central cities in the 1950s, and new town advocates, such as Lewis Mumford, were accused of wanting to solve the problems of cities by disbanding them into rural new towns (Glazer, 1958; Jacobs, 1961:17–25; Whyte, 1963 and others). This criticism was variously countered as a romantic ideology favoring an anachronism of the close, dense life of working class "urban villages" or life in the classical European city as the ideal models of contemporary American urban life (Greer, 1972:265–279; Elazar, 1966). There was merit on both sides of the debate. But what must be recognized now is that the central cities have and will continue to decentralize, and that we must begin to think in terms of finding the good city in a new urban texture of the metropolitan community.

The new towns being built by private enterprise, however, do not often pursue this goal in the planning of suburbs, but in some respects exacerbate the social problems associated with the suburban trend. Now that planners and developers have turned their attention to the suburbs, a more subtle anti-urban ideology is to be found underlying many new town proposals.[1] The visionary planners' image of suburbia and the adaptation of that image by developers can best be elucidated by an examination of modern anti-urban ideology in new town planning theory and in the suburban social movement. Finally, we can see how the two lines of thought merge with the presentation of American new towns as the conventional Suburban Dream.

It is the argument of this essay that the ideological overtones of new town promotional themes have and will find a fertile field in suburban America, for the abandonment of the city in favor of the suburbs has its roots deep in anti-urban sentiments. Most new town developers in this country have compromised the ideals and potentials of real "Garden Cities" as places of urbanity and pluralism. The naïve sociological content of contemporary new town advocacy, especially as it has evolved in this country, is in fact suburban ideology—the celebration of middle-class suburban life styles and a reaction to the idea of the city. Simply put, the social planning aspects of many new town proposals are conservative utopian models of suburban communities.[2] Suburbs are small-town surrogates in a nation ambivalently dependent on cities. New towns are the *mise en scène* of a small-town America of a mythical past, and new town proposals echo the disappointments that Americans found in the cities and have now developed in their suburbs.

In all fairness to the exceptional developer who sets out with high, though often too sanguine, communal ideals to build the good suburban community, such as James Rouse did for Columbia, there are heavy pressures from competition and potential buyers that conspire to turn ideal new towns into conventional suburbia. And the early residents themselves, demanding that suburbia, can wrest control from the developer (Brooks, 1971, 1974). Most developers, however, anticipate this, or have no such ambitions, and they offer suburbia from the outset.

Anti-Urbanism and the Early New Town Movement

Anglo-American anti-urban traditions in social thought, their influence on early sociological theory, the influence of both intellectual traditions on new town planning thought, and finally the building of experimental new towns in the 1920s and 1930s in England and America were parallel and related developments. Urban planning ideas are born of a cultural context and their articulation by planners and developers of new towns may be expected to reflect these traditions, as well as the developers' perceptions of public tastes in housing and neighborhood flavor.

Anti-urbanism, as the term will be used here, is a fundamental rejection of the city as an *idea* (Hadden and Barton, 1973). It is related to, but not identical with, the ideology of agrarianism. It is, rather, a singular and negative valuation of the degree of loosened social control, sophistication, cosmopolitanism, and pluralism in city life compared to what is believed to exist in small towns. There is a tendency to react against city life and a preference, realized by many, for a simple, homogeneous, small community, typified by the *ersatz* small towns of suburbia. Anti-urbanism is the expression, often recorded at the ballot box or in an exodus from the cities, of indifference or even fear and hostility toward the city and its people— one important reason the nation appears to have turned its back on the great cities. The anti-urban ideology has its antithesis in the suburban utopia. The pertinence of anti-urbanism for contemporary new town proposals is best understood in terms of what is being *sought* in a social movement, rather than what is being fled. Thus, one can speak of *suburban* ideology as synonymous with *anti-urban* ideology.

The new town movements in England and America were closely related. Indeed, Dyckman (1962) even suggests that the influence of American agrarian ideology on Ebenezer Howard was so great that "Americans, in fact, gave the garden cities back to the English via Howard." Anti-urbanism was deeply imbedded in nineteenth century Anglo-American social thought and a century of writing fulminating against the industrial city and its problems culminated in the acceptance of the social policy expressed in Howard's (1898, 1902) Garden City proposal at the turn of the century (Armytage, 1961:370–440; Glass, 1968; Petersen, 1968). The Garden City movement has been analyzed by Reissman (1964:39–68) as a full-fledged social movement or collective-behavioral phenomenon, which may be said to have been "institutionalized" by Britain's 1946 New Towns Act. Glass (1968) has argued that anti-urbanism still influences British town planning theory and, as well, some British academic sociology. Contemporary British town planning, however, has moved far away from the ideas of Howard and even from many ideas of the 1947 system (e.g., Hall, et al., 1973).

America had a related tradition of nineteenth century anti-urbanism, but its interpretations have varied widely (cf. White and White, 1962; Freidel, 1963; Elazar, 1966, and Glaab and Brown, 1967:53–81). This ideology is related to American romantic agrarianism, but it would be too simplistic to attribute it to that alone. But it is clear, whatever the cause, that Americans have had a love-hate relationship with their cities. White and White (1962) have shown that this relationship, as was the case in Britain, had an influence on urban planning theory and academic sociology, particularly the Chicago school of sociology. A highly rationalized anti-urbanism infused sociological theory by two related routes. A *native* line of influence came from the agrarian orientations and sentiments of certain early sociologists (Mills, 1942). The other line was the classical romantic *European* heritage of Durkheim, Weber, Toennies and Simmel, best displayed in Wirth's (1938) summary essay, "Urbanism as a Way of Life." Classical mass-society theory also had its impact on urban planning theory, including the thought of Lewis Mumford.

It has been endlessly debated whether Howard and his followers, Lewis Mumford in particular, are "anti-urban" or romantic agrarians who include cities in their scheme of things (see Goist, 1969). An elucidating comparison may be made between Mumford and Louis Wirth, who share a similar ambivalence about the social organization of urban-industrial society. But it would be incorrect to say that either dislikes the *idea* of the city or the potentialities of the good city. Dyckman (1962) describes both Mumford and Wirth as urban romantics deeply influenced, on one hand, by American agrarian ideology and, on the other, by classical European sociology.

In the last 35 years sociology has moved to a more qualified view of the mass-society, which is to say of metropolitan society, by a continued "rediscovery of the primary group" in every area of urban and suburban life. Yet a primitive and half-understood mass-society imagery, with an implicit suburban bias and anti-city sentiments, continues to pervade new town advocacy and promotional themes in the 1970s. Planners, such as Sinding (1967), Whyte (1968:224–43) and Alonso (1970), have alluded to the mass-society bias in the developer's proposals, but the implications of, and the motivations for, this bias have never been explored. The emphasis, I believe, is in selling the new town concept for the wrong reasons and thus betraying the realistically attainable ideal of new towns as places of urbanity and pluralism.

Fava (1973) has argued that new towns have succeeded suburbs as the focus of "pop" sociology in the '60s and '70s. She writes that "Suburbs were the focus of community pop sociology in the period of public awareness of metropolitan emergence; New Towns are the expression of community pop sociology in the era of the mature metropolis." New town policy, she observes, addresses the same set of needs as the pop image of suburbia, "the same anti-urbanism, the same fear and distrust of the city, . . . the same concern with diversity, the containment of conflict and the maintenance of outward harmony and equality."

The Suburban Migration and the Developers' New Towns

Reissman (1964:39–68, Wood (1958:3–19, Dobriner (1963:61–80), Elazar (1966), Donaldson (1969:23–44, 78–90) and Hadden and Barton (1973) have variously treated the migration to suburbia in this country as a *social movement* and agrarianism and anti-urbanism as its guiding ideologies. Hadden and Barton (1973) explored the roots of anti-urban ideology and concluded that the middle-class ideals of rural retreat and intense familism were the ideological impetus leading to the abandonment of the American city. The suburbs were the middle ground between the city and country, the best of both worlds. This anti-urban ideology, they argued, encouraged the federal policies in the 1950s and 1960s that led to the extreme decentralization of the city, a course to which we are now irresistibly committed. The future of urban America, indeed, is in the suburbs. A Gallup (1972) poll showed that four of every five residents of cities of over half a million population would prefer to live outside the city, mostly in the suburbs. The central city can be described as a stored ideological energy that was finally released by technological and economic incentives resulting in mass suburban migration.

Fogelson (1967:186–204) has written of the disappointments that the settlers of Los Angeles, the prototypical suburban city, found in their suburban quest and their reaction to those disappointments in the first decades of this century. The native white majority from the beginning settled the city as a collection of suburbs in an effort to find rusticity and a cohesive community through homogeneity and to deny the complexity of the metropolis and its problems. Fogelson writes that "the permanent thus became the utopian"—a reaction to the spatial mobility in Los Angeles. But they failed to find the "community" they sought and "Finally, these people intensified, rather than renounced, their commitment to homogeneity and rusticity; and instead of turning toward an activism that encouraged radical alternatives, they drifted toward a personalism that discouraged involvement per se." Much of what they were fleeing, of course, was the growing ethnic diversity of Los Angeles in those years.

Donaldson (1969:23–44) writes of the great compatibility between the ideals present in American suburbs and the idea of new towns. "Howard's Garden City represented the apotheosis of the suburban dream, places which were at once *real* communities, collections of people who would work and live together in civic and social harmony, and at the same time totally self-sufficient units, made up of discrete individuals able and willing to pursue their private goals." Howard's Garden Cities and the new towns of his followers, Donaldson writes, were to be a "happy marriage" between town and country. It was such a happy marriage that Americans sought in suburbia. Many people did, indeed, find contentment in suburbia. But many suburbs have come to embody the worst, not the best, of city and country. They are a "Paradise Lost."

If the British Garden Cities movement, including its transplantation to this country in the first half of the century, was a reaction to the predominant mode of urban life, then the contemporary American new town movement in the second half of the century is, also—except that the predominant mode for the middle-class masses is now suburban. Much of the public interest in new towns, I suspect, is a continuation of the suburban quest. New town ideology is the semiarticulated ideology of suburbia and of the suburban migration raised to the level of a utopian model, and both are based on the same elements of sociologically naïve mass-society ideology. The new towns will be "Paradise Regained," or this is what the developers seem to be suggesting.

Actually, the equation of new towns with suburbs is not new in American planning thought. Lubove (1967:11) writes that Americans, as early as the 1920s and 1930s, did a disservice to the Garden City idea by identifying it "with almost any variety of low-density suburban subdivision whether or not it satisfied Howard's criteria." It may be fair to say that the new town idea has been absorbed as yet another vehicle for the suburban quest.

Greer (1972:265-79) has characterized the ideology and utopian thoughtways of urban redevelopment, describing as "liberal utopian" such proponents of new towns as Mumford. Sinding (1967), however, describes the contemporary new towns of the developers as "conservative," for they are a reaction against modern urbanism and an attempt to return to community forms of the past, even of a mythical past. This is the difference, I think, between the new towns of the urbane utopians and those of the developers which reflect a distinctly conservative attitude toward social change.

Around 1950, when sociologists intensified the critical and empirical analysis of their deductive hypotheses about the nature of city life, intellectuals, journalists, planners and other critics—some sociologists among them—began creating the "myth of suburbia" (Berger, 1960:1-14). This myth, another deductive fallacy derived from a popularized image of the mass-society, held the burgeoning suburbs of the 1950s to be homogeneously middle-class, split-level traps of conformity, consumerism, status anxiety, child-centeredness, and neurosis (See, Dobriner, 1963:5-28 and Donaldson, 1969: 1-22).

The mass migration to the suburbs was, of course, the pursuit of the American Dream. The myth of suburbia that ensued was an expression of the intellectual's contempt for that Dream (Berger, 1966). One pertinent facet of this myth was the belief that the move to suburbia made people change their life styles. Sociologists, such as Ktsanes and Reissman (1960), Berger (1960), and Dobriner (1963), exploded the myth and showed the suburbs to be as various in class and life styles as the neighborhoods of central cities, which are their proper comparisons. Moreover, they showed that people are largely satisfied with the suburbs and that their life styles were ones they brought with them or aspired to before the move.

There was in that myth the idea that there was something in the built environment of low-density tract developments that made people change and take on new and lesser forms of community. This, of course, is a naïve belief in physical determinism, the idea that spatial arrangements can meaningfully affect social arrangements—for better or worse. The fallacy of physical determinism is a sociological truism; the limits of the built environment to shape behavior are well known (Michelson, 1970:168-90). Yet new town planners and developers, now arguing for a "positive" design effect, persist in the face of all evidence in suggesting that plans can produce new psychologies and social organization, especially those that enhance "community."

There is evidence (Gans, 1967:408-33) that people do live somewhat differently after moving to a new town, but it is largely because the new town permits them to realize some life style change, which is often the reason they moved. When middle-class people move from the city, they bring their life style with them, and when working-class and ethnic groups move *en bloc*, their subcultures largely survive any influence of the suburban environment. Gans (1967:409) writes: "New towns are ultimately old communities on new land, culturally not significantly different from suburban subdivisions and urban neighborhoods inhabited by the same kinds of people, and politically much like other small American towns." But as Berger (1966) writes, "myths are potent enough to survive evidence; they are not disarmed by understanding."

Berger (1966), in discussing the functions of the myth, says that "realtor-chamber of commerce interests ... could use the myth to reaffirm the American Way of Life." City planners, architects, and urban design people used the myth to make war on tract developments as "the urban slums of tomorrow." And we know, too, that new town advocates have pointed to that myth in terms of the human costs of uncontrolled urban sprawl. Berger notes, further, that the planners believed that "there was somehow a direct relationship between the physical structure or the esthetic shape of a residential environment and the sort of values and culture it can possibly engender." Some planners and developers apparently still abide by this aspect of the myth, for they are suggesting they can eliminate the bad part of suburbia by changing the physical plan—making new towns the American Dream finally realized. The developers are saying that design, land-use plans, and service facilities can foster neighborhood and community and can engender happiness. Gans (1967:408-32) and other sociologists have repeatedly shown that neighborhood and community spirit, regardless of the quality of that community, are mainly the result of class and age homogeneity, but developers have often taken this to be a design effect and, thus, confirmation of their belief in physical determinism.

The content of the new life style is, of course, prescribed by the ideology. The life style the developers want to foster by design is that of the small town surrogate of the Suburban Dream, which is yearned for by urbanites still in the cities and never quite realized by suburbanites who fled the cities in its pursuit. Warren (1972:81) has written that suburbs are a reaction to social change in cities. "The suburbs are the small town's last stand. They represent the last great hope for preserving small-town values within the ever growing metropolitan orbits."

The ideal model of suburbia has always been that of the small town. People move to suburbia principally for housing and neighborhood amenities, especially those that enhance childrearing. The Dream is of a small town, even a rural flavor of community, access to open-space recreational facilities, and a scale of community simple and small enough to permit meaningful participation. They sought this Dream in a community that was relatively independent of the city, at least for all but the most basic needs of employment and specialty services. Political autonomy was essential and Wood (1958:3-18) has described suburbia as "republics in miniature." The suburbs were to be a romantic cocoon enclosing and encircling life and protecting it from the ethnic and class variety of the metropolis. Moreover, the life style was to be an eminently middle-class one. Family life, togetherness, and child rearing were to be at the core of it. The developers have seen to it that their new towns fill that bill. Developers are not offering a new form of community, as they suggest, but are selling old wine in new bottles—the old suburbs in a new package. They are not candidly selling new suburbs that would avoid some of the troubles of the old, but too often cater to irrational beliefs and dark fears about the loss of community, and to fears of the overwhelming pluralism of metropolitan life.

New Towns as Models of the Suburban Dream

New town developers in this country are admittedly in business to make money. They must sell houses and make new towns a paying enterprise. This means selling to a public seeking not only better housing but also what it considers better community amenities. To sell houses, developers must also sell the idea of new towns, for people buy neighborhoods and communities as well as housing. The internal land-use plan of new towns, so contrary to the familiar house and private lot of the tract suburbs, is a notion that some prospective homeowners—especially those of a freeholding, agrarian mentality—resist at first. But the promise of essential services lacking in the tract suburbs often sways them. The sales promotion stresses the theme of "community" and "neighborhood" and how the new town will foster them. These are themes the buying public apparently wants to hear. The rhetoric of new town advocacy and of its promotional literature consistently and repetitively share certain explicit and implicit themes that sociologists have shown underlie the suburban quest.

The themes of building "true" community, increasing social participation, reducing alienation, and rediscovering the pleasures of neighboring are ones that permeate new town proposals. Themes of a loss of community and a quest for true community are, of course, characteristic of both liberal and conservative ideologies and they are to be found, correspondingly, in the ideologies of utopian visionaries and new town promotion.

A typical physical plan calls for "neighborhoods" or "villages" of several thousand persons.[3] The focal point of each neighborhood is usually an elementary school and sometimes a neighborhood center designed for the whole family, facts which themselves attest to the familistic values being catered to. The school-centered neighborhood is an idea developed in 1920 by Clarence Perry, who adapted it directly from Ebenezer Howard. In new towns, the school-centered neighborhood does not take into account the many non-territorial bases of community in urban society—especially for middle-class people—that have been the object of recent interest among sociologists and planning theorists. And the fact that new towns are being planned primarily for middle-class people suggests a wish to escape to some pristine community form of the past. More than assuming that propinquity and territory are adequate bases for community, the "neighborhood" implicitly fosters the two-parent, nuclear family model of the Suburban Dream. It further implies that the commonality of having children in the same school (and it seems to assume most will) and getting to know the parents of a child's playmates is an adequate and desirable catalyst of community.

Conventional new town plans assume that most residents will want to pursue this one kind of family-centered life style, that of the isolated nuclear family and of traditional sex roles. Truly urbane new town plans would encourage a pluralism in the patterns of social and family life. Goldstein (1975) has criticized the relevance of new town plans for women and concludes that they often structure the occupational mobility potential of women and restrict role choice.

New town developers typically speak of the "culture"—the fine arts—that will blossom in their communities. There is, however, little reason to believe that there will be any more culture in new towns than in any other middle-class suburb of about the same size—and for the same reasons. The presence of cultural facilities and interests in a community is closely related to the number of well-educated, middle-class residents, especially those who patronize and create culture as a life style; and a college in the community is an important factor (Allen, 1968). New town residents will continue to rely upon the city for threatre, music, and the dance, as do most suburban communities. As Gans (1967:424-25) points out, many of the culture-bearing middle class have already relocated into suburbs and the cities, as cultural centers, have not declined as a result, for these suburbanites return to the city to use its facilities and have generated some suburban facilities as well.

Roszak (1967) believes that new towns in the Bay Area, by drawing off San Francisco's middle class, will diminish public financial support for the city's cultural facilities. New town residents are no longer fiscally responsible to the city, but its facilities are available to them nonetheless if they are willing to commute. This is but one example of how suburban new towns will exploitively rely on central city facilities as do most residential suburbs. It appears that the talk of culture in new towns is to assure prospective residents that they will have to pay only a minimum price in the lost urban amenities that result from the physical and social isolation of suburban new towns. It is a compliment that vice pays to virtue.

New town social planning themes reflect a reaction to the degree of mobility and rootlessness inherent in urban life. New town schemes often speak of "balancing" the community by providing housing to accommodate all stages of the life cycle, not only to lend an age-mix from the outset, but so that there is no need to leave the new town once ensconced in it. Thus, a three-generation community is offered with the connotations of a new extended familism—a middle-class commune. Here, again, emerges the suburban value of familism and togetherness in new town ideology. But the *potentialities* of planning for age pluralism and extended-family life styles should not be dismissed lightly.

Sandberg (1973), Grigsby (1973), and Mead (1973) have discussed the necessity of planning for age pluralism and extended familism or, at least, not discouraging the latter possiblity. The network of kin is often one important social and psychological mooring for some ethnic minorities. Urban sociologists have long been appreciative of this use of community. But the only pluralism that the developers are now promoting is that of age, and even that is dangerously close to three-generation togetherness rather than a genuine pluralism and understanding among age groups.

Gans (1973), however, doubts that age integration is attainable because of ever-widening cultural differences between age groups. But that probably varies for different classes and ethnic groups.

A cherished myth of suburban communities is that they are self-contained islands in a disagreeable metropolitan sea. They find a rationalization of the illusion in their fierce political autonomy and they find new evidence of autonomy in the continuing suburbanization of jobs, institutions, and daily service facilities; the interdependencies of "primary" community relations or of face-to-face interaction have, in fact, diminished. But they fail or refuse to understand the equally important interdependencies of "secondary" community relations to the city and other suburbs, those "invisible" ties of economic and class relations that bind suburban neighborhoods into the complex of metropolitan systems. Gans (1967:418-19) commented in a similar vein on the anti-pluralism of Levittowners. In viewing their homes as the center of life they have used a societal model of agrarian America which denies that they live in a pluralistic national society with a great complex of interdependencies.

The developers' emphasis on the "balanced" and "self-contained" features of new towns, I think, sometimes deliberately fosters the illusion of functional and, by implication, moral autonomy of suburban new towns. New towns, as the finest of the visionaries have conceived them, would stress the *interdependencies* of new towns in the metropolitan system, not the illusion of functional autonomy. The classical new town concept of "regionalism" visualizes the metropolitan community as a *system* of small and large cities. Among the urban amenities that flow from interdependencies are contact, social variety, intensified communication—all truly traits of urbanity. And this is not necessarily contradictory to the notions of "self-containment" or "balance," for both these features were meant to achieve completeness of community, not to be the apparatuses of escape and civic denial that some developers seem to suggest.

It is the bitterest irony of all, as Roszak (1967) so aptly noted, that the developers have turned Mumford's criticism of the suburbs into their principal promotional appeal. Mumford (1961:493-503) called the early Romantic Suburbs "an asylum for the preservation of illusion" and he later remarked that "what the [mass] suburb retains today is largely its original weakness: snobbery, segregation, status-seeking, political irresponsiblity." Mumford also, it must be admitted, is swayed to some extent by the "myth of suburbia," possibly because it is congenial to his mass society thinking.

Mumford's new towns were to be the antithesis of the physical form and the mentality of the mass suburbs he so deplores. But the commercial developers are dangerously close to appealing to the darkest motivations of class and ethnic segregation and to the fear of diversity that brought people to the mass suburbs. Kaplan (1973) reports that fully 70 percent of the survey respondents in the new community of Flower Mound near Dallas say a "safe environment" is the first or second most important consideration in their purchase decision. The spectacle of barricaded, literally fenced, walled and guarded, "new communities" appearing around some large cities is evidence of the ugliest motivation behind the suburban quest, and they are evidence that some developers will cater directly to it.

Ethnically Pluralistic New Towns

Ideally, new towns should be relatively small, manageable, and workable microcosms of the metropolitan community with all its age, class, ethnic, and racial heterogeneity and, yes, its share of responsibility for the attendant social problems. But almost all commercial new town proposals, because of high housing costs and also because of the perceived tastes of prospective house buyers, cater to homogeneous segments of the population, middle-class people in the child-bearing and rearing years. The sense of community that is so dear to the planners is a result of this homogeneity. In this and other ways new town developers promote those community amenities that are wrought by homogeneity, not pluralism.

Berger (1966) spoke of a deeper function of the "myth of suburbia," the attempt to render suburbia as a homogeneous, culturally unified America without a trace of ethnicity. The myth of suburbia, then, is a part and parcel of "Melting Pot" ideology or an assimilationist model of American society. In reality, individual suburbs, as any urban neighborhood, tend toward class and sometimes ethnic homogeneity. The implicit image of suburbs as the new Melting Pot is also reflected in new town plans. The developers' new towns are not planning for cultural pluralism. Not only do housing costs preclude class variety, but the housing styles and the services promised all too often reflect the developer's anticipation of white middle-class, perhaps even "Protestant" tastes.

If new towns are ever to be places of genuine urbanity and pluralism, something more than middle-class suburbs, they will have to be deliberately planned to be such places. I believe that genuine pluralism and the attendant variety of community is the key to urbanity in new towns. But this is not part of the Suburban Dream to be redeemed in new towns, and I predict a pluralist alternative in new towns will be hard fought against. Some urbanists, nonetheless, have recently begun an important dialogue concerning planning for racial, class, and ethnic pluralism in new towns (Gans, 1973; Sandberg, 1973; Grigsby, 1973; Mead, 1973; Greenbie, 1975 and others). Present and past efforts at class and race integration in new towns and HUD guidelines stress a random, salt-and-pepper scattering, which has an implicit majority-normative or assimilationist perspective rather than a true pluralist, nonsegregation approach that provides for voluntary enclave living.

Mead (1973), in particular, has made an eloquent plea for the pluralist alternative in new towns. She argues against the ethnocentric idea of integration or giving minorities the opportunity to become like the majority. She says "If people are not given some device through which those with common social and cultural backgrounds can live close together, share each others' cooking smells and lullabies and jokes, there is no hope of their children growing up with a relationship to their pasts that they will be able to transmit to children." She favors "designing neigh-borhoods in ways that produce clusters of ethnic or life style seclusion within larger areas that provide contact with many other kinds of people, allowing for choice of neighbors and friends instead of for atomization. . . . "

If new towns are ever to be places of urbanity and pluralism, they must take account of the growth of separatist thinking in the 1970s among blacks and some white ethnic minorities and make its accommodation a major planning goal. Many Americans who are black, Puerto Rican, Mexican (Chicano), Native American (Indian), Chinese and other Asian groups, and several European ethnic groups may well elect voluntary enclave living in new towns. A pluralistic community would not only create a greater community spirit within enclaves but would bring into sharper relief for all groups the real needs of the larger community such as schools, day care centers, health care services, and so on. Such a pluralistic new town would be a healthier urban place that could not easily delude itself about its functional relations to the rest of the metropolitan community. Among the advocates of pluralist living in new towns, Greenbie (1974; 1975, Chap. 12), in particular, has suggested the possibility of using new towns to relocate whole ethnic neighborhoods and extended families that have been displaced by urban renewal and highway building, rather than scattering such groups to the four corners of the metropolis and disrupting their community and life style. It would be much preferable to save or rebuild the neighborhoods and "ethnic villages" of the central cities with enlightened urban renewal and economic redevelopment, for the suburbanization of minorities creates many problems of commutation and access to jobs. But a wise and vigorous public policy of relocating when necessary or of allowing viable ethnic enclaves of limited size to develop in new towns could make those problems surmountable.

Conclusions

The finest of the urban visionaries and some or perhaps many community planners conceived of new towns as places of urbanity and pluralism, not as places devoid of race, class, or ethnicity or as places to indulge a selfish, simplistic view of the world. I have argued that most commercial developers of new towns *and the public* have conceived new towns as the Suburban Dream redeemed. Most developers have explicitly and implicitly advertised new towns as the *mise en scène* of the small town of a mythical past and catered to the anti-urban sentiments that precipitated the suburban stampede in the first place. Many developers have traded openly on the prestige of the new town idea to sell more suburban housing but, except for certain physical planning considerations, have betrayed its principles.

I believe the key to redeeming the new town concept and to making the suburbs good cities with the best amenities of urbanism as a way of life and a minimum of the social problems that plague urban-industrial society is to reconceive new towns fundamentally as crucibles of class and ethnic pluralism in metropolitan life.

I am afraid our national faith in the singular efficacy of private enterprise will deflect attention from the possibilities of new towns. It would be ideal to begin some earnest experiments with pluralistic living in federally subsidized new towns. New towns would make ideal laboratories for one of the most important experiments in the history of urban redevelopment.

. . . .

Each of the thirteen essays that comprise this anthology was written before, some long before, this collection was begun. Taken together, they bring into relief the roles of ideology and utopia in the planning and building of new towns. The critical implications that emerge may be taken as policy recommendations to new town planners, developers, and to government policy makers that they endeavor to let new towns realize their full potential and social responsibility. Parts II through IV of this volume group essays that examine aspects of the Suburban Dream and how planners of suburbs and new towns have tried to realize it. Several of the essays do not deal explicitly with suburbs that are also new towns, but juxtaposing them to essays that do emphasizes the oneness of the two phenomena. Each of the four Parts is concluded by a short list of "Further Readings" that deal with related themes by yet other authors appears on pages 280-81.

Part II is opened with an essay by Jeffrey K. Hadden and Josef J. Barton that explores in depth the history of the ancient and lingering ideology of anti-urbanism and how it affects thinking about cities and their problems today. William Petersen makes a case study of the British new town movement, in some ways the precursor of the American movement, and examines the influence of nineteenth century anti-urban ideology on the new town concept and their planning. Scott Donaldson discusses how new towns were to have been the happy marriage of city and country and how agrarian ideology is common to both suburbanization and new towns. Part II is concluded with an essay by Sylvia F. Fava that makes the case that new towns have succeeded suburbs as the focus of "pop sociology" in the 1970s, and she discusses the implications of this for new towns policy.

Part III sets in parallel two essays that develop the idea that suburbanization and the new town movement are analyzable as the collective-behavioral phenomenon of a social movement. William M. Dobriner writes of ideology and utopia in the suburban search. The late Leonard Reissman analyzed the urban planning visionaries and, in particular, the new town movement as a complete social movement by all sociological criteria.

Part IV brings together three essays by three prominent planning theorists who are also critics of new towns; William Alonso, William H. Whyte, and Edward P. Eichler. While their critical analyses vary in important respects, all three agree that new towns are, in effect, suburbia. Each is pessimistic about the prospects of new towns meaningfully alleviating metropolitan problems. While the impetus to collecting this volume is the belief that new towns hold the potential for realizing the urbane community in at least some suburbs, these critics need a careful hearing if future new towns are to avoid the pitfalls of most present ones.

The final objective of the anthology is to bring together essays that evaluate contemporary suburban development proposals with respect to the ideal of the pluralistic good community. Part V opens with an essay by Bennett M. Berger who was an early observer that the "myth of suburbia" in one respect served to deny the fact of class and ethnic pluralism in American society. Margaret Mead's essay makes an appeal for new towns to be planned to accommodate voluntary enclave living for ethnic groups thereby enabling them to transmit their ethnic cultures from generation to generation. Barrie B. Greenbie examines the principle of territoriality and its importance in planning to maintain the integrity of ethnic cultures, especially when ethnic groups may be disrupted by relocation into the suburbs. Finally, there is an essay by Neil C. Sandberg that takes a hard look at the feasibility of integration in new towns and concludes that suburban new towns ought to provide opportunities for voluntary enclave living, as well as providing integrated areas, and that new-towns-intown should be aimed at keeping white "ethnic villages" intact and viable as ethnic communities.

The discussion of ethnic pluralism in America is likely to continue as a major theme of social criticism in the '70s and '80s, and new town planning theory and commentary will inevitably be engaged with it.

NOTES

Author's note:
   The introductory essay is a revision and expansion of an article published in *Sociological Symposium,* Fall Issue, 1974, under the title, "New Towns and Suburban Ideology: Selling the American Dream." It is used here in revised form by permission of the publisher.
1. When I speak of "developers" and their promotional themes, I have deliberately created an amalgam of themes, all of which probably do not characterize the promotion of any given new town and probably none of the themes characterize a few new towns. The themes are variously present and stressed, depending on the beliefs, tastes, and market perceptions of developers. Moreover, I use the term "developer" because the person or the corporate entity is the source of final issuance of promotional themes, which obviously also reflect the views of their advisors, consultants, planners and federal government policy. I have no interest in characterizing particular developers, but only an interest in analyzing the tenor of popular themes in the new town movement of the '60s and '70s.
2. The methods of my study for this essay are those of an informal content analysis of documents of personal observation. Documents include promotional literature for new towns and content analyses by others of similar promotional literature (e.g., Sinding, 1967; Whyte, 1968; Alonso, 1970; and others), which have, it should be observed, tended toward negative appraisals of promotional themes. My interpretation of promotional themes has also been influenced by many articles by developers and their supporters and spokesmen. My general impressions have, moreover, been corroborated by an enormous advocacy literature by persons who, for the most part, are not associated with any particular new town development.
3. I have wondered if it is entirely a faithfulness to established usage that American planners and develpers kept the British term "new *town*" or whether it was because "town" in American English connotes *small* town. It is also telling that some developers prefer, especially in the case of smaller developments, the term "new *communities.*" "New *cities*" found favor for a while but never caught on, perhaps because it connoted large size or citification, and the term now seems restricted to free-standing new cities.

REFERENCES

Allen, Irving Lewis.
　1968　"Community size, population composition and cultural activity in smaller communities." *Rural Sociology* 33 (September): 328–38.
Alonso, William.
　1970　"The mirage of new towns." *The Public Interest* 19 (Spring): 3–17.
Armytage, W. H. G.
　1961　*Heavens Below: Utopian Experiments in England, 1560–1960*. Toronto: University of Toronto Press.
Berger, Bennett M.
　1960　*Working-Class Suburb: A Study of Auto Workers in Suburbia*. Berkeley, Ca.: University of California Press.

　1966　"Suburbia and the American dream." *The Public Interest* 2 (Winter): 80–91.
Brooks, Richard Oliver.
　1974　*New Towns and Communal Values: A Case Study of Columbia, Maryland*. New York: Praeger Publishers.
Dobriner, William M.
　1963　*Class in Suburbia*. Englewood Cliffs, N. J.: Prentice Hall, Inc.
Donaldson, Scott.
　1969　*The Suburban Myth*. New York: Columbia University Press.
Dyckman, John W.
　1962　"The European motherland of American urban romanticism." *Journal of American Institute of Planners* 28 (November): 277–81.
Elazar, Daniel J.
　1966　"Are we a nation of cities?" Pp. 89–114 in Robert A. Goldwin (ed.), *A Nation of Cities: Essays on America's Urban Problems*. Chicago: Rand McNally and Co.
Fava, Sylvia F.
　1973　"The pop sociology of suburbs and new towns." *American Studies* 14 (Spring): 121–33.
Fogelson, Robert M.
　1967　*The Fragmented Metropolis: Los Angeles, 1850–1930*. Cambridge, Mass.: Harvard University Press.
Freidel, Frank.
　1963　"Boosters, intellectuals, and the American city." Pp. 115–20 in Oscar Handlin and John Burchard (eds.), *The Historian and the City*. Cambridge, Mass.: M. I. T. Press.
Gallup, George and Associates.
　1972　"The Gallup Poll." *Washington Post* (December 12).
Gans, Herbert.
　1962　"Urbanism and suburbanism as ways of life: a re-evaluation of definitions." Pp. 625–48 in Arnold M. Rose (ed.), *Human Behavior and Social Processes*. Boston: Houghton Mifflin.

　1967　*The Levittowners*. New York: Random House.

　1973　"The possibilities of class and racial integration of American new towns." Pp. 137–58 in Harvey S. Perloff and Neil C. Sandberg (eds.), *New Towns: Why-& for Whom?* New York: Praeger Publishers.
Glaab, Charles N. and A. Theodore Brown.
　1967　*A History of Urban America*. New York: The Macmillan Company.
Glass, Ruth.
　1968　"Urban sociology in Great Britain." Pp. 47–73 in R. E. Pahl (ed.), *Readings in Urban Sociology*. London: Pergamon Press.
Glazer, Nathan.
　1958　"Why city planning is obsolete." *Architectural Forum* 109 (July): 96–98.
Goist, Park Dixon
　1969　"Lewis Mumford and 'anti-urbanism.'" *Journal of American Institute of Planners* 35 (September): 340–47.
Goldstein, Joan.
　1975　"Planning for women in new towns: new concepts and dated roles." A paper presented at the Annual Meeting of the American Sociological Association, San Francisco, August 29.
Greenbie, Barrie B.
　1974　"Social territory, community health and urban planning." *Journal of the American Institute of Planning* 40 (March): 74–82.

1975   *Design for Diversity: Planning for Natural Man in the Neo-technic Environment; an Ethological Approach.* New York and Amsterdam: Elsevier Scientific Publishing Company.

Greer, Scott.
1972   *The Urbane View.* New York: Oxford University Press.

Grigsby, J. Eugene.
1973   "Views on the feasibility of integration." Pp. 189–94 in Harvey S. Perloff and Neil C. Sandberg (eds.), *New Towns: Why-& for Whom?* New York: Praeger Publishers.

Haar, Charles M.
1972   *The End of Innocence: A Suburban Reader.* Glenview, Illinois: Scott, Foresman and Co.

Hadden, Jeffrey K. and Josef J. Barton.
1973   "The image that will not die: thoughts on the history of anti-urban ideology." Pp. 79–116 in Louis M. Masotti and Jeffrey K. Hadden (eds.), *Urbanization of the Suburbs.* Beverly Hills, Ca.: Sage Publications, Inc.

Hall, Petet, et al.
1973   *The Containment of Urban England* (Two volumes). Beverly Hills, Ca.: Sage Publications.

Howard, Ebenezer.
1898, 1902 (1965) *Garden Cities of To-Morrow.* Cambridge, Mass.: M. I. T. Press.

Jacobs, Jane.
1961   *The Death and Life of Great American Cities.* New York: Random House.

Kaplan, Marshall.
1973   "Social planning, perceptions, and new towns." Pp. 130–36 in Harvey S. Perloff and Neil C. Sandberg (eds.), *New Towns: Why-& for Whom?* New York: Praeger Publishers.

Ktsanes, Thomas and Leonard Reissman.
1960   "Suburbia—new homes for old values." *Social Problems* 7 (Winter): 187–95.

Lubove, Roy.
1967   *The Urban Community: Housing and Planning in the Progressive Era.* Englewood Cliffs, N. J.: Prentice-Hall, Inc.

Mead, Margaret.
1973   "New towns to set new life styles." Pp. 117–29 in Harvey S. Perloff and Neil C. Sandberg (eds.), *New Towns: Why-& for Whom?* New York: Praeger Publishers.

Michelson, William H.
1976   *Man and His Urban Environment: A Sociological Approach.* Reading, Mass.: Addison-Wesley Publishing Co.

Mills, C. Wright.
1942   "The professional ideology of social pathologists." *American Journal of Sociology* XLIX (September): 165–80.

Mumford, Lewis.
1961   *The City in History: Its Origins, Its Transformations, and Its Prospects.* New York: Harcourt, Brace & World.

Petersen, William.
1968   "The ideological origins of Britain's new towns." *Journal of the American Institute of Planners* 34 (May): 160–70.

Reissman, Leonard.
1964   *The Urban Process: Cities in Industrial Society.* New York: The Free Press.

Riesman, David.
1957   "The suburban dislocation." *Annals* (Fall): 123–46.

Roszak, Theodore.
1967   "Life in the instant cities." *The Nation* 204 (March 13).

Sandberg, Neil C.
1973   "The realities of integration in new and old towns." Pp. 179–88 in Harvey S. Perloff and Neil C. Sandberg (eds.), *New Towns: Why-& for Whom?* New York: Praeger Publishers.

Sinding, Monica K.
1967   *The Philosophic Basis for New Town Development in America.* Chapel Hill, N. C.: Center for Urban and Regional Studies, University of North Carolina.

Sobin, Dennis P.
    1971   *The Future of the Suburbs: Survival or Extinction?* Port Washington, N. Y.: Kennikat Press.

Warren, Roland L.
    1972   *The Community in America.* Second edition. Chicago: Rand McNally.

White, Morton and Lucia.
    1962   *The Intellectual Versus the City: From Thomas Jefferson to Frank Lloyd Wright.* Cambridge, Mass.: Harvard University Press and M. I. T. Press.

Whyte, William H.
    1963   "The anti-city." Pp. 45-58 in Elizabeth Geen, Jeanne R. Lowe and Kenneth Walker (eds.), *Man and the Modern City.* Pittsburgh, Pa.: University of Pittsburgh Press.

    1968   *The Last Landscape.* Garden City, N. Y.: Doublday & Co.

Wirth, Louis.
    1938   "Urbanism as a way of life." *American Journal of Sociology* 44 (July): 1-24.

Wood, Robert C.
    1958   *Suburbia: Its People and Their Politics.* Boston: Houghton Mifflin Company.

PART TWO
SUBURBIA, NEW TOWNS, AND
THE ANTI-URBAN ANIMUS

JEFFREY K. HADDEN AND JOSEF J. BARTON

AN IMAGE THAT WILL NOT DIE: THOUGHTS ON THE HISTORY OF ANTI-URBAN IDEOLOGY

IT IS THE PURPOSE OF THIS ESSAY to trace the history of man's thought about cities and suburbs. We take as axiomatic that man, in his yet short experience, still struggles to accommodate himself to the reality of the urban revolution. Without denying the significance of the political, economic, technological, and organizational dimensions of urban problems, we argue that the negative *image* man holds of the city looms as a major obstacle to the maturation of urban civilization. In substantial measure, the discontents of urban civilization are a function of man's deep-seated and fundamental rejection of the city as an *idea*.[1]

The suburb is, in part, merely a consequence of rapid population expansion along the lines of least resistance toward cheaper land at the fringes of cities, facilitated by expanding technology's ability to transport men greater and greater distances between place of residence and place of work. But the suburb is also an attempt to compromise the imperatives of the industrial revolution, to re-create the pastoral rapport between man and nature, at least on weekends and holidays.

The Urbanization of the Suburbs, Vol. 7 *Urban Affairs Annual Reviews* ©1973. L. H. Masotti and J. K. Hadden, Editors. Pp. 79-116 reprinted by permission of the publisher, Sage Publications, Inc., the editors, and the authors.

We have known that some—indeed, many—men of history disliked the city, but scholars have only recently begun to explore the implications this has. It is now rather thoroughly documented that many of the key figures in the framing of this nation held city life and all that cities represent in utter disdain (Rourke, 1964). Similarly, research has pointed to the like disaffection of many intellectual giants of the American past (White and White, 1962). The historical roots of anti-urbanism remain, however, inadequately plumbed. Nor can such a sweeping topic be comprehensively explored here. Our task, thus, is exploratory, a seeking to establish only the plausibility of a line of reasoning, and thereby hopefully stimulate others to join in more thorough research.

Our analysis proceeds in three distinct directions. First, we attempt to establish plausibility for the proposition that anti-urban sentiment is as old as cities themselves. Second, we examine the objective conditions and consequences of the early industrial-urban revolution. And third, we explore in some detail the mosaic of several complex ideological threads in American history which have interacted to preserve and give peculiar shape to a negative image of cities and the consequent suburbanization of our own culture. Underlying each of these tasks is a theoretical assumption that man's basic value orientations—i.e., his taken-for-granted assumptions about the nature of reality—significantly mold the physical environment he creates.

THEORETICAL ORIENTATION

The theoretical heritage of the sociology of knowledge informs our inquiry, particularly as this perspective has been elaborated by Berger and Luckmann (1966). Reality is socially constructed. Man the creator is in turn molded and continually reshaped both by the objective structures of his creation and by the meanings he internalizes about social reality. Man created the city and gave meaning to his creation. But this product is in turn an objective reality which, on the one hand, imposes restraints and limitations and, on the other hand, presents new vistas and opportunities. In wrestling with the possibilities and meanings of the city with its sui generis realities, man is ever internalizing new meaning.

Thus, this task of world-building (city-building) is an ongoing process. Still, meanings once internalized in the collective human consciousness may transcend the generations. Meanings internalized by men constitute the essential social bonds of human societies—that is, assumed truths about the nature of social reality. But that which is internalized as truth and the objective imperatives of social structures are not necessarily congruent. Man's capacity to create (invent) new artifacts results in a process of continually changing social structures. Meanings, thus, constantly shift to accommodate new realities. But, again, there is neither inherent necessity nor guarantee that meaning and structure will move toward harmony. Indeed, meaning and structure may drift apart to the point of ultimate collapse of a human group. But, more important for our purposes, meaning and structure can be unbalanced for long periods of time by mutually reinforcing the imbalance.[2]

To apply this to our task, we believe the meaning or image of the city developed in human history to be antithetical to the structural reality of the city. From the onset, man viewed the city as contrary to the "natural" relationship between man and environment. As man altered his nomadic life style for more permanent or quasi-permanent settlements, he came to define the wilderness as "unnatural." But to his subsequent transition from this pastoral-agrarian environment to an urban environment, he did not bring a parallel redefinition of the meaning of "natural" environment. Momentarily we will attempt to show some compelling objective reasons for this failure to reconstruct reality. For the present, however, we wish simply to postulate the initial imbalance between meaning and structure and to further suggest the reciprocal nature of the incongruity. Early cities were not only a departure from the natural as man had come to define it, but also the very structure of urban life lent objective reason for man's dislike and distrust. This internalized meaning, in turn, affected the ongoing process of city-building by structuring and restructuring the city in a manner to reinforce rather than reduce estrangement. City builders have been men *in* but ideologically not *of* the cities—that is, not attuned to the proposition (or internalized meaning) of cities as man's "natural" habitat. Hence, efforts to utilize man's resources to create an ideal urban milieu have hardly even been attempted. Stated otherwise, man has approached the city as an unnatural and unpleasant environment and has thus contributed to a self-fulfilling prophecy. Moreover, the circuit's effects are felt *both* in terms of the physical structure of the city and in terms of man's feelings toward this environment.

Let us hasten to add that the history of man's thought about the city has not been monolithic. Greek philosophers loved their cities, as have some other men of history. Many have viewed the city as the locus of nearly all man's intellectual, ideological, cultural, and technological achievements (Spengler, 1928: 90). Indeed, the words city and civilization have a common origin in the Latin *civis.* But to acknowledge that some men have liked the city and that many, if not most, of man's achievements have occurred in the city is not to disqualify the proposition that anti-urban sentiment has undergirded and dominated man's thinking about the city.

INEQUALITY AND
THE EMERGENCE OF CITIES

Answers to the questions of where, when, and how cities emerged can never be known with certainty. But the space-time/order-of-magnitude aspects of these questions now seem in reasonable focus (Hammond, 1972; Mumford, 1961; Sjoberg, 1960). While the fairly immediate ancestors to homo sapiens may have been around for millions of years, physically modern man seems to date back some forty to fifty thousand years. Cities did not appear until roughly five or six thousand years ago. The process of transition from permanent farming villages to "real" cities was in one sense very gradual. Still, in a relative sense, it happened very quickly. The transition from food-gathering to food production, implying the first permanent settlement, did not occur until the Mesolithic period, roughly ten to twelve thousand years ago. Evidence of the embryonic foreshadowings of cities are apparent by 4000-3500 B.C. and by 2400 B.C. there is evidence of well-developed urban culture (Hammond, 1972).

It is neither central nor essential to our task to elaborate the necessary and sufficient conditions for the existence of cities (Childe, 1950). Rather, we will discuss only those conditions having a bearing on man's image of the city.

In our view, the development of organizational principles radically different from those previously existing stands as *the* critical imperative for the emergence and development of cities. Central to this process was the development of principles of hierarchy not based on kinship. In embryonic form, some cities may well have involved organization along the lines of elaborate kinship systems. But leaders of extended kin networks were necessarily caught in a role conflict between their fellow kinsmen and the imperatives of urban development as perceived by those at the pinnacle of the hierarchy. Only as the influence of kinship declined was it possible to develop the elaborate division of labor which distinguishes a city from a large village.

The second characteristic of urban organization was simply the accentuation of the principle of hierarchy. Cities generated not only a greater division of labor than existed in farming settlements, but the stratifying of people by function also produced a more elaborate hierarchy. In short, the emergence of cities engendered greater inequities than existed in villages organized along lines of kinship. Moreover, leaders demanded new bonds of allegiance, sans kinship ties. The creation of new gods and other ideological principles no doubt served to legitimize emerging hierarchies, but old gods and old traditions died slowly. The memories of other social arrangements lingered, especially among those who gained the least (or suffered the most) from the new principles of organization.

It is reasonably clear that more than natural increase among inhabitants accounts for city growth. Promise of opportunity lured some, but a substantial proportion of the growth occurred as men were brought to the city in bondage. Other probabilities for providing new residents are territorial disputes and nomadic bands. In some instances, nomadic bands conquered cities and wandered on leaving them leveled. In other instances, they remained as conquerers, imposing their superior military organization upon the social organization already present. It is possible that the first cities emerged as powerful nomadic bands settled down to reap the benefits of the conquest of agricultural villages.

Theories on the emergence of cities abound. However it happened, the very nature and growth of cities almost inevitably implies an intensification of the principle of hierarchy and, hence, marked inequality (Childe, 1954). Those at the bottom of the totem pole, and there is reason to believe they constituted a sizeable proportion, must necessarily have viewed the city as an inferior environment.

The emergence of cities also demanded a stable working relationship with an agricultural hinterland. This, again, raised a problem of new forms of social organization. How such relationships were initially established leaves much room for conjecture. Perhaps contractual agreements between free men were sufficient at first, but the survival of a growing urban population required more than an assumption of continuing good will between farmers and artisans. Without reasonable guarantee of a continual flow of food from the hinterland, the settlement of large aggregates of people is inconceivable. It seems, thus, reasonable to speculate that such assurances were achieved by superior strength—that is, the ability to impose sanctions for failure to comply with the needs and expectations of the city. But this guarantee of food is minimum. As cities grew in size and strength, many of them must have demanded more from their hinterland and for diminishing compensation. Moreover, the conditions which gave rise to a city must have resulted in several cities within the same area. As cities grew, they required larger hinterlands and struggles to claim the same territory must have ensued, with the agrarian peasants being caught in the cross-fire.

In short, the emergence of cities not only resulted in heightened inequalities for those within them, but also imposed radically different social relationships among those within the range of a city's hinterland. It is not inconceivable that some farmers profited from cities, but, on balance, the cities imposed disturbing restraints on herders, fishermen, and agriculturists. Hence, another possible source of anti-urban sentiment emerges from those beyond the city gates but nevertheless deeply affected by the city.

An elaborate accounting of life in early cities and of the relationships between cities and their hinterlands is unnecessary. Our major point is that the emergence of cities demanded a more marked system of stratification than was previously the case. This argument is, of course, speculative, as we have no known written records of the earliest cities. The earliest written records available, however, indicate rigid stratification with a sizeable proportion of the population in bondage. In the Greek city-state, the concept of citizen applied to only a small minority. It is our position, thus, that the emergence and growth of cities depended on the development of new principles of organization involving significant intensification of hierarchical principles. While many within and outside the cities profited from the new social order, a very large proportion did not. And from those victimized rather than benefitted, there emerged dislike, distrust, and fear of the city.

Important as this proposition may be in tracing sources of anti-urbanism, we cannot ignore the possibility that many who experienced status enhancement in the city may also have found urban life repugnant, or at best a mixed blessing. Cities were dirty and noisy; disease was more easily contracted. At least a small minority found the city an escape from the sanctions of informal social control in the village or clan—i.e., they were more likely to cheat or steal. In short, in miniature scale, all of today's urban shortcomings existed. Personal success in the city did not, then, necessarily reflect personal satisfaction with the environment.

BIBLICAL EVIDENCE OF ANTI-URBANISM

Though cities may have provided fertile turf for the spawning of anti-urbanism, people's early feelings about cities remain yet an empirical question. That is, is there any evidence attesting to a negative image of the city from its beginning? Public opinion surveys were nonexistent, very little of detailed development records have been uncovered, diaries and memoirs are unavailable, and, further, it is unlikely that the early philosophers whose work remains extant reflected or represented the populace.

Probably the nearest we come to possessing a social history of the masses are the books of the Old Testament. While recognizing its limitations, we can yet defend the Bible as an embodiment of popular opinion by virtue of its prestige as the most influential document in Western Civilization. It emerged from and carried on a folk wisdom. We may view religious values as the most basic of human values, orienting one's total *weltanschauung*. Thus, the Judeo-Christian tradition, including its reflections on the city, has affected Western man's thinking.

The scholarly literature on cities contains a few passing references to anti-urbanism in the Bible (e.g., Ericksen, 1954: 68), but not until recently has anyone explored it in depth. Jacques Ellul, French philosopher and author of the controversial and provocative book, *The Technological Society* (1964), has recently undertaken this task in a volume entitled *The Meaning of the City* (1970).

The city, as viewed by Ellul (1970: 8, 58) is a hiding place man created to escape the judgment of God, and as such remains forever cursed:

> [The] city was, from the day of its creation, incapable, because of the motives behind its construction, of any other destiny than that

of killing the country, where God put man to enable him to live his life as best he could. . . . The City was built as protection for man. It turns out that she is nothing other than his ruin: the word of God pierces her ramparts and she takes all her inhabitants down with her in her destruction, precisely because man hoped that the city would shelter him from destruction. Condemned herself, the city brings on man's destruction. He is not directly condemned but is implicated in her crime by having sought her protection.

There is a remarkable parallelism between Ellul's earlier treatment of *la technique* and his analysis of the city. Man is incapable of controlling either technology or the city. Now, in *The Meaning of the City,* Ellul lays bare his own theological presuppositions in explanation: God's judgment allows both to rage out of control until, at the time of the second coming, His grace will restore order.

Such a view may reassure those professing benign neglect as an appropriate policy for dealing with urban problems. Similarly, were they inclined toward reading, fundamentalist preachers would delight in learning of Ellul's "text-proof" of God's condemnation of the wicked city. But can any serious scholar view this work as anything other than a diatribe by an angry and disillusioned man whose mind and soul belong to another era?

Harvey Cox (1965), one of America's most prominent theologians, says yes. "Jacques Ellul," writes Cox (1971: 357), "is neither a purblind Luddite nor a quaint religious fanatic. Though his theology has some serious thin spots and even some holes here and there, his instincts are usually dependable. He cannot be ignored." Cox quarrels mainly with Ellul's preoccupation with human evil to the neglect of grace and redemption promised in the New Testament. But of Ellul's tedious explication of anti-urbanism in the Bible, Cox feels the argument is neither strained nor out of context.

Few social scientists will accept Ellul's interpretation of the *meaning* of this anti-urbanism—i.e., an indicator of God's condemnation of the city and of the futility of man's attempts to change this. But his personal presuppositions notwithstanding, *The Meaning of the City* stands as a bench mark in illuminating the historical depths of anti-urbanism. Moving back and forth from Ellul to his scripture citations, one suspects that Ellul's exuberance has occasionally led him to quote passages out of context. But the strength of Ellul's scholarship lies not in particulars but rather in demonstrating the consistency with which the Bible regards cities.

Ellul's argument begins with the story of creation. Adam and Eve bore two sons, Cain and Abel. After Cain slew his brother, God sent him forth, a fugitive, wandering the face of the earth. God promised, however, to protect him from revenge seekers. But Cain refused this protection. He went, rather, to the land of Nod, where he built and named the first city after his son Enoch. Thus, the first murderer is also the first city builder. The city is man's attempt to control his own destiny in defiance of God. Symbolically, the city stands as a fortress where man attempts to hide from God's judgment.

Nimrod, who appears in the tenth chapter of Genesis, was the first mighty man of earth and builder of many cities. Descended from Ham, he bore a curse for the latter's improprieties. Again, the censured man builds the city which in turn shares his condemnation. It was in the most famous of Nimrod's cities where the Babylonians attempted to build a tower to the heavens to become as gods. And, of course, the Lord's response was to confuse their tongues, to cause babbling and misunderstanding. The city, hence, became a place where men lived in discord and hostility.

The Israelites themselves were a nomadic people who knew nothing of cities until as captives in Egypt they were forced to build them. From that day forth,

> when Israel built their own cities, it was always for them the sign of a curse, and the proclamation of slavery renewed. . . . Israel bound herself to slavery, and, even more, to the land of sorrow and sin; by the cities she built, cities that were always the imitation of what she had learned in Egypt, before the deliverance. For the greatest significance is in the fact that Israel was initiated in this art by a king other than God. The people whom God chose for himself obeyed a worldly king, a king whose power was the most impressive of his time, the king of the land of Mizraim. And the power of this king forced the chosen people into ways not meant for a people of God [Ellul, 1970: 25].

The plight of the Israelites echoes our earlier argument that those brought to the city in bondage have an objective basis for their dislike of the urban environment. Yet the grasp of the city loomed mightier than the mere locale of captivity. Delivered from Egypt, the Israelites built their own cities and bound themselves to repeated violation of God's covenant.

Jericho is probably the most familiar instance. The Israelites, having broken God's covenant, found their beloved Jericho besieged and miraculously destroyed by a small band following Joshua, who then promised a curse on he who would rebuild the city. "At the cost of his first-born shall he lay its foundation/ And at the cost of his youngest son shall he set up its gates" (Josh. 6 : 26). And later Hiel of Bethel did indeed rebuild Jericho and paid the price prophesied by Joshua (I Kings 16 : 34).

Again and again the Old Testament recounts the breaking of God's covenant in the city and the judgment of God which follows. The city appears as an environment of disobedience to God, presumably because the city is an "unnatural" setting created by man in defiance of God's will.

The New Testament contains fewer negative references to the city. Yet, if not preoccupied with cities, the New Testament magnifies the Old Testament lessons. The eleventh chapter of Matthew contains Jesus Christ's strongest reproachment of cities, but nonetheless the Gospels reflect a subtle—and sometimes not so subtle—rejection of urban life throughout. At no point does Jesus speak favorably about cities. He often retreats to the countryside to teach and pray. Frequently he admonishes typically urban behavior and life styles. And, in the end, a big-city boss releases him to an unruly urban mob to be crucified.

Ellul (1970: 123) summarizes his interpretation of the scriptural message about cities as follows: "If man keeps up Cain's reaction, if man continues to take the city as his port and as his security, then Jesus' work is in vain—or, rather, man will forever be ignorant of his true port and his true security." Such a conclusion is altogether unacceptable as social scientific scholarship. But a careful reading of the scores of texts Ellul cites can leave little doubt as to the Bible's pervasive negative sentiment toward cities. From Genesis to Revelations, the Bible denounces the city. Such consistency cannot be dismissed as incidental or insignificant.

The Scriptures lend credibility and plausibility, though certainly not proof, to our thesis that the very nature of social organization in early cities contained seeds for anti-urban sentiment. We will now postulate a further logical link between contemporary anti-urbanism and the earliest cities. The validity of our thesis, however, does not depend on absolute and specific conclusions here. To repeat our earlier stated goal, we are trying simply to establish plausibility for the thesis that anti-urbanism stems from roots deeper than the late industrial revolution; its origins are far older—perhaps, indeed, as old as cities themselves.

We predicate our argument on the assumption of persistent anti-urban ideology over the millennia. To trace the pattern in broad strokes, we know that Greek and Roman philosophers were urbanists by residence and sentiment. Yet in their writings we find repeated cautions against the dangers of urban life and affirmations of the virtues of farmers. Plato, for example, models his Republic in an agrarian setting. His utopian city would have contained only 5,040 people. As Mumford (1961: 180-181) notes, "No city could have shrunk into the form Plato desired without ceasing to be a city." Though the urban philosophers do govern, the agriculturists garner much prestige while trade, money-lending, commerce and other urban occupations do not even rank in this vision. An aristocratic distrust of the urban masses underlies his ideal state. Aristotle, too, rated farmers as superior to the urban riff-raff. Excluding them from the governing class reflected his belief that governing required special skills, not his sentiments on farmers' worth. Clearly the health of the city-state depended on protecting and fostering the vitality of the farming class. Like Plato, Aristotle distrusted merchants and artisans, viewing their life style as "ignoble and inimical to virtue." Seneca similarly felt the vitality of the city-state depended on the well-being of the agrarian population. In his *Epilogue,* he notes that farmers make superior soldiers and chastises urban dwellers for laziness.

The quest for salvation of the soul dominated men's thought in Medieval times, and no scholar was more significant than Saint Augustine. Of his more than one hundred titles, none carried influence equal to *The City of God.* He began by refuting a popular notion of his time which traced the fall of the Roman Empire to the establishment of Christianity as the state religion and the con-comitant disobedience of the "pagan" gods of Rome. He then posited that only the Christian God offered immortality, and followed this with the development of a radical dichotomy between the city of God and the cities of man. Cain, the first city builder, and Romulus, the founder of Rome, were both murderers. The cities of man, thus, are founded in sin. They manifest demonic forces and deserve the epithet "city of the Devil." Immortality, however, proceeds from renouncement of materialism, worldly power, and the pleasures of the flesh. In other words, the achievement of immor-tality and a place in the city of God depends upon one's disciplined rejection of the cities of the world.

Harvey Wheeler (1971: 10-11) refers to Augustine's absolute separation of heaven and earth as "the Christian heresy": "one effect of the Augustinian maneuver was to secularize nature, giving the things of this world a monopoly of evil and visiting the heavenly city with a monopoly of virtue." Having so defined reality, man could waste and ravage this evil environment with impunity. "The consummation came," Wheeler (1971: 11) argues, "with the industrializing Protestants, who interpreted their Christianity as giving them free license to indulge themselves in the merciless exploitation of man and nature alike." And, we would argue, this merciless exploitation masked a total disregard and disdain for attempts to create inhabitable cities.

The Judeo-Christian tradition can claim no monopoly on anti-urban underpinnings. One of history's most intriguing statements about cities comes from Ibn Khaldun, a fourteenth-century Muslim. A great thinker, Khaldun was a city dweller who won favor with many political regimes and thereby shared the riches and pleasures of urban civilization. Yet he saw the city as fundamentally corrupting of mind and body. In his three-volume classic *The Muqaddimah*, he devotes more than a hundred pages to analyzing the differences between nomads and sedentary urban people.[3]

Urban civilization constitutes the pinnacle of human development, but, once attained, the populace becomes corrupted and degenerate, incapable, even, of caring for their own necessities. They eat and drink to excess. They indulge in sexual perversions which result in the inability to replenish population (homosexuality) and in loss of community (because promiscuity makes it impossible to identify kinsmen). For Khaldun, the maintenance of a strong sense of community equates with the highest human virtues. Nomadic people, in contrast to urbanites, must work hard for the necessities of life. They are physically stronger, braver, more loyal to their kinsmen and community, and more faithful to their moral and religious heritage. Cities, however, must continually ingest nomad populations, who, in turn, assimilate the corrupting influences of urban life. Though a highly original thinker, Khaldun's writing probably reflects accurately the *zeitgeist* of the broader Arab world. The veil of anti-urbanism stretches beyond the Judeo-Christian world.[4]

HUMAN CONSEQUENCES OF
THE URBAN-INDUSTRIAL REVOLUTION

With the breakup of the Roman Empire, urban life in the West gradually disintegrated. By the ninth century, cities as large political, administrative, commercial, and religious centers had largely vanished (Pirenne, 1956: 17). Besieged by repeated invasions, cities became essentially fortresses for protection. Though the twelfth and thirteenth centuries witnessed a resurgence of trade centers struggling for autonomy from feudal lords, the fourteenth century brought political anarchy, and most of Europe slipped again into urban and economic coma until the sixteenth century.

The Industrial Revolution kindled the first serious and extensive city-building. The forces were a long time in mustering sufficient cohesiveness and direction, but by the late eighteenth century the components had gathered together and thrust the Western world into a phenomenal surge in urban growth.

People were pushed as well as pulled into the city. The guild system had largely broken down. Craftsmen working for merchants under a putting-out or domestic system experienced increasing exploitation. Expanding competition intensified the plight of the artisans to the point of hopeless indebtedness to merchants who required more production for less compensation. The emerging factory system had already made many crafts obsolete and thus forced village workers into cities. Agrarian peasants suffered similar difficulties, and tens of thousands chose to cast off rural impoverishment for the dream of urban prosperity.

Concomitant with burgeoning urbanization and industrialization came unprecedented population growth. Demographers have traditionally attributed rapid population increase to improved food supplies and health conditions which lower mortality rates. William Petersen (1960) has argued persuasively, with historical data from the Netherlands, that the population expansion more likely reflects increased fertility resulting from the breakup of the joint family household, which had previously functioned to restrict marriage and fertility. Urbanization meant a larger proportion of the population marrying, possibly at a younger age. In the Netherlands, a significant decline in mortality does not occur until the last decade of the nineteenth century (see also Eversley, 1965).

While cities eventually produced a sizeable middle class, they initially offered mainly misery to the large majority of their inhabitants. Living conditions were deplorable. The tiny flats which helped destroy extended families soon overflowed in unrestrained fertility. Cities could not cope with the pace of migration and fertility, and the crowded results were hothouses for communicable diseases. Petersen (1960: 340) reports that, in some urban locales, infant mortality ran as high as one-third to one-half.

Early factories were dens of inhumane work and wage conditions. To escape starvation, a large proportion of the population sent their children into the mills at a very young age, often by six or eight. These children, working twelve to sixteen hours a day, six days a week, could expect severe beatings for tardiness and a strap across the back for drowsiness or dreaminess over machines they could barely manage. In England, an investigation of the working conditions of children conducted by Michael Sadler (1832) helped enact the Factory Act of 1833, which regulated child labor practices.[5] While somewhat effective in reducing the long hours and mistreatment, it failed to remove many children from the labor force. By the end of the century, a large proportion of children still worked.

In 1889, Charles Booth classified 35% of the population of London as poor.[6] His category of "regular standard earnings—above the line of poverty" consisted of 42% of the population, but these families typically maintained this level by sending their children into the labor force (Fried and Elman, 1968: 18). In addition to the impoverished, a small proportion of the population was absolutely dispossessed and without any means of livelihood. Booth estimates this group as only about one-and-one-quarter percent of the population, but hastens to clarify this as a "very rough estimate, as these people are beyond enumeration" (Fried and Elman, 1968: 11). Given our own difficulties in calculating certain groups within the urban poor, we can reasonably assume Booth's tally to underestimate actual percentages. Clearly, such a population roaming the streets, begging, and stealing would generate fear and more suffering.

Poor housing, despicable working conditions, poverty or marginal subsistence, high rates of disease and mortality, rampant crime, and the like made cities hell incarnate. During the nineteenth century, millions migrated to the United States seeking more than their factory or peasant existence in Europe. But, for many, the American city offered little solace, only more factories and tenements.

Eventually, in Europe and the United States, the impoverished achieved middle class and escaped the slums, leaving them for others to overcome. But scars remained. And the image of the past lingered as a memory of dirty, crowded, crime-ridden streets, cold, rat-infested walk-up tenements, and noisy, inhumane mills.

Millions came to the cities by need rather than choice. Often the realities they then faced magnified their deepest apprehensions. Objective conditions notwithstanding, they constructed a nostalgic image of a village or pastoral environment where life was better and simpler. The centrifugal growth of cities was as much an ideological movement to escape the city as it was a natural pursuit of cheaper land. The city alienated her majority long before she could offer them the joys of the culture, variety, and excitement of urban living. But the roots of anti-urbanism in America run deeper than the objective conditions suffered by millions of immigrants. America, the new world, had been shaping her identity since the seventeenth century, and threads of her ideals had gradually formed a complex pattern of philosophic thought which now reacted to the reality of industrial cities.

IMAGES OF
CITY AND COUNTRY IN AMERICA

When J. Hector St. John de Crevecoeur ringingly asked in 1782, "What then is the American, this new man?" he partially responded with a vision of the American appearing in a middle landscape, a place midway between the primitive and the civilized. He saw this new man following a path to a village, "where, far removed from the accursed neighborhood of Europeans, its inhabitants live with more ease, decency, and peace, than you imagine; where, though governed by no laws, yet find, in uncontaminated simple manners all that laws can afford." This system of life, this pastoral setting, encompassed enough "to answer all the primary wants of man, and to constitute him a social being, such as he ought to be in the great forest of nature" (Crevecoeur, 1912: 211).

This image of the self-sufficient American in the plenitude of the garden blossomed into one of the dominant symbols of nineteenth-century American culture, a collective representation defining the promise of American life. "The master symbol of the garden," as Henry Nash Smith (1950) reminds us, "embraced a cluster of metaphors expressing fecundity, growth, increase, and blissful labor in the earth." The image of an agricultural paradise, dominated by the heroic figure of the frontier farmer and embodying memories of an earlier, simpler, and happier state of society, long forged a strong bond between memory and desire. "So powerful and vivid was the image," Smith (1950: 123) adds, "that down to the very end of the nineteenth century it continued to remain a representation in Whitman's words, of the core of the nation, 'the real genuine America.' " Never oblivious to life across the ocean, America sought to define herself, and perhaps thus actually mold herself, differently.

This powerful image early became associated with an American animus toward the city. But this cluster of memories and desires represented more than a simple distrust of the city and its ways (White and White, 1962). The pastoral representation of the American landscape also reflected the dissonance created by urban growth and constituted an effort to resolve the conflict between urban and rural values. The mythic figure of the farmer and the poetic map of the middle ground between the wilderness and the city merged into American ideology because they resolved a profound conflict between the values of the "real genuine America" and the attraction of the city and its cluster of new technologies (Marx, 1964: 22-23, 29-32; Empson, 1950: 11-19). As the city threatened to break down the deeply held valuation of the countryside, the pastoral ideal reconciled Americans to the emergence of a new world.

Jefferson's (1955) *Notes on the State of Virginia*, written in 1785, furnishes the most famous use of the yeoman farmer as the vehicle of truly American values. In an answer to a query about the present state of manufactures in Virginia, Jefferson wonders whether man should improve the vast countryside, or whether half should devote their energies to manufacture and crafts. His answer, which has fascinated Americans as much as Crevecoeur's question, resolves the problem forthrightly:

> Those who labor in the earth are the chosen people of God, if ever He had a chosen people, whose breasts He has made His peculiar deposit for substantial and genuine virtue. It is the focus in which He keeps alive that sacred fire, which otherwise might escape from the face of the earth. Corruption of morals in the mass of cultivators is a phenomenon of which no age or nation has furnished an example. It

is the mark set on those, who, not looking up to heaven, to their own soil and industry, as does the husbandman, for their subsistence, depend for it on casualties and caprice of customers. Dependence begets subservience and venality, suffocates the germ of virtue, and prepares fit tools for the designs of ambition [Jefferson, 1955: 164-165].

The farmer was safe from the gross vices of the city dweller, for the agriculturist lived with his hands, rather than with his head. To work with one's hands meant independence; to live by artifice signaled moral degeneracy. Let the workshops remain in Europe, wrote Jefferson (1955: 165), for "the mobs of great cities add just so much to the support of pure government, as sores do to the strength of the human body" (see also Boorstin, 1948: 147). Jefferson nevertheless recognized the restless striving of Americans and, despite misgivings, later resigned himself to the necessity of industry and cities. But his image of "those who labor in the earth" magnified to continental size the cardinal image of American aspirations (Marx, 1964: 124-144).

The Jeffersonian equation of virtue and agrarianism continued to fascinate Americans during the nineteenth century. For the Jacksonians, though they lived in the midst of an industrial revolution, "the real people" were farmers and planters, the mechanics and laborers—in short, the productive classes, in the peculiar Jacksonian meaning of the term. This "bone and sinew of the country" was simple and stable, self-reliant and independent, honest and plain-dealing. Andrew Jackson's America, as described in his first inaugural address, was a happy countryside of "flocks and herds and cultivated farms, worked in seasonal rhythm and linked in republican community" (Meyers, 1957: 24). Look toward the West if you seek examples to follow, urged a Fourth of July orator in 1831: "There we can behold how the young American grapples with the wilderness and thence we can return and imagine how our fathers lived" (Ward, 1955: 39). The Jacksonians, then, never reconciled themselves to economic change and urbanization, but instead seized the enchanting Jeffersonian version of an agrarian society just as it threatened to slip away. And as they attempted to restore the world they had lost, they breathed new life into the pastoral ideal (Peterson, 1960: 84-85).

The political potential of Jeffersonian agrarianism slowly petered out in the late nineteenth century. A brief revival of the radical side of the tradition accompanied the rise of Populism in the 1890s. But the exhaustion of creative potential in Jeffersonianism is nowhere more apparent than in the last few years of Tom Watson, an agrarian rebel whose only rest seemed to come when he was near the earth. The world of the twentieth century, however, would not yield to agrarian solutions, and Watson spent his last few years in his Georgia household, spying everywhere the shadow of the Pope and the conspiracy of the international Jew. This biographer of Jefferson ended his days by releasing much of the rural malice which found its vehicle in the Ku Klux Klan (Peterson, 1960: 256-258; Woodward, 1938: 346, 416-450). The vexations of a rural world in flux found an ethnic, urban focus in anti-Semitism; but as rural America was increasingly integrated into the national culture, even this last perversion of Jeffersonianism disappeared (Higham, 1966: 249-250). However important these political varieties of Jeffersonian agrarianism may have been, the more important version of pastoralism has been the domesticated rural ideal of the urban middle class. This domestic pastoral had its roots in the Romantic evaluation of rural life as the point of equilibrium between the wilderness and urban civilization. This revolution in understanding found its intellectual expression in Henry Thoreau's *Walden* (1854), its popular form in the landscapes of Thomas Cole, and its occasional realization in summers in the Adirondacks (Nash, 1967: 61-62, 78-83, 90-95). Comfortable urban dwellers hung the landscapes of Cole, Asher Durand, and Thomas Doughty over their fireplaces because they sought a tamed wilderness, scenes in which man and nature recovered a lost goodness (Miller, 1967: 180-181). And so the American wilderness entered the urban home just as urban homes invaded the rural landscape around Boston, New York, and Philadelphia.

We can see this ideological current at work by tracing the rise of a new domestic architecture and its use in early American suburbs. Andrew Jackson Downing (1815-1852) provides, in his architectural career, one way to lay bare the ideal image of American society implicit in these early suburban developments. Downing valued above all the tranquilizing effect of landscape, for "under its enchanting influence, the too great hustle and excitement of our commercial cities will be happily counter-balanced by the more elegant and quiet enjoyments of country life." What was needed was a domestic architecture of equipoise in order to assuage the effects of American urban life, an environment to serve "for a counterpoise to the great tendency towards constant change and the restless spirit of emigration." Unable to put down roots anywhere, the American needed, in Downing's estimation, "the security and repose of society, the love of home" so that his unsettling energies might be kept within bounds. Downing thus translated a widespread concern about the boundless energies of American character into a domestic architecture (Ward, 1969: 270-281). And it was this domestic architecture, scattered on the peripheries of growing American cities, which would define the new suburban dimension (Scully, 1953; 1955: 1-18, 71-90).

The garden suburb of the second half of the nineteenth century was the logical outcome of this domestication of nature. In Llewellyn Park, New Jersey (1853), in Lake Forest, Illinois (1857), in Riverside, Illinois (1969), in Shaker Heights, Ohio (1910), the mid-twentieth-century suburb had its origins (Reps, 1965: 339-348; Gowans, 1964: 309-315). What was there in these rural and open suburbs to provide a sense of life in man's world, an association of the feeling of art and community? "There wants to be something in a city that produces a sense of its being a world in itself," wrote the American theologian Horace Bushnell (1864: 313) as he wondered about the growth of cities at mid-century. Frederick Law Olmsted provided a distinctively American answer to the theologian's disturbed questioning, a response which signals the emergence of a characteristic urban community. The suburb was to exhibit, Olmsted wrote in his 1868 plan for Riverside, "in regard to those special features whereby the town is distinguished from the country . . . the greatest possible contrast which is compatible with the convenient communication and pleasant abode of a community." The essential feature of a suburb was domesticity; all other aspects of community life were subordinate to the "domestic indoor and outdoor private life" of the family (Sutton, 1971: 299-300, 303).

American images of the city, then, were rarely simply anti-urban. Rather they were a bridge, a middle ground between the wilderness and urban civilization. Only occasionally did this ideology animate a pure hatred of the city, as in the novels of Thomas Dixon, Jr. Author of *The Clansman* (1905), the novel which furnished the script for D. W. Griffith's "The Birth of a Nation" (1915), Dixon spent ten frustrating years as a Baptist minister in New York. "In the roar of this modern Babylon," cried this Jeremiah, "is religion increasing its hold on man?" No. So he fled, first to an "airy apartment," then to a suburb, on to a five-acre place on Staten Island, finally to a stately colonial manor 200 years old, from which he poured forth his wrath in popular racist novels (Dixon, 1896: 13, 1905: 1-8). The intractable urban world vexed his Protestant moral sensibilities, as it also irked Tom Watson, so he sought shelter in a rural bastion. But the more general outcome was the suburb, a new Arcadia, where, as a promoter observed in 1915, urban dwellers hoped "to obtain attractive homes at a modest cost, to get into the genuine unspoiled country, to take their own social life with them, to restore to the land its elemental charm" (Schmitt, 1969: 18). The dream had its roots in the ancient promise of the garden, where a fecund earth produced under the hand of an honest toiler. The persistent attempt to redeem this promise of plenitude mediated the American response to the city.

PROMISE OF PLENTY

This people of plenty held to a second promise, equally as important as their search for the garden. The self-made man, the mobile American, stood beside the yeoman farmer, a hero of iron will who reconciled Americans to the city's production of social inequalities. At first glance, this mythical representative of equality should have been an urban figure, and so he was in his first appearance. But the apostles of the self-made man made him also a vehicle for rural values, and therein lies his significance for our account of suburbanization. For as a repository of pastoral virtue, the American entrepreneur broadcast a profound distrust of the city. As this ideology trickled down into the ranks of businessmen and clerks after 1850, the American middle classes acquired a distinctly anti-urban attitude.

The roots of the nineteenth-century myth of the self-made man lie in the career of Benjamin Franklin. A provincial in colonial Philadelphia, Franklin was nevertheless practiced in the arts of urbanity. Here Franklin found, like James Boswell, another famous eighteenth-century provincial in the big city, "the satisfaction of pursuing whatever plan is most agreeable, without being known or looked at" (Boswell, 1950: 69). This was a world of voluntary association, in which the main problem was to prepare men "to enter the World, zealously unite, and make all the Interest there can be made to establish them" (Franklin, 1959: vol. 3, 400). When Franklin wrote this in 1749, the problematical shape of American character was already evident: the individual was not born to an identity, but had to create one for himself. Hence the various associations of Philadelphia were Franklin's life enlarged and extended; this extension and enlargement furnished the material for myth (Van Doren, 1938: 77-78). In a pamphlet published in 1751, "Idea of the English School," Franklin projected his own experience to continental size. After having described a thoroughly innovative curriculum for an urban school, Franklin concluded with a remarkable judgment on the probable effects of this education: "Thus instructed, Youth will come out of this school fitted for learning any Business, Calling or Profession" (Franklin, 1959: vol. 4, 108). Change in status and occupation, not continuity, seemed to Franklin the common experience. This emerging attitude reflects, as Bernard Bailyn (1960: 36) has noted, "the beginnings of a permanent motion within American society by which the continuity between generations was to be repeatedly broken."

The rise of the city and the spread of the factory, as we have already pointed out, were dissonant elements in this hopeful creed. To accommodate themselves to the troublesome new inequalities of industrial cities and to the threat of disorder, Americans supplied themselves with a conservative version of Franklin's promise of mobility. The exponents of self-improvement in the age of Jackson and Lincoln tried to balance traditional values and innovation. The status of rich or poor was impermanent, these apostles insisted; a mobile, freely competitive society would give every man an opportunity to rise to his merited status. But success also grew out of a man's moral character. The secrets of success lay in the practices of industry and economy and in following a simple maxim: spend less than you earn. The morally meritorious always succeeded, yet there were weaknesses in the creed. Luck sometimes played an embarrassingly large part in success, as in the novels of Horatio Alger. And even the most hidebound exponent of self-help admitted that environment and institutions helped men to succeed. The big emphasis, however, falls on the conservative function of the myth of the self-made man. The heroes achieve, but they achieve through fidelity to their employers and by acquisition of a middle-class competence (Cawelti, 1965: 46-55, 101-123; Thernstrom, 1964: 56, 66, 72-79).

The tensions of urban life, however, produced pressures on the middle class which led to a transformation of the self-help gospel. For one thing, as the editor of the *Nation* pointed out in 1865, the myth of the self-made man left no room for decorum and for the deference which successful men expected (Godkin, 1896: 42-43). The very honorific nature of status, the constant threat of loss as well as gain, induced the proponents of success to seek some means of consolidating their positions. But as the businessmen of the late nineteenth century flaunted symbols of success, they also brought down criticism for introducing the very emblems of the inequality which the mobility ideology was to efface (Kirkland, 1956: 29-49; Wyllie, 1954).

More importantly, the persistent tension between the ideals of frugality and abstinence, and the virtues of conspicuous consumption, both necessary to status in the city, led to a modification of the mobility ideology. A. D. Mayo captured this tension well in 1859:

> All the dangers of the town may be summed up in this: that here, withdrawn from the blessed influence of Nature, and set face to face against humanity, man loses his own nature and becomes a new and artificial creature—an inhuman cog in a social machinery that works like a fate, and cheats him of his true culture as a soul [Wohl, 1969: 106-107].

The tradition of rural virtue lay ready at hand to reclaim the urban dweller from his fate, and to accommodate him to life in the city. For the exponents of success, urban life appeared too complex, too difficult, too hazardous for Americans. So they adapted a rural tradition which would define an accommodation between the promise of success and the desire for order (Wohl, 1969: 110, 139, 155). Urban society was a neutral arena within which each individual was free to pursue the main chance, then, but it was also fraught with the tensions of individualism. Hence the society trumpeted rich and conspicuous success, but continued to yearn for a lost rural society in which the country boy made his way through a simple world (Williams, 1958: 325; Wohl, 1953: 394; Cawelti, 1965: 125-164).

Urbanization, mobility, migration—all these social developments left Americans with a deep sense of loss. There was no longer in New England, Charles Eliot Norton lamented in 1889, a "common stock of things taken for granted" (Solomon, 1956: 21). Rather the competition for prestige and success, a struggle symbolized in the

self-made man, had eroded social order. The status rivalries characteristic of late nineteenth-century society found a convenient vehicle
in anti-immigrant and anti-urban ideologies. Hence as the Irish and
Jews began to crowd the social ladder—to claim the dream of success
as their own—they suffered anti-Catholic and anti-Semitic outbreaks.
Americans expected immigrants to become Americans, but not too
fast (Higham, 1958: 151-152, 156, 1966: 243-246). The loss of
confidence which these status rivalries provoked, and the consequent
unleashing of anti-immigrant and anti-urban hysteria, reveal the
persistent tensions which American society could not overcome. The
vexations of an assertive society found an urban and ethnic focus in a
series of campaigns against the immigrants, from the American
Protective Association in the 1880s to the Immigration Restriction
League of the 1910s (Kinzer, 1964: 58, 80-84, 91-94, 180; Higham,
1963: 52-87, 158-186). One of the major sources of anti-urban
ideologies, then, has been the conflict induced by the rapid
assimilation of immigrant groups.

The clerks and stockboys of American cities dreamed of success,
but when they woke they began to flee the site of their success. The
urban origins of the self-made man wore off as the hidden costs of
mobility became obvious in the late nineteenth century. Success
became more and more closely linked to the preservation of an older,
simpler world, and many of the urban reform movements of the
1890s looked to the restoration of an agrarian society. We see again,
then, how the myth of rural virtue accommodated Americans to the
strange new world they were busily building in the city.

FAMILY LIFE AND SUBURBS

These images of the good life performed their conciliatory
function in the setting of middle-class households. Within the circle
of bourgeois family life, as Andrew Jackson Downing noticed, the
love of country was linked to the love of home. Whatever led a man
to assemble the comforts of rural life in his household also
strengthened the family. Here again we find the theme of restoration: "And as the first man was shut out from the *garden*, in the
cultivation of which no alloy was mixed with his happiness, the
desire to return to it seems to be implanted by nature, more or less

strongly, in every heart" (Downing, 1844: ix). The battle of life is carried on in the cities, where mobile men incessantly struggle to achieve the promises of success. But the temper of life, Downing wrote, "is, for the most part, fixed amid those communings with nature and the family, where individuality takes its most natural and strongest development." The family hearth must symbolize "the dearest affections and enjoyments of social life," where "that feverish unrest and want of balance between the desire and fulfillment of life, is calmed and adjusted by the pursuit of tastes which result in making a little world of the family home, where truthfulness, beauty and order have the largest dominion" (Downing, 1850: v-vi, 23). The suburban home was a refuge where the ambitious American could "keep alive his love for nature, till the time shall come when he shall have wrung out of the nervous hand of commerce enough means to enable him to realize his ideal of the 'retired life' of an American landed proprietor" (Downing, 1853: 111, 212).

"A little world of the family home," for the "retired life." These hopes would provoke contemptuous criticism a hundred years later, but, in the mid-nineteenth century, they expressed the triumph of the middle class. A confidence in the civilizing mission of the bourgeois home, the achievement of equipoise between the anti-institutionalism of American life and the widening compass of middle-class decorum signaled an important reorientation of American culture after 1850 (Elkins, 1959: 27-37; Higham, 1969; Fredrickson, 1965). And it was in the suburbs that this middle class pursued its need for a stable and organized environment.

The major problem, then, is to grasp the relationship between an emerging middle-class family and the cumulation of individual decisions which created the characteristic American suburb. In order to do this, we shall have to make a frankly speculative foray into the history of the American family. Since the American literature is thin, some of our material comes from the abundant writing on the English and French middle-class family. Nonetheless, this effort in hypothesis provides a crucial connection between the ideologies of pastoralism and romantic capitalism and their realization in the suburb.

The origins of the link between middle-class aspirations and the residential development of American families lies in the changing relationship between family and community. The boundaries between family and community in the eighteenth century were ill-defined, so there was no distinct sphere of family life. We can see this most clearly in the variety of communal sanctions against early marriage. A recent study of Andover, Massachusetts, furnished an extraordinary insight into the nature of communal controls on the life of the family (Greven, 1970: compare Demos, 1970; Laslett, 1965: 53-106). Greven shows that the first generation of settlers created a stable social order and established a patriarchal family system. The population of the town as a whole grew very rapidly during the first three generations. Husbands and wives lived together longer than they had in England and shared the responsibilities of parenthood well into old age. The survival of large numbers of their children into adulthood meant that they must have land and houses to establish households. The fathers accomplished this by delaying their granting of land to the sons until they were mature and well-established. Thus more than 25% of both the second and third generations married after thirty years of age. The stability of this kind of control over fertility depends, however, on the persistence of communal institutions. The fourth generation of Andover's population effectively subverted the whole system. The sons reached maturity sooner, married younger, established their independence more effectively and earlier in life, and migrated from the community much more frequently than earlier generations. Thus the small farmers of the 1750s had set into motion the same constant break in communal and generational links which Benjamin Franklin celebrated in Philadelphia. In the loosening of the ties binding men to their parents and to their families of origin, the fourth generation of Americans also broke communal controls over family life.

Before the industrial revolution, then, the community exercised sanctions over the family, while, during the nineteenth century, such social controls disappeared, and family limitation—a matter of personal decision—became much more common. The dramatic fall in the birth rate during the nineteenth century illustrated the effectiveness of family limitation. During the sixty years from 1830 to 1890, a very sharp reduction occurred in American fertility. The crude birth rate dropped from 50 to about 28 per thousand, and the death rate fell from about 25 to 15 per thousand. Thus, the annual rate of reproductive increase fell from 25 per thousand in 1830 to 13 per thousand in 1890. The rate of reproductive increase was, in short, cut in half. Thus Americans reduced their fertility by half in the space of two generations, and without the expensive appliance of modern birth control (Potter, 1965: 631-688).

The decisive fact in this remarkable fall in fertility was the emergence of the modern, middle-class family. In 1790, the mean size of American households was about 6.5 members; discounting slaves reduces the figure to 5.8. Not until the early years of the twentieth century does the size dip to 4.75 members, which was the average size of English households during the nineteenth century. Within the upper-income levels, however, the small modern family was making its appearance early in the nineteenth century. Rather than live in the large households which characterized American society before 1850, these affluent families were cutting themselves off from the world around them and gathering into isolated groups of parents and children. All the effort of these families was directed toward helping the children to rise in the world, individually and without any collective ambition for the household; the children, rather than the whole family, became the center of the household. At first, this type of family was limited to the merchant aristocracy, the middle class, and the richer artisans. In the mid-nineteenth century, a large section of the population, the poorest and biggest part, still lived in extended households under the old dependencies. But the fact remains that, by the end of the eighteenth century, the modern family had appeared, and it has changed very little since. The important change in the nineteenth century was the gradual extension of this modern form of household life to other social strata. Late marriage, the precariousness of employment, the difficulty of finding shelter, the mobility of laborers, and the continuation of the tradition of apprenticeship—all these were obstacles which the evolution of the family would eventually remove. So family life finally embraced nearly the whole of society, to such an extent that historians and sociologists have forgotten its middle-class origins (Ariès, 1962: 365-406; Carey, 1830: 456; Jaher, 1968: 205-208; Warner, 1968: 63-78).

But how does this transformation of family life affect the whole of society? A tentative answers lies in the outcome of the remarkable population debate of the nineteenth century. The population controversy in the nineteenth-century Atlantic community—first, the argument between Thomas Malthus and Richard Godwin, then the reopening of the argument by Francis Place in the 1820s—revealed an important practice of middle-class families, the delay of marriage until self-sufficiency was achieved. The parties to the population controversy were engaged chiefly in setting up the prudential behavior of the middle class as an ideal for the rest of society. In doing so, the exponents of bourgeois morality made into an explicit ethos what had been merely a practice. If a man's ambition is awakened, wrote an American moralist in the 1850s, "he will become prudent not only in his expenditures, but in contracting any relations which may become a burden to him . . . In a normal state, then, the inclination of people to marry is controlled by the opinion of the effect which marriage will have upon their position in life" (Bowen, 1850: 155-156). This calculation was directly linked to the structure of middle-class careers. Unlike the workingman, whose maximum earnings were reached in early adulthood, the middle-class father could anticipate a steady series of income increases at least until middle age. Postponement of marriage was necessary for four or five years, until the clerk or businessman was established, but then children came at a fairly rapid pace. Families continued to be fairly large, then, until the 1880s, when contraception began to be widely practiced (Himes, 1938: 209-285; Calhoun, 1965: 1-19, 178-197).

What provoked a search for a new setting for this emergent family life was the tension following the economic and social crises of the 1870s and 1880s. The burgeoning growth of American cities, the threatening expansion of ethnic groups into middle-class neighborhoods, and the sense of economic restriction furnished powerful motives for the attempt to assimilate the whole of society into the economy of bourgeois family life (Banks, 1954; Sennett, 1970a; Kennedy, 1971: 36-107). Middle-class family life became the model for a whole generation of urban reformers in their attempt to bring order into the formless cities of the nineteenth century. Temperance campaigns, charity organization, the standardization and integration of school systems and police forces all sprang from the attempt to uplift the "dangerous classes" into middle-class family life (Gusfield, 1963: 79, 85; Bremner, 1956: 31-66; Katz, 1968: 39-40. 91; Lane, 1967: 118-141). This steady enlargement of the area of family life created the characteristic domestic suburb of the late nineteenth and early twentieth century.

ANTI-URBAN IDEOLOGIES AND SUBURBANIZATION: A TRIAL BALANCE

The rural ideal and the pleasures of private family life—these were the two images which encouraged the middle class to build the modern suburb. Before the streetcar and the automobile, two houses, one in the city and one in the country, were necessary to realize the "retired life." But the streetcar and automobile suburbs opened up a whole continent to settlement by middle-class homesteads. New transportation technology enabled families to move beyond the old city into the countryside. The result of thousands of family decisions was a weave of small patterns which created the social geography of the modern city. The activities of middle-class householders and small lenders and builders shaped the metropolis into a discontinuous series of residential neighborhoods segregated by income and ethnic identity. The poor, the immigrants and the blacks inherited the inner city; the affluent and white dispersed throughout the residential suburbs (Warner, 1962; Schnore, 1965: 222-241, 255-272; Taeuber and Taeuber, 1965: 43-62). The logical outcome was a new creation, a city like Los Angeles, a metropolis which was, as a city planner gushed in 1930, "a federation of communities coordinated into a metropolis of sunlight and air." It was toward this ideal that American cities would move until, as another Angeleno hoped in 1910, the metropolis spread to meet the country, "until beautiful forms of urban life blend[ed] almost imperceptibly into beautiful forms of rural life" (Fogelson, 1967: 163).

What gave shape and meaning to this protean growth of the American city was the juncture of the powerful ideal of rural virtue and the growing vexation with the assertiveness of urban society. The rural ideal promised relief from the "rasp and graze of splintered/ normality," from the "clamors of collision." Though it was a dream more than a little false, the rural ideal recovered the link between pastoral and family life whose loss Americans had begun to mourn in the 1830s. Thus the movement outward of the middle class was not simply an escape from the city; it was more importantly an attempt to find a pleasing context in which to enjoy the newly discovered pleasures of family life. These pleasurable haunts of family life were continually disturbed, however, by another myth, that of the self-made, mobile American. A creature of nature and custom, so the parable went, found the rural world restrictive and left at the first chance for the city. But while he found success and approval, he was haunted by dreams of peace and wholeness which must, he imagined, have been realized somewhere in the past of the village. So the self-made American returned to the countryside in the suburb, where he could find solace in the delights of family and in the rhythms of nature.

When we discover what a tenuous balance Americans have struck between pastoral dreams and urban realities, it should come as no surprise to find a welter of anti-urban ideologies in American culture. Americans have associated virtue with nature, and freedom with open space. Their ideals of family life and individualism have seemed incompatible with the impersonal character of the new urban world. Hence, when urban problems have impinged too much upon their retreats, they have lashed out at the dangers and corruptions of the city in hundreds of reform campaigns. But these campaigns never approached the city as a functioning community, but rather as a collection of evils. These reform efforts, typically dominated by the older middle class, sought to forcibly uplift working-class urban dwellers to the level of 100% Americans (Hofstadter, 1955; Huthmacher, 1962). The older Americans, still enchanted by pastoral dreams, felt no need to accept the city and make it livable. Rather, they thought to make it over into the rural village of their memories.

While the charter Americans remained deeply distrustful of the city, a new group of Americans, especially from eastern and southern Europe, were coming to terms with their urban world. "We *had* to live in it," a second-generation immigrant wrote in 1930, "and learn what it chose to teach us" (Gold, 1930: 19). This the immigrants and their children were prepared to do, for their own cultures had a long tradition of viewing cities as the intellectual and cultural heart of their society, while simultaneously placing far less emphasis on rural life and individualism than did the Anglo-American community. Thus, these immigrants, in shaping a livable urban habitat, took the lead in organizing trade unions and in creating a welfare state. While accommodating themselves to the city in these ways, the immigrants, and especially their children, were also forging a new urban mass culture to meet the needs which their broken communal life could no longer fulfill (Higham, 1968; Holli, 1969: 157-181; Huthmacher, 1968; Juergens, 1966). In some measure, then, as John Higham (1968: 103) has recently written, these immigrants taught the older Americans how to live with the city. But before the new immigrants could fully overcome the handicaps of high-density living and develop its potentials, the centrifugal growth of the city was already assured (Warner, 1962).

Throughout the course of the twentieth century, numerous forces have interacted to push and pull immigrants from the communal life of their ethnic neighborhoods. In some measure, the desire of second and third generations of immigrants to assimilate into the mainstream of American culture resulted in their conscious loss of accent, a change of name, and residence outside their ethnic ghettos. More important to the demise of ethnic communities was the systematic development of public policy which encouraged suburban development while reaping havoc on inner-city neighborhoods. For example, Cleveland's rapid transit system, built in 1917 to shuttle the city's elite between downtown and the elegant suburban Shaker Heights, destroyed Slovak and Polish neighborhoods.

Urban renewal, beginning with the Housing Act of 1937, no doubt razed much slum housing that was in a condition of hopeless disrepair. But as the program gathered steam, after World War II, it bulldozed indiscriminately through neighborhoods which could easily have been rehabilitated, and even leveled areas with little substandard housing (Rossi and Dentler, 1961). And, more tragically, the urban renewal agency uprooted thousands of urban poor whose fondest possession was a sense of identity and belonging in their neighborhood (Gans, 1962). Later, the nation's multi-billion-dollar superhighway program gobbled up thousands of acres of inner-city land, shattering hundreds of neighborhoods.

Urban renewal and expressways are hardly the only public policies which have functioned to encourage suburbanization while destroying inner-city neighborhoods. It is more difficult to obtain a full FHA or VA mortgage in aging residential areas than for new suburban housing. Since the larger proportion of the full mortgage is interest, and, hence, tax deductible, millions of Americans have found it economically possible to buy in the suburbs where they could not afford comparable housing in the central city. Moreover, rehabilitation of inner-city housing is certain to bring an appraiser and result in higher taxes. While many suburbs have higher mean property taxes than the mean for their parent city, the balance of tax laws favors the choice of suburban housing rather than the purchase and rehabilitation of an older, central-city house.

To this must be added the large influx of blacks into the central cities. Prejudice and fear have unmistakably played a role in encouraging the exodus of whites from the central city, but, equally important, the decline of municipal services and the conscious neglect of deteriorating, absentee-owned rental property have taken a heavy toll. Those who chose to stay and protect their neighborhoods were fighting high odds against the encroachment of malignant urban decay.

In short, the complex maze of public policies, the influx of another wave of poor immigrants, and thousands of individual decisions militated against the maturation and preservation of community life in the inner cities. Those individuals and groups who sought to preserve their neighborhoods gradually learned it was easier to switch than fight.

Finally, we must remember that the dominant cultural ideology professed the virtue of the suburb as an ideal urban life style. This ideology not only encouraged the policies which resulted in centrifugal growth, but its final crushing blow was to enter the consciousness of immigrants who for one brief shining moment believed they were building their Camelot in the heart of the metropolis.

CONCLUSION

Perhaps the experience of the past two hundred years is sufficient to account for man's dislike of cities. We have attempted in this paper to sketch an argument for the proposition that dislike and distrust of urban life is as old as cities themselves. Whether further research will refute or reinforce this proposition, there can be little question of the persistence of anti-urbanism in the American experience. We have tried to trace some of the unique features of American culture which have reinforced this sentiment. Recently, the Gallup organization asked the American public "If you could live anywhere in the United States that you wanted to, would you prefer a city, suburban area, small town or farm?" (Gallup, 1972). Only thirteen percent responded that their ideal place to live would be the city. Of those who live in a city of a half-million or more, four out of five would prefer not to live in the city.

We have tried to trace some of the unique features of American culture which have contributed to this anti-urban sentiment. While there are objective reasons why large proportions of our population should not like cities, these are criss-crossed and reinforced by an underpinning of agrarian philosophy which, as it were, never gave the cities a chance. It is our view that cities have been the birthplace of nearly everything we value in human society, but if the city has been the liberator of man, this has not occurred without a heavy price.

And that price, reinforced by agrarian philosophy, lingers closer to human consciousness than the realization that cities have made men free.

Only a tiny proportion of elites have ever realized the potential of high-density living. But, for the most part, they developed that potential only for themselves. In some measure, late-arriving immigrants made their peace with the city and found it a good environment, but their romance with the city was short-lived, for they were powerless to fight the tide of exodus and the encroachment of decay. By the time planners and other visionaries realized the potential of a high-density core, their efforts were too little and too late to prevent the inevitable flow of population to the periphery of the metropolis. Little by little, the great old neighborhoods have been engulfed by the malignancy of urban decay. And every year more and more ideologically urbane give up their dream of a city where art, culture, and culinary delight are at their doorstep and join the army of commuters who seek the promised land in the suburbs.

Those who imagine the city as a high-density repository of culture, maximum opportunity, and the fulfillment of man's highest aspirations will not find their city in this century—at least not in the United States. We are becoming an urban civilization without cities. Our commitment to sprawl is irreversible in this century.

This sprawl is not so bad as some have tried to portray. It is not easy to find the ideal-typical suburb so vociferously portrayed by journalists and academics alike during the 1950s and 1960s. Suburbia, while highly segregated along marginally differentiated cost lines, is not one endless row of homogeneous, split-level traps inhabited by a conforming middle class that is hyperorganized and hypersociable. On the whole, they are less organized and less sociable than the high-density ethnic ghettos of the late nineteenth and early twentieth centuries. If there is excessive drinking, adultery, divorce, and mental illness in the suburbs, it is not easy to draw a causal link to suburbanization. The suburbs may not be the Buelah Lands many expected, but there can be no question that the overwhelming majority of suburbanites prefer being where they are to high-density city life. The expectations of many planners that large numbers of affluent suburbanites beyond the child-rearing age would return to luxury apartments in the central cities has simply not materialized. We are reshaping urban America in the form of suburban sprawl because this is what Americans want.

But what of the future? Suburbs, too, will grow old and decay. The tiny shopping centers conveniently scattered throughout the suburbs will become increasingly hard-pressed to stay alive in the face of growing competition from giant shopping malls. As this happens, we will be forced to spend more and more time on increasingly congested concrete arteries which are obsolete before completion. And, in the long run, it is questionable whether the decentralization of commerce and industry will reduce the time/ distance ratio of the journey to work. And what will be the long-range consequences of isolation in relatively homogeneous neighborhoods? Will people, as Richard Sennett (1970b) suggests, become less capable of coping with diversity and dissent in a pluralistic culture? Or is this just another shibboleth of a disheartened urbanist who grieves the passing of the city?

Perhaps there is no compelling reason for urban civilization to have high-density cores. We may succeed in suburbanizing fine restaurants, theatres, museums, orchestras, and professional athletics without destroying their vitality. And, in time, we may tear down those horribly decaying centers and make suburbs of them also (Banfield, 1970).

But if it is aimless nonsense to prolong nostalgia for the kind of city we have only imagined as we climbed Telegraph Hill, or strolled carelessly through the Vieux Carre, or whiled away a Sunday afternoon in Washington Square, it is also dangerous to fail to be hard-nosed about the long range implications of the new city we are creating. As individuals and as a society, we are captives of our images. Except for a small minority, our image of the high-density city has been negative. And now we are working at a frantic pace to create a new city on the fringe of the old. But we should recognize that the new creation is no more than a facsimile of what we had envisioned. What it will ultimately be is as problematic as the visionaries' image of a vertical city, which was never realized. But our new city most assuredly will come into full fruition. Suburbia is the new American frontier. We are too deeply committed to reverse the trend. But while we are completing the task, it is perhaps appropriate for some to ponder the question what happens next if we discover that the environment we have created has the advantages neither of urban nor of rural living, and the disadvantages of both?

NOTES

1. The concept "discontents of urban civilization" is taken from Irving Kristol (1970a). In an article, Kristol argues that it is the absence of human values which are appropriate and applicable to urban civilization that has created the "urban crisis." "The challenge to urban democracy," he writes, "is to evolve a set of values and a conception of democracy that can function as the equivalent of the 'republican morality' of yesteryear" (Kristol, 1970b: 47). In short, the urban crisis is essentially "a moral-philosophical one, and . . . it cannot be dealt with simply by a 'practical' pragmatic, matter-of-fact approach" (Kristol, 1970b). This is implicitly the argument of this paper.

2. This discussion is also informed by the writings of Kenneth Boulding. We view Boulding's (1956) proposal for a science of *eiconics* as substantially in the same genre of theoretical thought as developed by Berger and Luckmann (1966). The concept's meaning and image as used in this paper are essentially interchangeable.

3. The longest single passage on urban and nomadic life is in Volume 2 (1958: 233-307), but passing references to the character of men of the city and the country are scattered throughout the three volumes. See also Volume 1 (1958: 250-267, 308-310).

4. The literature on the emergence of cities in the Oriental world is sparse in comparison with that available for the Occidental world. We hesitate, at this point, to apply our argument to cities of the Far East, although there is evidence which tends to support both our assumptions and conclusions. For example, cities of the Shang Dynasty during the second millennium B.C. were politically organized as theocracies with a political order replacing kinship organization (Wheatley, 1971). Similarly, the evidence points to rigidly stratified social organization (Wright, 1967). But it is also clear that cities of the Orient were of a significantly different character from those which emerged in the West (Mote, 1970; Balazs, 1964). To conclude, either the presence or absence of anti-urbanism is premature.

5. Excerpts from this remarkable report are reprinted in Beatty and Johnson (1958: 534-543).

6. Charles Booth's first volume, which was thrice revised, on the social and economic conditions of London was published in 1889. The third edition of *Life and Labour in London* was 17 volumes (1902-1903). The materials cited here are from an edited volume of Booth's work (Fried and Elman, 1968).

REFERENCES

ARIES, P. (1962) Centuries of Childhood. New York: Alfred A. Knopf.

BAILYN, B. (1960) Education in the Forming of American Society. Chapel Hill: Univ. of North Carolina Press.

BALAZS, E. (1964) Chinese Civilization and Bureaucracy. New Haven, Conn.: Yale Univ. Press.

BANFIELD, E. C. (1970) The Unheavenly City. Boston: Little, Brown.

BANKS, J. A. (1954) Prosperity and Parenthood: A Study of Family Planning among the Victorian Middle Classes. London: Routledge & Kegan Paul.

BEATTY, J. L. and O. A. JOHNSON [eds.] (1958) Heritage of Western Civilization. Englewood Cliffs, N.J.: Prentice-Hall.

BERGER, P. L. and T. LUCKMANN (1966) The Social Construction of Reality. Garden City, N.Y.: Doubleday.

BOORSTIN, D. J. (1948) The Lost World of Thomas Jefferson. New York: Holt, Rinehart & Winston.

BOOTH, C. (1902-1903) Life and Labour of the People of London. London and New York: Macmillan.

——— (1889) Life and Labour of the People. London and Edinburgh: Williams & Norgate.

BOSWELL, J. (1950) London Journal, 1762-1763. New York: McGraw-Hill.

BOULDING, K. E. (1956) The Image. Ann Arbor: Univ. of Michigan Press.

BOWEN, F. (1856) The Principles of Political Economy. Boston: Little, Brown.

BREMNER, R. H. (1956) From the Depths: The Discovery of Poverty in the United States. New York: New York Univ. Press.

BUSHNELL, H. (1864) Work and Play; or Literary Varieties. New York: Harper.

CALHOUN, D. H. (1965) Professional Lives in America: Structure and Aspiration, 1750-1850. Cambridge, Mass.: Harvard Univ. Press.

CAREY, M. (1830) Miscellaneous Essays. Philadelphia: Carey & Hart.

CAWELTI, J. G. (1965) Apostles of the Self-Made Man. Chicago: Univ. of Chicago Press.

CHILDE, V. G. (1954) What Happened in History. Baltimore: Penguin.

——— (1950) "The urban revolution." Town Planning Rev. 21: 3-17.

COX, H. (1971) "The ungodly city: a theological response to Jacques Ellul." Commonweal (July 9): 351-357.

——— (1965) The Secular City. New York: Macmillan.

CREVECOEUR, J. H. J. (1912) Letters from an American Farmer. London: J. M. Dent.

DEMOS, J. (1970) A Little Commonwealth: Family Life in Plymouth Colony. New York: Oxford Univ. Press.

DIXON, T., Jr. (1905) The Life Worth Living: A Personal Experience. New York: Doubleday, Page.

——— (1896) The Failure of Protestantism in New York and its Causes. New York: Strauss & Rehn.

DOWNING, A. J. (1853) Rural Essays. New York: Leavitt & Allen.

——— (1850) The Architecture of Country Houses. New York: D. Appleton.

——— (1844) A Treatise on the Theory and Practice of Landscape Gardening. New York: Wiley & Putnam.

ELKINS, S. (1959) Slavery: A Problem in American Institutional and Intellectual Life. Chicago: Univ. of Chicago Press.

ELLUL, J. (1970) The Meaning of the City. Grand Rapids, Michigan: Eerdmans.

——— (1964) The Technological Society. New York: Alfred A. Knopf. (Originally published in French in 1954 as La Technique ou l'enjeu du siècle by Librairie Armand Colin.)

EMPSON, W. (1950) Some Versions of the Pastoral. London: Chatto & Windus.

ERICKSEN, E. G. (1954) Urban Behavior. New York: Macmillan.

EVERSLEY, D.E.C. (1965) "Population, economy and society," in D. V. Glass and D.E.C. Eversley (eds.) Population in History.

FOGELSON, R. M. (1967) The Fragmented Metropolis: Los Angeles 1850-1930. Cambridge, Mass.: Harvard Univ. Press.

FRANKLIN, B. (1959) Papers. New Haven, Conn.: Yale Univ. Press.

FREDRICKSON, G. (1965) The Inner Civil War: Northern Intellectuals and the Crisis of the Union. New York: Harper & Row.

FRIED, A. and R. M. ELMAN [eds.] (1968) Charles Booth's London. New York: Pantheon.

Gallup, G. and Associates (1972) "The Gallup poll." Washington Post (December 12).

GANS, H. J. (1962) The Urban Villagers. New York: Free Press.

GODKIN, E. L. (1896) Problems of Modern Democracy. New York: Charles Scribner's.

GOLD, M. (1930) Jews Without Money. London: N. Douglas.

GOWANS, A. (1964) Images of American Living: Four Centuries of Architecture and Furniture as Cultural Expression. Philadelphia: J. B. Lippincott.

GREVEN, P. J., Jr. (1970) Four Generations: Population, Land and Family in Colonial Andover, Massachusetts. Ithaca: Cornell Univ. Press.

GUSFIELD, J. R. (1963) Symbolic Crusade: Status Politics and the American Temperance Movement. Urbana: Univ. of Illinois Press.

HAMMOND, M. (1972) The City in the Ancient World. Cambridge, Mass.: Harvard Univ. Press.

HIGHAM, J. (1969) From Boundlessness to Consolidation: The Transformation of American Culture, 1848-1860. Ann Arbor: William L. Clements Library.

——— (1968) "Immigration," in C. V. Woodward (ed.) The Comparative Approach to American History. New York: Basic Books.

——— (1966) "American Anti-Semitism historically reconsidered," in M. H. Stember (ed.) Jews in the Mind of America. New York: Basic Books.

——— (1963) Strangers in the Land: Patterns of American Nativism, 1860-1925. New York: Atheneum.

——— (1958) "Another look at nativism." Catholic Historical Rev. 44: 147-158.

HIMES, N. E. (1938) Medical History of Contraception. Baltimore: Williams & Wilkins.

HOFSTADTER, R. (1955) The Age of Reform. New York: Alfred A. Knopf.

HOLLI, M. G. (1969) Reform in Detroit: Hazen S. Pingree and Urban Politics. New York: Oxford Univ. Press.

HUTHMACHER, J. J. (1968) Senator Robert F. Wagner and the Rise of Urban Liberalism. New York: Atheneum.

——— (1962) "Urban liberalism and the age of reform." Mississippi Valley Historical Rev. 49: 231-241.

JAHER, F. C. (1968) "The Boston Brahmins in the age of industrial capitalism," in The Age of Industrialism in America. New York: Free Press.

JEFFERSON, T. (1955) Notes on the State of Virginia. Chapel Hill: Univ. of North Carolina Press.

JUERGENS, G. (1966) Joseph Pulitzer and the New York World. Princeton: Princeton Univ. Press.

KATZ, M. (1968) The Irony of Early School Reform: Educational Innovation in Mid-Nineteenth Century Massachusetts. Cambridge, Mass.: Harvard Univ. Press.

KENNEDY, D. M. (1971) Birth Control in America: The Career of Margaret Sanger. New Haven, Conn.: Yale Univ. Press.

KHALDUN, I. (1969) The Maquaddimah. Princeton: Princeton Univ. Press.

KINZER, D. L. (1964) An Episode in Anti-Catholicism: The American Protective Association. Seattle: Univ. of Washington Press.

KIRKLAND, E. C. (1956) Dream and Thought in the Business Community, 1860-1900. Ithaca: Cornell Univ. Press.

KRISTOL, I. (1970a) "Urban civilization and its discontents." Commentary (July): 29-35.

——— (1970b) "Is the urban crisis real?" Commentary (November): 44-47.

LANE, R. (1967) Policing the City: Boston, 1821-1885. Cambridge, Mass.: Harvard Univ. Press.

LASLETT, P. (1965) The World We Have Lost. New York: Charles Scribner's.

MARX, L. (1964) The Machine in the Garden: Technology and the Pastoral Ideal in America. New York: Oxford Univ. Press.

MEYERS, M. (1957) The Jacksonian Persuasion: Politics and Belief. Stanford: Stanford Univ. Press.

MILLER, P. (1967) Nature's Nation. Cambridge, Mass.: Harvard Univ. Press.

MOTE, F. W. (1970) "The city in traditional Chinese civilization," in J.T.C. Liu and W. Tu (eds.) Traditional China. Englewood Cliffs, N.J.: Prentice-Hall.

MUMFORD, L. (1961) The City in History. New York: Harcourt, Brace & World.

NASH, R. (1967) Wilderness and the American Mind. New Haven, Conn.: Yale Univ. Press.

PETERSEN, W. (1960) "The demographic transition in the Netherlands." Amer. Soc. Rev. 25: 334-347.

PETERSON, M. D. (1960) The Jefferson Image in the American Mind. New York: Oxford Univ. Press.

PIRENNE, H. (1956) Medieval Cities. Garden City, N.Y.: Doubleday.

POTTER, J. (1965) "The growth of population in America, 1700-1860," in D. V. Glass and D.E.C. Eversley (eds.) Population in History. London: Arnold.

REPS, J. W. (1965) The Making of Urban America: A History of City Planning in the United States. Princeton: Princeton Univ. Press.

ROSSI, P. H. and R. A. DENTLER (1961) The Politics of Urban Renewal. New York: Free Press.

ROURKE, F. E. (1964) "Urbanism and American democracy." Ethics 74: 255-268.

SADLER, M. (1832) The Sadler Report, Report from the Committee on the Bill to Regulate the Labour of the Children in the Mills and Factories of the United Kingdom. London: House of Commons.

SCHMITT, P. J. (1969) Back to Nature: The Arcadian Myth in Urban America. New York: Oxford Univ. Press.

SCHNORE, L. F. (1965) The Urban Scene: Human Ecology and Demography. New York: Free Press.

SCULLY, V. J., Jr. (1955) The Shingle Style: Architectural Theory and Design from Richardson to the Origins of Wright. New Haven, Conn.: Yale Univ. Press.

——— (1953) "Romantic retionalism and the expression of structure in wood: Downing, Wheeler, Gardner, and the 'stick style'." Art Bull. 35: 121-142.

SENNETT, R. (1970a) Families Against the City: Middle Class Homes of Industrial Chicago, 1872-1890. Cambridge, Mass.: Harvard Univ. Press.

——— (1970b) The Uses of Disorder: Personal Identity and City Life. New York: Alfred A. Knopf.

SJOBERG, G. (1960) The Preindustrial City, Past and Present. New York: Free Press.

SMITH, H. N. (1950) Virgin Land: The American West as Symbol and Myth. Cambridge, Mass.: Harvard Univ. Press.

SOLOMON, B. M. (1956) Ancestors and Immigrants: A Changing New England Tradition. Cambridge, Mass.: Harvard Univ. Press.

SPENGLER, O. (1928) The Decline of the West. Volume 2 of Perspectives of World-History. New York: Alfred A. Knopf.

SUTTON, S. B. [ed.] (1971) Civilizing American Cities: A Selection of Frederick Law Olmsted's Writings on City Landscapes. Cambridge, Mass.: MIT Press.

TAEUBER, K. E. and A. F. TAEUBER (1965) Negroes in Cities: Residential Segregation and Neighborhood Change. Chicago: Aldine.

THERNSTROM, S. (1964) Poverty and Progress: Social Mobility in a Nineteenth-Century City. Cambridge, Mass.: Harvard Univ. Press.

VAN DOREN, C. (1938) Benjamin Franklin. New York: Viking.

WARD, J. W. (1969) Red, White and Blue: Men, Books and Ideas in American Culture. New York: Oxford Univ. Press.

——— (1955) Andrew Jackson: Symbol for an Age. New York: Oxford Univ. Press.

WARNER, S. B., Jr. (1968) The Private City: Philadelphia in Three Periods of its Growth. Philadelphia: Univ. of Pennsylvania Press.

——— (1962) Streetcar Suburbs: The Process of Growth in Boston, 1870-1900. Cambridge, Mass.: Harvard Univ. Press.

WHEATLEY, P. (1971) The Pivot of the Four Quarters: A Preliminary Inquiry into the Origins and Character of the Ancient Chinese City. Chicago: Aldine.

WHEELER, H. (1971) "The phenomenon of God." Center Magazine (March/April): 7-12.

WHITE, M. and L. WHITE (1962) The Intellectual Versus the City. Cambridge, Mass.: Harvard Univ. and MIT Presses.

WILLIAMS, R. (1958) Culture and Society, 1750-1950. New York: Columbia Univ. Press.

WOHL, R. R. (1969) "The 'country boy' myth and its place in American urban culture: the nineteenth-century contribution." Perspectives in Amer. History 3: 77-156.

––– (1953) "The rags to riches story: an episode of secular idealism," in R. Bendix and S. M. Lipset (eds.) Class, Status and Power. New York: Free Press.

WOODWARD, C. V. (1938) Tom Watson: Agrarian Rebel. New York: Macmillan.

WRIGHT, A. F. (1967) "Changan," in A. Toynbee (ed.) Cities of Destiny. New York: McGraw-Hill.

WYLLIE, I. G. (1954) The Self-Made Man in America: The Myth of Rags to Riches. New Brunswick, N.J.: Rutgers Univ. Press.

WILLIAM PETERSEN

THE IDEOLOGICAL ORIGINS OF BRITAIN'S NEW TOWNS

The notion that no solution to urban problems is possible within the framework of the metropolis and that, therefore, it must be sought through a mass transfer of large-city residents to small towns, is on the face of it unreasonable. The idea of New Towns, however, culminated a century of anti-urban writings, and after this ideological preparation even the Garden City struck Britons as good social policy.

It is difficult today to see the existence of the New Towns as problematic, to grasp the improbability that in something under half a century Ebenezer Howard's utopian proposal for the Garden City would blossom into full-fledged government policy. Much of the explanation may be found in the reaction against nineteenth-century industrial cities.

Ashworth has described how, with the growth of industrial cities, new problems arose or, by their great concentration in working-class urban quarters, were more clearly recognized. "Overcrowding and congestion, poverty, crime, ill health and heavy mortality were shown to be conditions commonly found together." Responding to the stimulus of an enlightened minority, the nation passed a series of precedent-breaking laws; but, despite these efforts, "mid-Victorian society as a whole never came within sight of overtaking those problems." A beginning of a more complete solution came only with the first Town Planning Act (1909), which was based on the premise that "suburbanization was to be the salvation of the town."

The type of town development which was chosen ... was in many ways curious for an urban nation. ... It was as though people ... had decided that they could

Journal of the American Institute of Planners, Vol. 34, No. 3 (May, 1968), 160–170. Copyright © 1968 by the American Institute of Planners. Reprinted by permission of the author and publisher.

be reconciled to an unavoidable urban existence only if ... their towns were made as untownlike as possible.[1]

The line of subsequent development, from the Garden City movement to the planned dispersal of sizable portions of Great Britain's metropolitan population, constitutes a major direction of British planning. There is, however, no clear, rational line from urban problems to this "solution." Although we can hardly be surprised that Victorian England's tradition of social reform should be continued in today's wealthier nation, with its more demanding populace and more egalitarian government, and that efforts to improve the environment have focused more and more on cities, now the home of most Britons, what demands explanation is that the government operates, at least in part, on the premise of the Garden City movement. Garden City planning, based on the postulate that urban problems are insoluble within the framework of the metropolis, in effect denotes *anti-city* planning. It is only in the context of a long ideological preparation that this extraordinary realization of the New Town myth could have been brought about.

Garden City: The Blueprint

A less prepossessing leader of a social movement than Ebenezer Howard could not be imagined.[2] Born in 1850, the son of a small shopkeeper, he started work as a clerk at fifteen and over the next six years drifted "from one insignificant job to another." Then he emigrated to the United States, acquired a homestead plot in Nebraska, tried to farm it, and ended up a "dismal failure." Five years later he was back in England, where he set up a business partnership, and failed again. Having learned shorthand, he then became a parliamentary reporter; and until the Garden City scheme brought him fame, an adequate income, and eventually even knighthood, he earned his living by this means. His avocation was mechanical invention; and in later years, when he could afford it, he usually employed a mechanic to work out his ideas in a small workshop. Though he was obsessed by his inventions, they brought in less money than they cost to develop. George Bernard Shaw, who was well disposed toward him,[3] said that Howard seemed to be an "elderly nobody, whom the Stock Exchange would have dismissed as a negligible crank." A nonconformist churchman, Howard moved in the earnest circles of religious enthusiasts, whose overlapping plans on how to conquer poverty and urban squalor were generally based on novel tax systems or the nationalization of land. The most important single literary influence was Bellamy's *Looking Backward*, which Howard tells us he "swallowed whole."

In his Garden City concept, originally published in 1898, Howard offered a means of achieving what he termed "a healthy, natural, and economic combination of town and country life." He provided an illustrative example, an ideal community with two interacting portions—a town of 30,000 built on 1,000 acres, and a surrounding agricultural belt of 5,000 acres with a population of some 2,000. Since the farmer has a market at his doorstep and can thus eliminate the costs of transportation and the profits of middlemen, and since the town's refuse can be used to fertilize the agricultural land, the farmer will prosper greatly, not only competing successfully with the extensive grain agriculture of America and Russia but possibly even growing under glass such exotic products as tea and coffee, spices, tropical fruits, and sugar.

In a diagrammatic form, the town is a circle a mile and a half across, transgressed by "six magnificent boulevards," but very little of its design is spelled out. The physical layout is starkly schematic, and the social structure reflects all too clearly the author's life experience. There is a long discussion, for instance, of how the number of retail shops might be limited to avoid wasteful competition; there is some earnest reflection on temperance reform. The town's basic economy, on the other hand, is covered by a mere listing of "factories, warehouses, dairies, markets, coal yards, timber yards, etc., all fronting on the circle railway which encompasses the whole town." Similarly, the population of the town is "engaged in various trades, callings, and professions."

The most detailed analysis in Howard's book is of the new community's finances. The whole scheme was based on the premise that the town was to be built on land "at present purely agricultural"; and as commercial developers everywhere know, farmland is a bargain when it is converted to urban uses. In Howard's ideal community, moreover, some of the costs of social welfare were to be eliminated by offering private "charitable and philanthropic institutions" the opportunity of establishing themselves "in an open healthy district." As a consequence of these several types of saving, Howard estimated that the resident of the Garden City would have to pay an average of only £ 2 annually both in rent to the municipality, which was to be the sole owner of the land, and in local taxes.

The abstract formulas of nineteenth-century visionary groups, many of which combined nonconformist religion with anti-urban populism in a recipe reminiscent of Howard's, were tested in the utopian oases that spattered the countryside of New England, New York State, and parts of the Midwest.[4] Actually to have founded two Garden Cities did not distinguish Howard's group from its humdrum predecessors; in retrospect, Letchworth and Welwyn are disproportionately important only as the prototypes of New Towns. During its first year, the company formed to build Letchworth was unable to sell enough shares even to cover the cost of the site, so that the construction was paid out of mortgages, which entailed heavy interest and administrative expenses. The original shareholders waited twenty years for their promised 5 percent dividend. The financing of Welwyn Garden City was also based less on business investment than the support of well-to-do ideologues, and even so this second project had to be rescued by a grant from the government. The workers' cottages built by the Letchworth company had to be leased for rents that the lowest paid laborers could not afford, so that this social class, whose amelioration had constituted a telling argument for the whole scheme, could be accommodated only after the district council was induced to use the better credit facilities of a public authority.[5] The commercialization of the first Garden City was finally averted only in 1962, by public acquisition.[6]

Though he does not spell out the contention, Howard suggests that he envisaged the Garden City not merely as an alternative to metropolitan living but ultimately as a substitute for it. "There should be an earnest attempt to organize a migratory movement of population from our overcrowded centers to sparsely settled rural districts," beginning slowly so as to avoid unnecessary difficulties but then gathering momentum under government sponsorship. In his view, this movement would soon begin to feed itself: as some leave the city, its "ground values will fall enormously," making necessary an increase in municipal taxes, which will induce still others to move out. Ultimately, the former city will be emptied over large areas, which can then be torn down and converted into parks.

The social values that derive from urban concentration (if indeed in Howard's view there are such values) would be preserved by the planning and building of "town clusters." "For administrative purposes there would be *two* cities [or more]; but the inhabitants of the one could reach the other in a very few minutes, . . . and thus the people of the two towns would in reality represent one community." But presumably many will use the easy access so provided as a means of commutation, in which case the Garden City will not be a tiny self-contained social-economic unit but the residential suburb of a metropolitan center.[7] Even at that time this seems to have been the relation between Adelaide and North Adelaide, the Australian communities Howard cited as an example of a town cluster. A functional unification of several towns with their continued separation "for administrative purposes" curiously reverses the correct statement of the issue. "The major problem was, and still is, to transform the limited corporate jurisdictions of cities like London, Liverpool, Manchester, and Birmingham into more efficiently organized metropolitan regions."[8]

Initially no component of the developing Labor Party, neither trade unionists nor London intellectuals, responded favorably to the petty bourgeois ideals of a visionary stenographer. Apart from Shaw, already mentioned, and Raymond Unwin, who wrote a Fabian tract on country cottages, the Fabians were hostile or, more often, indifferent. Thus Howard's future seemed to lie with the neglected utopian writers. Instead, as Mumford wrote in the introduction to *Garden Cities,* this "has done more than any other single book to guide the modern town-planning movement and to alter its objectives." This judgment comes from a zealous proponent of Howard's ideas, but so forthright an adversary as Jane Jacobs, for instance, has the same opinion of his importance.[9]

Howard's support came from associates and successors, such as Lewis Mumford, Patrick Geddes, and Frederic Osborn, and from the Town and Country Planning Association, scarcely the model of an efficient pressure group. From its inception the Association was hampered—or should have been—by the basic contradictions built into its structure and functioning. The Association spoke in the name of the urban poor, but its membership was drawn from the comfortable middle class. It professed humanist ideals and extolled the virtues of totalitarian planning in the Soviet Union. Supposedly an organization fostering democracy, it appealed neither to the mass of the electorate nor even to political parties, but exclusively to what

Frederic Osborn, as Howard's successor in the movement, termed "influential people." Allegedly speaking for greater social efficiency, it nevertheless consisttently deprecated cost as one criterion of feasible reform.[10]

Why has Britain, a nation whose greatness resides in her cities, accepted the thesis that to solve urban problems the state must move city people to small towns? Since the Garden City movement alone was not effective enough to bring about this improbable conversion, the explanation must be that England's educated classes, the planners and legislators who made the key decisions realizing this policy, were influenced by a century of anti-urban animus. The literary works that Englishmen study in school and, as adults, read for pleasure, almost all speak with one voice, saying that cities are evil. From the beginning of the nineteenth century, while Britain grew great from her cities and industry, her poets, novelists, and essayists pictured this development as a deterioration from a preindustrial golden age.

On the Myth of Victorian Smugness

The characterization of Victoria's England as a land of certainty and self-assurance, which is no longer taken seriously among specialists in the period, remains an enduring folk belief. The post-1914 critics of their Victorian forefathers were so busy uncovering the false notes in pomp and circumstance marches that they often overlooked the fact that their denigration of Victorian society merely echoed the dominant mood of Victorian letters, and even the inner voice of some of the minority that were outwardly in tune with their time. Even planners, whose social view derives in part from earlier social critics, are probably seldom aware that they are in the conformist mainstream of English intellectual history, legitimate heirs to the greatest nineteenth-century writers.

It is true that such types as Andrew Ure carved their niche in history books by a fatuous defense of indefensible elements in early English industrialization; and there were, later and more importantly, men like Joseph Chamberlain, who as mayor of Birmingham was proud of his city and its achievements.[11] But if we try to substantiate the notion of a self-satisfied century from the works of men whose names we remember without the promptings of specialized historians, we must also come to doubt the validity of the stereotype. In any list of optimists, the first name that comes to mind is likely to be Macaulay's. But like such other early Victorians as Disraeli and John Stuart Mill, Macaulay spoke with a public voice expressing belief while his private one in letters or diaries expressed doubt. Around 1830 the best writers were struggling to maintain their optimistic faith, but by the end of the century the pessimistic, subjective, relativist, and detached view also emerged as the dominant public voice.[12]

If, nevertheless, we count Macaulay as an optimist, who could be added to him in order to support the stereotype of a self-satisfied age? T. H. Huxley's virtually one-man campaign on behalf of Darwin's new biology and against its belittlers reflected the optimism that the prowess of science can engender. Walter Bagehot was more than a bit complacent about the stable society he saw in middle class England, which he analyzed in a modern style. Among novelists, George Eliot (also a "modern") most clearly had the same brand of cool detachment; the half-nostalgic attachment to the rural past in *Adam Bede,* her first extended work of fiction, disappeared from her mature works, which reflected a rare objectivity based on a wide-ranging erudition.

Other seeming examples of Victorian smugness, however, do not really validate the stereotype. The Manchester economists defended the status quo with such pervasive gloom that their discipline came universally to be known by Carlyle's famous epithet, "the dismal science." Herbert Spencer, in spite of his doctrine of progress, was too much the anarchist, too restive with what he termed "the coming slavery," to be an effective advocate of his time. In some of his writings Bentham might fit the optimistic pattern if he were altogether a nineteenth-century figure; but then not all the utilitarians would, and in particular, as we shall note, not John Stuart Mill. Among the writers of belles lettres, one thinks of Browning, whose best remembered line may be "God's in his heaven—all's right with the world!" But those who cite this as the *reductio ad absurdum* of Victorian fatuity forget that this refrain was intended to reflect not a just opinion but Pippa's childlike naïveté, and that Browning's compromise with his real world covered over, or rather did not quite cover over, a great conflict of conscience.[13] And Tennyson, perhaps the most representative poet of Victorian England, had little of the supposedly typical pride in the age's economic and scientific progress. "The Tennysonian theme is frustration, and his poetry offers an analysis of its symptoms rather than the cure."[14]

Contrasted with the list headed by Macaulay, however one expands it, is the main body of English intellectuals, from the Romantics at the beginning of the century to the Victorians and beyond, from Coleridge to Matthew Arnold to today's angry young men; encompassing the full political range from Marx to Carlyle; including poets and essayists, historians and novelists. Almost all rejected, either *in toto* or in some decisive part, the democratic urban-industrial society that developed in nineteenth-century England. An era that made it possible, for the first time in history, to conquer early death has been condemned for its lack of sanitation. An era during which literacy and suffrage first became universal has been condemned for its sharpened class relations. An era that produced a hundred years' peace from 1815 to 1914—a phenomenon unheard of in the annals of Western civilization—has been denounced for "the resurgence of economic nationalism and national imperialism," for being the "seed-time of totalitarian nationalism."[15]

Some English intellectuals of the nineteenth century were "democrats" (a new word then), who celebrated the broadening of the political base in America and France, and then in England; others, conservatives, defended traditional society and criticized the premises of democratic theory. But almost all reacted negatively to perhaps the greatest of the revolutions of the time, the establishment of England's urban-industrial society. Over the whole range of English public opinion, the rise of smoking factories and the congregation of large numbers in cities were seen as cancerous. Thus, some of the major themes of nineteenth-century letters, developed for their own sake, in various ways implicitly identified urban with evil. The most obvious instance, perhaps, is Wordsworth's veneration of "nature," and the discussion of how this relates to our theme leads into an analysis of the "community," as man's "natural" abode.

Nature v. the City

The theme of the nature poets most directly relevant to this topic is William Cowper's maxim, "God made the country, and man made the town." The meaning that the Romantics gave "nature" was not limited, of course, to denigration of the city, but other themes fitted in with this. Wordsworth's "mystical faith in the goodness of nature," his "diffidence in repect of the merely intellectual processes of the mind," his "trust in the good that may accrue to man from the cultivation of his sense and feelings,"[16] can be matched with other nineteenth-century examples. Thus, every "companion" of St. George's Company, Ruskin's private organization of men of "Rousseauian" goodwill, had to sign an eight-point creed, of which the second article asserted his naïve trust in "the nobleness of human nature, the majesty of its faculties, the fullness of its mercy, and the joy of its love." For Hazlitt, as another instance, nature was simply "company enough"; he derived satisfaction from looking out a window or from his broccoli plants and kidney beans. In Wordsworth, our prime example, the contrast between "nature" and the city is constant. In an atypical mood, he exclaimed that "earth has not anything to show more fair" than a fine London morning ("Composed upon Westminster Bridge"). More usually, he glorified nature by pointing to the city's "lonely rooms" ("Tintern Abbey"), "turbulent world" ("Prelude"), and "trivial pomp" ("Blest Is"). He congratulates Coleridge on the fact that though "reared in the great city," he had "long desired to serve in Nature's temple" ("Prelude"). Love cannot exist "among the close and overcrowded haunts of cities, where the human heart is sick" ("Prelude"); for the city has turned to false gods—"rapine, avarice, expense"—and "plain living and high thinking are no more" ("London, 1802").

In other contexts the "nature" of the Romantics transcended physical reality altogether. Indeed, some assert that this is the essence of the movement: "Romantic literature is a dream-picture of life, providing sustenance and fulfillment for impulses cramped by society or reality."[17] In this more complex variant, "nature" exemplifies critics' generalizations that the yearning of all the major Romantics "to lose identity must have arisen from common distaste for their identities,"[18] and that nineteenth-century poetry in general "was characteristically preoccupied with the creation of a dream-world."[19] "Nature" in this sense was like medievalism or the romanticized Middle East—another vehicle to escape from nineteenth-century England.

If for Wordsworth and the Romantics generally "nature" was often an escape from reality, it is also true that this was too elementary a device to survive unscathed beyond the Romantic period. The point is neatly made by comparing several of Wordsworth's compositions with parallel poems of Matthew Arnold, where the same theme is used to give a new meaning. For example, in both Wordsworth's "Tintern Abbey" and Arnold's "Resignation," the scene is the Lake Country, the situation is a mature poet's discourse to his sister. Wordsworth's poet, "a worshiper of Nature," voices his simple creed: "Nature never did betray the heart that loved her." But for a Victorian intellectual, this is *too* simple. In Arnold's poem "an emotional faith in Nature is qualified by the wider intellectual view afforded by scientific skepticism, historicism, and 'Culture.'"[20]

But not all of the impact of the nature poets' doctrine was dissipated; it was given some permanence by the practice of fashioning new meanings for some of the key words at issue. The meaning of *nature* in Wordsworth is rather clearcut; it is the antithesis of towns, of science and arts, of books, of man and things man-made. It is essentially, but not merely, a synonym for *rural* or *rustic;* and though this usage is not logically rigorous, it is not wholly objectionable. The primary meaning of *nature* for the Romantics was the countryside—the opposite of the city. Villages, country lanes, and lakes were good because they were "natural," all that there is (or ought to be), and in accord with "human nature."

Community

The *natural* man lives in a functionally integrated societal unit called a *community*. In one sense, Robert Nisbet is correct in asserting that "the quest for community" is a fashionable pastime of the modern age,[21] but the search has been for a number of contradictory values and on the part of social thinkers who in fact agreed on little or nothing. Marx and, in some contexts, Engels seemed to view capitalist society as a disorganized interregnum between the feudal community of the past and the socialist community of the inevitable future. Sociological theory, both in its nineteenth-century beginnings and its present-day ramifications, is typically based on one or another paraphrase of the thesis that human life, once integrated in a familylike *Gemeinschaft* (or community), has increasingly degenerated into a corporationlike *Gesellschaft* (or society). Not surprisingly, several versions of the same theme have been current in the writings of English literati.

The fascination with medieval life in much nineteenth-century poetry and fiction exemplifies this manner of thinking. To seek new roots in the past can be an attempt to escape from the present, or to understand it, or to refashion it after different models. Just as the eighteenth-century *philosophes* leaped over the Christian era and derived new moral guidance from the Stoics, so a surprising range of nineteenth-century intellectuals tried to ignore the Enlightenment and to revivify the Schoolmen. Cobbett, for example, for all his idiosyncracies and biases, might seem to be the pinnacle of British common sense; his usual norm was "the England into which I was born." Yet according to Raymond Williams, Cobbett was "responsible for a large share of the idealization of the Middle Ages": his *History of the Protestant Reformation*, which was mainly based on a single Catholic source, had "a huge circulation."[22] Coleridge, in many respects the antithesis of Cobbett, was far more important in reviving medieval ideas. He early suspected that the Dark Ages were less dark than they had been pictured. On reading Duns Scotus, he wrote to Southey: "I mean to set the poor old Gemman [gentleman] on his feet again; and in order to wake him out of his present lethargy, I am burning Locke, Hume, and Hobbes under his nose."[23] For Coleridge, the attraction of the Middle Ages was the institutional arrangement of feudalism. The purposes of the state, he wrote in "A Lay Sermon," should be wholly parallel to those of agriculture. A true gentleman is less interested in his marketable produce than in the rural population serving him—"I mean a healthful, callous-handed, but high and warm-hearted tenantry, twice the number of the present landless, parish-paid laborers, and ready to march off at the first call to their country with a son of house at their head." Land should be held on the feudal system, as a trust in return for the performance of duties associated with one's office. The "sound conception of the right to property" implies and demands "the performance of commensurate duties"—each different according to one's station in life.[24]

While the defense of medievalism can be followed in the writings of many nineteenth-century conservatives, it is more striking when one finds it, or a close approximation, in the writings of those otherwise opposed to the Coleridge tradition. If one had to choose a representative liberal work of the mid-nineteenth century, one might select John Stuart Mill's *On Liberty,* yet Mill was much in sympathy with Coleridge's type of conservatism in the early and again in the latter portion of his life. Bentham represented for him, he wrote, an important partial truth, to which the "Germano-Coleridgian doctrine" was a useful reaction, "less extreme" than the utilitarian view it opposed. "These two sorts of men, who seem to be, and believe themselves to be, enemies, are in reality allies," so that "an enlightened Radical or Liberal ought to rejoice over such a Conservative as Coleridge." Coleridge is to be honored, first, for his support of religion; second, for having vindicated "the principle of an endowed class, for the cultivation of learning, and for diffusing its results among the community."

Perhaps, however, the greatest service which Coleridge has rendered to politics in his capacity of a conservative philosopher ... is in reviving the idea of a *trust* inherent in landed property. The land, the gift of nature, the source of subsistence to all, and the foundation of everything that influences our physical well-being, cannot be considered a subject of *property* in the same absolute sense in which men are deemed proprietors of that which no one has any interest in but themselves —that which they have actually called into existence by their own bodily exertion.[25]

Is it too much to contend that one route to the twentieth-century Labor Party's demand that land be nationalized, as contained in such documents as the Uthwatt Report, lay from Duns Scotus, to Coleridge, to Mill after his "mental crisis," to his present-day admirers?

The Influence of Kingsley and Ruskin

In the atmosphere of revivified Anglo-Catholicism in Victorian England, one might have expected such echoes of Coleridge as Keble's description of the nation as "by Mammon's touch new molded o'er and o'er," or Pusey's expression of his "acute distaste for the social atmosphere of towns."[26] These were the so-called "Tracts for the Times," but neither the Tractarians who wrote them nor most of the Christian Socialists worked out a substitute for the liberal capitalism that they rejected which was more definite than Maurice's "assertion of God's order." Of the proponents of the movement that did specify their Christian purpose, the most influential acquired the epithet "muscular Christianity."[27] The most interesting proponent of this school of thought was Charles Kingsley. A theologian, the author of execrable poetry and moralizing novels hardly readable today, Kingsley was a paradoxical combination, strange even by the standards of Victorian noncon-formity. By the end of his life he was for feudalism in its full sense, with every tenant bound to his landlord and every social being responsible to his superior in a fixed hierarchical order. Yet in some facets of his thought he was more "modern" than his companions in the movement, or even than the secularist reformers of his day.

In "Great Cities and Their Influence for Good and Evil," originally a lecture delivered in 1857, Kingsley set forth an "idea of something like the Garden City movement of the present century."[28] "The social state of a city depends directly on its moral state," he asserted, which in turn depends largely "on the physical state of that city; on the food, water, air, and lodging of its inhabitants." When pestilence used to strike "the jolly city," the inhabitants fasted and prayed, but in vain. Pestilence was truly a judgment of God, but they failed to see what it was God was judging: "foul air, foul water, unclean backyards, stifling attics, houses hanging over the narrow street till light and air were alike shut out." Drunkenness, similarly, is not "a cause of evil, but an effect," brought about mainly by "bad air and bad lodging."

Reformatories, ragged schools, even hospitals and asylums, treat only the symptoms, not the actual causes, of the disease; and the causes are only to be touched by im-proving the simple physical conditions of the class; by abolishing foul air, foul water, foul lodging, overcrowded dwellings, in which morality is difficult and com-mon decency impossible. You may breed a pig in a sty, ladies and gentlemen, and make a learned pig of him, after all; but you cannot breed a man in a sty, and make a learned man of him; or indeed, in the true sense of that great word, a man at all.[29]

This is the faith not so much of a Christian moralist as of a human ecologist. The Chicago sociologists of the interwar decades elaborated on this thesis in a series of classic works, but even they seldom put forward in such forcefully direct language the postulate that all of man, his spiritual as well as his physical well-being, is a direct and simple function of this habitat.

The same ideas were advocated by the medievalist-socialist, William Morris. "As a Socialist, he worked for the future, but his heart was in the past. He both advocated revolution and founded the Society for the Protection of Ancient Buildings."[30] This link between past and future was most clearly manifested in Morris' two utopian novels, *The Dream of John Ball* (1887) and *News from No-*

where (1890), both written originally for publication in *Commonweal*, the journal of Morris' Socialist League. According to a progressive critic of the 1930's,

> it is astonishing ... how Morris's picture corresponds to the indications given by Marx on the *Gotha Program*, and even anticipates some of the features already beginning to show themselves in embryo in the present transition to socialism in Soviet Russia.[31]

The implication that Morris would have supported the country of hyperrapid industrialization through Stalin's five-year plans is, of course, nonsense; but it is at least arguable that Marx's vision of the future socialist society, to the degree that we can decipher it from his scanty allusions, has important parallels with that of all the intellectuals, left or right, who attacked commercialism and profit-mongering, and all who sought to rescue individuals from urban alienation by refashioning them into a stronger community.

The theme of medievalist socialism was expounded in greater and more influential ramifications by John Ruskin, who is one of the key persons in the argument of this paper. His ideal society, which would assure "honest production and just distribution," was to be led by three estates: at the top, landowners; then merchants and manufacturers; and then "scholars and artists," equivalent to Coleridge's "clerisy." All would be educated by the state and employed by it as civil servants. Below these would be the skilled workers, organized in "guilds,"[32] and below them a class performing the "necessary inferior labor." Such a society would rest "upon a foundation of eternal law, which nothing can alter nor overthrow."[33]

Ruskin's hatred of the city was expressed in very forceful language. "The great cities of the earth ... have become loathsome centers of fornication and covetousness, the smoke of their sin going up into the face of Heaven like the furnace of Sodom." The main reason for the low state of the arts is "the hot fermentation and unwholesome secrecy of the population crowded into large cities. ... The resulting modes of mental ruin and distress are continually new; and in a certain sense, worth study in their monstrosity." "There is some excuse, indeed, for the pathologic labor of the modern novelist in the fact that he cannot easily, in a city population, find a healthy mind to vivisect." The influence even of Paris on the young would-be artist is deleterious, for there "no purity of nature is accessible, but only a terrible picturesqueness, mingled with ghastly, with ludicrous, with base concomitants." Even architects "ought not to live in our cities," whose "miserable walls brick up to death men's imaginations." Send the architect rather "to our hills, and let him study there what nature understands by a buttress, and what by a dome." Indeed, a good citizen will not only refuse to live in a city but will not even visit it.[34]

Ruskin's extensive influence[35] can be inferred from two essays defending his views, one by J. A. Hobson, the left-liberal author of *Imperialism*, on which Lenin based his better known work of the same title, and the other by Patrick Geddes, whom city planners still respectfully cite as one of their pioneer thinkers.[36] Both point out that his ideas were superior to the main body of nineteenth-century economic theory, which in Geddes' view was "little better than an air-castle of medieval metaphysics, collapsing at [Ruskin's] slightest breath of scientific criticism." The trouble with orthodox economists, by this view, is that they study the production and consumption of commodities in relation to the market, with no attention to such products with "intrinsic value" as, to cite Ruskin's examples, a sheaf of wheat, a cubic foot of pure air, and a cluster of flowers. In Hobson's exegesis—

Capitalism would be able to maintain its worst tyranny, that of subdivided and dehumanizing toil, by concessions as liberal as they had to be upon the wages question. This, Ruskin clearly saw, would in itself be no solution of the social problem. It would leave degraded human beings with more money to apply to the satisfaction of degraded tastes. The whole problem of luxury or bad wealth, "illth," would remain unsolved.[37]

Liberalism, Conservatism, and Social Conscience

Principled proponents of "the community," especially when this was identified with some more or less fanciful reconstruction of the rigidly structured social unit of the Middle Ages, would hardly be likely also to advocate democracy; or so one might suppose. Actually, many of the intellectuals associated with either political orientation were ambivalent about the extension of the suffrage to the rapidly growing urban mass. Some of those on "the right" supported "progressive" measures, either on principle or in order to give the Conservative Party a broader electoral appeal; and some on "the left" derived their social norms, as we have seen, from medieval models.

This confusion in social values was reflected in the fundamental change in meaning of both party names. Take, for example, the word *liberal*. In its original connotation, *Liberalism* indicated an advocacy of freedom from the bonds of the mercantilist state and the fully established church. But the lack of state control came to be seen as discriminatory against those classes unable to take advantage of their freedom, and such mid-century Liberals as T. H. Green began to advocate a fundamental shift in ideology. When he argued for universal suffrage, he was extending earlier Liberal principles, but when he fought for the full protection of factory workers or for a preliminary version of the welfare state, the link is rather to twentieth-century liberals (for convenience, with a small initial letter), who are defined first of all by their demand for broader and deeper state intervention in all social processes. As one of the men who initiated this change in English Liberalism, Green derived some of his philosophical underpinnings from Burke and "the Germano-Coleridgian school," and on the other hand he attacked such typical progenitors of progressive thought as Locke, Rousseau, Spencer, and Bentham.[38] The break with classical Liberal thought was made, in other words, by appealing in a new perspective to Conservative authorities.

It is no easier to classify a *conservative*. By one frequent criterion in the late eighteenth or the nineteenth century—one's attitude toward the French Revolution—Edmund Burke was the forefather of all modern conservatives. This simple equation, however, did not apply to Green or to many other individuals: for the French Revolution, a complex entity from which arose much of the modern impulse to nationalism, militarism, and terrorism as well as *liberté, egalité et fraternité,* cannot be an efficient litmus to measure subsequent political opinions. A second index of classical conservative thought was the thesis that the class structure is immutable, so that efforts to change it will benefit no one but only harm the good society; thus, poverty is like death, an unpleasant fact but a fact, a permanent element of the human condition. What Burke saw as new was not the misery of the poor but the unreasonable reaction to this misery, the neglect of the principle than an orderly society is founded on the interdependence, and thus the cooperation, between the rich and the poor.[39] This prime tenet of the old conservatism, that poverty is inevitable, virtually disappeared during the nineteenth century; political spokesmen promised a better living for all and advocated policies supposedly designed to bring it about.[40]

It is obvious, despite the above, that the complexity and variety of nineteenth-century English politics cannot be encompassed in any dichotomous classification. This is especially so since the opposition between Liberal and Conservative in a narrow political sense was established in large part by the struggle to repeal the Corn Law, which protected English agriculture with tariffs that raised the price of food for the urban population. Richard Cobden and John Bright, the two principal leaders of the Anti-Corn Law League, were representatives of the new generation of manufacturers, and as such they appealed to the urban working class for an alliance against the rural gentry. Here the opposition (blurred in other contexts) was sharp between rural-Conservative and urban-Liberal, while that between manufacturer and industrial proletariat was bridged through their common urban interests.

It is not sufficient, in other words, to identify the typical attitude toward the city with some general political orientation. Consider such a judgment as this:

The industrial town was identified with the working class: it was feared so strongly because the working class was so frightening. This was the persistent theme of Victorian literature, . . . [and] the memory of this fear has continued to be a reason for British animosity against urbanism.[41]

This analysis by Ruth Glass, while it represents a portion of the truth, also falsifies. Opposition to the industrial city, and to the industrial working class that became its archetypal inhabitants, was not restricted to any political grouping. While early anti-urban themes—the adoration of nature and of the unspoiled villager—continued in representative statements of the Conservative Party (including Disraeli's novels and the Young England pronouncements), and while the fear of the city poor, in line with Glass' thesis, was expressed by both Conservatives and Liberals, the city was attacked also from—in Marxist terms—"the left." The irrelevance of a general political stance to the anti-urban theme can be illustrated by the Romantics who began as radicals and later approached the Burkean position, mainly because the promise of the French Revolution was not fulfilled. The works of Wordsworth, for example, fall into two periods: up to 1805, when he was thirty-six, he was the nature poet par excellence; in 1805, the year that the Pope crowned

Napoleon as Emperor, he wrote the "Ode to Duty," and from that time on his tone of "sedate and sometimes conventional moralizing" celebrated the principles of order.[42] But before 1805 and after, Wordsworth's hostility to urban life was evident. As we have seen, Cobbett and Coleridge alike charged that agriculture was being overwhelmed by commerce, to the detriment of English society. Godwin, to take another example, disagreed sharply with Burke about whether human misery is subject to social control; but in their denunciation of the new commercial class and the ascendancy of the individual pursuit of gain, and at least by implication, of the new cities this class was building, Burke and Godwin echoed each other. Similarly, the socialist denunciation of capitalism, of the manufacturing and commercial classes, sometimes included a denunciation of the cities that reflected the new industrial order.

Opposition to "Mass Society"

To understand fully the opposition to the mass of people congregating in the cities of the nineteenth century, we must look at the literary intellectuals who fostered it. The word *intellectual,* introduced into English around 1820, designated a new social type. Writers and other creative artists traditionally were craftsmen, dependent for their living on finding a patron and keeping him satisfied. And the system of patronage, for all its limitations, in the best instances gave at least a greater security than later could generally be found in reliance upon the uncertain tastes of a fickle public. The creative artist had to learn to cater not merely to the sometimes ignorant tastes of one sponsor, as before, but to new consumers' undeveloped appreciation of his products (which had become commodities); paradoxically he became, in his own estimate and also that of his society, a higher type of human. "In the second half of the 19th century the artist is gradually accorded a position of which no earlier century would have dreamed. . . . Naturally this process was accompanied by a great increase in the artist's self-confidence."[43] To "man"— or, in Wordsworth's term, "the People"—the writer owed "devout respect, his reverence"; but in fact the artist's public, who dared to judge his work, aroused his contempt. One finds this sentiment in artists of earlier eras, of course, but it is stronger in Keats ("I have not the slightest feel of humility towards the Public"), in Shelley ("Accept no counsel from the simple-minded"), of course in Ruskin or Wilde—in short, in every self-conscious artist who rejected the concept of his work as a product-commodity. Between those who marketed a piece of themselves and those who, very often, rejected it, antipathy was as "natural" as between those who paid wages and those who received them. Just when artists became financially dependent on those they deemed unworthy to judge their work, they also moved "beyond economics," as Karl Renner defines the status of intellectuals. To live with this contradiction is galling; intellectuals, almost by definition, criticize the society that seems to impose the contradiction on them.

In the eighteenth century the advocacy of universal education had been the first index of the radical critic of traditional society, for literacy was the key to social democracy. That Adam Smith and Malthus, in England two of the earliest proponents of free schooling for all, came to be denounced as conservatives is indicative of the transformation the literati were effecting. The utopian dreams were bound to bring disillusionment; if those who had learned to read did not to the man absorb the world's great works of literature and philosophy, then some who had anticipated this miracle doubted the worth of the instrument. Even earlier, the demand for education lost some of its appeal because Romantics saw as less important the rational qualities of the mind that, in the eighteenth-century view, can be established or enhanced by schooling. The Romantics' antithesis between rationality and sentiment was repeatedly converted over the following decades into an antithesis of machine and "nature," town and country. Carlyle, who coined the word *industrialism* to designate "this age of ours," described it as "the Age of Machinery, in every outward and inward sense of that word. . . . Nothing is now done directly or by hand; all is by rule and calculated contrivance." "Men were not intended," Ruskin tells us, "to work with the accuracy of tools, to be precise and perfect in all their actions. If you will have that precision out of them, . . . you must unhumanize them."

Just as Matthew Arnold was a central figure through which to view the transmuted version of Wordsworth's worship of nature, so it is instructive to see the concept of "mass culture" as he developed it from the comparatively naïve beginnings in Shelley's generation. Though one seldom thinks of him in those terms, Arnold was mainly an educational philosopher and administrator, for thirty-five years Her Majesty's Inspector of Schools. His key ideas can be reviewed most usefully through their most familiar medium, *Culture and Anarchy*.[44] It is read and enjoyed today because it propounds with great energy the paradoxical faith of the modern liberal intellectual. Arnold would merely be of historical interest if he had opposed the growth of social democracy from the aristocratic point of view. "I am a Liberal," he wrote, "yet I am a Liberal tempered by experience, reflection, and renouncement, and I am, above all, a believer in culture." A believer also in equality: "the men of culture are the true apostles of equality,...those who have had a passion for diffusing, for making prevail, for carrying from one end of society to the other, the best knowledge, the best ideas of their time." Yet, from this belief in culture and in equality, he defines himself as utterly "alien" from the society that, to a greater degree than any before in history, laid the material base and the spiritual one (in literacy, if nothing more) for what he advocated.

In spite of some important differences (religion, a key factor in *Culture and Anarchy*, is now often seen as of little or no importance), today's intellectuals are heirs to the tradition that Arnold did much to develop, or even to initiate. That such defenders of conservative values as, say, F. R. Leavis or T. S. Eliot have attacked the "mass culture" of the neoliterate one would have expected in any case. But the most vehement denunciation of "mass culture" has generally come from one or another type of liberal or Marxist, from men, that is, who might have been sympathetic with the gains implicit in universal literacy, as well as in some cases attuned to the relation between the "superstructure" and the base of broadening material prosperity.[45]

When Arnold used the word *culture* in the title of his book, both it and *civilization* were acquiring new meanings in English. The history of the two words is complex: in some periods they were only loosely related; at other times, in the works of some authors, they were near synonyms. When they wrote their poems and novels and even more their "lay sermons," as Coleridge termed his heuristic essays, literary intellectuals were acting as conscious social critics; their argumentation is at the surface, visible to every reader. But after they helped fashion new meanings for such words as *natural, culture,* and *civilization,* their point of view passed into the language, which then expressed it with seeming neutrality in others' mouths. This criticism-by-redefinition, once an expression of personal preferences about either literature or society, thus changed into a seeming description of these entities.

Conclusion

The industrial, urban, and democratic institutions of Western society have brought about a general welfare exceeding the dreams of previous ages. In most parts of the world the development of an urban industrial civilization has brought not only a rise in the standards of living but an improved status and greater political power for the lower classes. Health is better, life longer, and labor less onerous. Yet in most parts of the world the attitude toward these benefits is often ambivalent. One explains this attraction-repulsion in underdeveloped nations as hostility toward the former imperial powers combined with envy of their industrial prowess. In the Soviet Union, similarly, the demand to overtake the West is coupled with the assertion of an already existent superiority. A portion of these mixed feelings, however, undoubtedly reflects not the complex special circumstances of present-day societies, but rather cultural borrowings from nineteenth-century English intellectuals, who also came into the modern world with dragging feet. The judgment of English literati, in short, is more than just an early example of this sentiment. Together with the industry that first developed there, the attitudes of her intellectuals toward it have spread to the rest of the world.

The human potential in the technical inventions that we summarize with the metaphor "the industrial revolution" was realized only because the nineteenth century was also an "age of reform," a "triumph of reform," a period in which we find the "origins of the British welfare state."[46] If the men who fashioned this new society, or those who spoke in its name, had expressed a certain smugness at their achievement, this would have been an understandable sentiment. But according to a much reprinted end-of-century appraisal—

Select ten, say, of the greatest writers of the Victorian era, and attempt from the picture which they present to effect a reconstruction of the Victorian age. The product is a human society so remote from all benignant ways as to demand nothing less than the advent of a kindly comet which will sweep the whole affair into nothingness.[47]

When this kind of indictment is spelled out in detail, the specification is, in Buckley's words, a "confusion of contradictory charges." The Victorians were condemned by some for being complacent, by others for being torn by doubt; by some as crass materialists, by others as excessively religious. Some denounced them as excessively conventional, others as too ruggedly individualistic; some as sentimental humanitarians, others as hard-boiled proponents of laissez-faire; some as sexually inhibited, others as the parents of incredibly large families. Victorian art was criticized as hypocritical and as ingenuous, Victorian literature as didactic and escapist.[48] All of these qualities undoubtedly adhere to some persons and groups; the mistake is to suppose that they can be used to characterize the whole of a variegated and rapidly changing age. Industrialization was first of all a process of variation. In particular, "the first effect of early industrialization was to differentiate English communities rather than to standardize them."[49]

We have no written report directly from the mass of nineteenth-century Englishmen on whether they agreed with the predominantly negative verdict of the literati. But the rural population indicated its preference in the most dramatic fashion possible—by a mass exodus *to* the cities. The reasons, as summarized from a series of Royal Commission reports, were that the rural laborer suffered from unfavorable wage differentials and from comparatively inadequate housing and public accommodations, particularly in sanitary services.[50] The lot of the rural female was even less attractive. According to a census report of 1891, country districts had a relative scarcity of females of all ages from ten up, and in the whole country one girl in three between the ages of fifteen and twenty was in domestic service, the main route to an urban residence.[51] This does not mean that as measured against some ideal norm the new industrial cities were attractive social organisms, but it strongly suggests that for anyone who lacked aristocratic or upper middle-class comforts Victorian cities were a far better place to live than the countryside or even the small town.

This mass migration and the consequent rapid growth of the cities was undoubtedly one reason for the great discrepancy between the reality of urban life and British intellectuals' general perception of it. A change of scale seems to engender a new reality: the same situation acquired a new urgency when the poor and miserable collected in highly visible clusters and, though their proportion may have remained constant or even declined, grew in absolute numbers with the general increase in population.[52] It was during the nineteenth century, moreover, that the official perception and measurement of social phenomena gradually developed. Through the century the law-making process came more and more to depend on the reports, the blue books and white papers of select committees and royal commissions. The notorious self-interest of the Victorians was always mitigated by the demand of an effective minority that the social wrongs be uncovered, publicized, and put right; and it was this disinterested public service rather than its contrary that marked a change from earlier periods. Child labor, to take an important example, was not new in nineteenth-century England, but the perception of it as evil and the demand that it be abolished was new. The unsavory facts thus un-covered, especially about the towns, became the main empirical base for every critic of the new order, whether Engels or Carlyle.

The urban picture that all these new statistics and reports recorded, even if we adjust it for reformers' zeal and political propaganda, is by present-day Western standards dismal, especially in contrast with the supposedly golden age that the industrial era had supplanted. Such writers as Cobbett conjured up a merrie Eng-land peopled with happy peasants and sturdy, beef-eating yeomanry; and this vi-sionary reconstruction found its echoes in Coleridge; in Engels, amazingly enough; and in later commentators as different as the socialist Hammonds, say, and the Catholic economist Colin Clark.

The manner of perceiving social reality is of crucial importance, for it colored all reports of the industrial city. It is useful to distinguish "level of living," meaning real per capita income or some equivalent, from "norm of living," or the criterion by which this level is judged; the usual term, standard of living, connotes both meanings. It is a commonplace that a population whose welfare is improving soon comes to assume that betterment as given, and to measure its future trend always from a new base with an ever higher level of living; in short, the norm of living tends to rise faster than the level of living.

Again and again, the solution offered to all these ills was to subvert the city, and the culmination of the nineteenth-century ideology was the planned dispersal of metropolitan populations to the New Towns. In the ideology of British town planning, three important public functions can be distinguished.[53] The first, to pro-vide fair and consistent criteria for the proper use of Britain's limited and increas-ingly crowded land and thus to reconcile competing claims among aspirant users, is no longer very popular. Peter Self is not alone in denouncing this type of govern-ment neutrality, what he terms the "umpire view" of planning, as a "poison in the heart of the planning machine. . . . It is not the task of the planning authorities to 'reconcile' land-use conflicts in a judicial kind of way, but to impose policies of their own upon the pattern of development and land-use."[54] The other two functions—to provide a better physical environment to the cities by means of im-proved housing, more parks, better transportation, and so on; and to establish low-density residential areas in relatively small, functionally isolated, and thoroughly integrated towns in which an active community life can be successfully fostered— are less complementary than competing goals. That the New Towns exist, that their number grows from year to year, and that they pay their own way—all this denotes a particular range of success. But if official policy is to induce factory owners and workers to move from metropolitan centers to provincial towns, on the assumption that no other solution to metropolitan problems is realistic, efforts within the metropolitan framework to cope with deficiencies of housing, transpor-tation, "social disorganization," or other problems of whatever kind are less likely to be effective.

NOTES

Author's Note: *The research for this study was greatly assisted by a grant from the Institute of Urban and Regional Development, University of California, Berkeley.*

1. William Ashworth, *The Genesis of Modern British Town Planning* (London: Routledge & Kegan Paul, 1954), pp. 48, 62, 182, 187.

2. The biographical facts are borrowed from Frederic Osborn's laudatory preface to Howard's *Garden Cities of Tomorrow*, which is reprinted in the 1965 edition (Cambridge, Mass.: M.I.T. Press).

3. In *John Bull's Other Island*, Shaw advertised the scheme with the following exchange: "Have you ever heard of Garden City?" "D'ye mane Heavn?"

4. For an account of some British counterparts, see Ashworth, chap. 5.

5. C. B. Purdom, *The Building of Satellite Towns* (London: Dent, 1925), pp. 67, 164, 269–270, 302.

6. C. B. Purdom, *The Letchworth Achievement* (London: Dent, 1963).

7. In an essay introducing Howard's book, Lewis Mumford asserts with italicized emphasis that "the Garden City, as Howard defined it, is not a suburb but the antithesis of a suburb." Yet on the next page he states that "the ideas Howard expounded were to . . . influence the planning of Hilversum in the Netherlands, Ernst May's satellite communities in Frankfort-am-Main, and Wright and Stein's Radburn," as well as towns "created by the Resettlement Administration in 1936–not least Greenbelt, Maryland, itself." Purdom cites even Los Angeles with its "satellite towns" (in his usage a synonym for Garden Cities) of Hollywood, Pasadena, Inglewood, etc., as an example of incipient regional development according to the Howard model (*Building of Satellite Towns*, pp. 17–18). It seems strange that the antithesis of the suburb should inspire the best planners of three countries to create what are palpably the antithesis of this antithesis.

8. Lloyd Rodwin, *The British New Towns Policy* (Cambridge, Mass.: Harvard University Press, 1956), p. 27.

9. "Howard's influence in the literal, or reasonably literal, acceptance of his program" was important, she wrote, but this was "as nothing compared to his influence on conceptions underlying all American city planning today. City planners and designers with no interest in Garden City, as such, are still thoroughly governed intellectually by its underlying principles" (*The Death and Life of Great American Cities* New York: Random House, 1961), pp 17–18. With characteristic adeptness, Mumford manages to have it both ways. In the process of an attack on Jacobs for her "preposterous mass of historic misinformation," he states that, apart from a few towns and personages he mentions, "Howard's actual influence was nil." Developing this argument further, he refers to the "growing list of planners who have, consciously or unconsciously, adopted most of Howard's leading ideas and given them another name."

10. David N. Levinson, "British Pressure Groups: Three Case Studies," Harvard College Honors Thesis, 1957; Donald L. Foley, "Idea and Influence: The Town and Country Planning Association," *Journal of the American Institute of Planners*, XXVIII (February 1962), 10–17.

11. Cf. Asa Briggs, *Victorian Cities* (London: Odhams Press, 1963), chap. 5.

12. William A. Madden, "The Victorian Sensibility," *Victorian Studies*, VII (September 1963), 67–97.

13. E. D. H. Johnson, *The Alien Vision of Victorian Poetry* (Princeton: Princeton University Press, 1952), pp. 86-88.

14. Arthur J. Carr, "Tennyson as a Modern Poet," in Austin Wright, ed., *Victorian Literature: Modern Essays in Criticism* (New York: Oxford-Galaxy, 1961), pp. 311–333.

15. Carlton J. H. Hayes, *A Generation of Materialism, 1871-1900* (New York: Harper, 1941), titles of chaps. 6 and 7.

16. Emile Legouis, "William Wordsworth," in A. W. Ward and A. R. Waller, eds., *The Cambridge History of English Literature*, XI, *The Period of the French Revolution* (New York: Putnam, 1916).

17. F. L. Lucas, *The Decline and Fall of the Romantic Ideal* (Cambridge: University Press, 1963), pp. 35–36.

18. Mark Schorer, *William Blake: The Politics of Vision* (New York: Vintage, 1959), p. 391.

19. F. R. Leavis, *New Bearings in English Poetry: A Study of the Contemporary Situation* (Ann Arbor, Mich.: Ann Arbor Paperbacks, University of Michigan Press, 1960), p. 10.

20. U. C. Knoepflmacher, "Dover Revisited: The Wordsworthian Matrix in the Poetry of Matthew Arnold," *Victorian Poetry*, I, No. 1 (January 1963), 17–26.

21. Robert A. Nisbet, *The Quest for Community: A Study in the Ethics of Order and Freedom* (New York: Oxford University Press, 1953).

22. Raymond Williams, *Culture & Society 1780-1950* (Garden City, N.Y.: Anchor-Doubleday, 1960), p. 21.

23. Quoted in R. J. White, ed., *Political Tracts of Wordsworth, Coleridge and Shelley* (Cambridge: University Press, 1953), p. 271.

24. Ibid., pp. 109-110, 277n.

25. John Stuart Mill, *Essays on Politics and Culture,* ed. Gertrude Himmelfarb (New York: Doubleday, 1962), pp. 132-186.

26. K. S. Inglis, *Churches and the Working Classes in Victorian England* (London: Routledge and Kegan Paul; Toronto: University of Toronto Press, 1963), pp. 265-266.

27. One manifestation was Thomas Hughes' *Tom Brown's Schooldays,* possibly the most important book ever to be written about the English school system and another link (apart from the works of Matthew Arnold, his son) to the ideas we are examining from Dr. Thomas Arnold, the great Rugby headmaster and a partial model for his fictional counterpart in Hughes' book. At Rugby in the 1860's, of the twenty-two hours in the school week seventeen were spent on the study of Greek and Latin classics—a rather remarkable adoration of the past.

28. Guy Kendall, *Charles Kingsley and His Ideas* (London: Hutchinson, n.d.), p. 78.

29. Charles Kingsley, "Great Cities and Their Influence for Good and Evil," in *Works,* XVIII, *Sanitary and Social Essays* (London: Macmillan, 1880), pp. 196, 204-205.

30. Philip Henderson, *William Morris* (The British Council and the National Book League; London: Longmans, Green, 1952), p. 8.

31. Philip Henderson, *Literature and a Changing Civilization* (London: John Lane, 1935), p. 89.

32. Some of Ruskin's ideas were half realized by A. J. Pente, the founder of guild socialism. Deprecating "the prejudice against medieval society created by lying historians," he advocated, in alleged imitation of that society, "the establishment of self-government in industry through a system of national guilds working in conjunction with other democratic functional organizations in the community" (Williams, pp. 202-203).

33. John Ruskin, "Time and Tide," *Works,* eds. E. T. Cook and Alexander Wedderburn (London: George Allen, 1908), XVII, 438 ff.

34. Ruskin. "To the Clergy on the Lord's Prayer," XXXIV, 205; "Fiction, Fair and Foul," pp. 268, 281; "Rembrandt, and Strong Waters," XIX, 115; "The Seven Lamps of Architecture," VIII, 136; "The Baron's Gate," XXVII, 105, Ruskin himself conducted three "practical experiments" to combat urban influences: (1) He put the slum tenements he owned in charge of a woman who used some of the income to improve the prperty. (2) He hired a number of street sweepers, including "his gardener and a young shoeblack," and set them an example by using the broom himself. "The experiment did not last very long." (3) He opened a tea shop, run by two of his mother's old servants, where the tea was to be unadulterated and sold without profiteering. See J. H. Whitehouse, "Ruskin and London," ed. J. Howard Whitehouse, *Ruskin the Prophet and Other Centenary Studies* (London: Allen & Unwin, 1920), pp. 135-145.

35. One might note what Ruskin's admirers inevitably pass over—that certain of his ideas and mannerisms were linked to psychopathic tendencies. See Gaylord C. LeRoy, "John Ruskin," ed. Austin Wright, *Victorian Literature: Modern Essays in Criticism* (New York: Oxford-Galaxy, 1961), pp. 268-283.

36. J. A. Hobson, "Ruskin as Political Economist," in Whitehouse, *Ruskin the Prophet,* pp. 81-98; Patrick Geddes, *John Ruskin, Economist,* The Round Table Series, 3 (Edinburgh: William Brown, 1884).

37. The depreciation of "mere" increased production is echoed in Galbraith's well-known contrast between America's wealth in privately produced goods and its poverty in public services. Even some of his examples recall passages in Ruskin: efficient vacuum cleaners v. street cleaners who are regarded as "an unfortunate expense," or the demand that city residents should have "a non-toxic supply of air." John Kenneth Galbraith, *The Affluent Society* (Boston: Houghton Mifflin, 1958), pp. 134, 252.

38. John R. Rodman, "Introduction" to T. H. Green, *The Political Theory of T. H. Green: Selected Writings* (New York: Appleton-Century Crofts, 1964).

39. Edmund Burke, "Thoughts and Details on Scarcity (1795)," in *Works* (Boston: Little, Brown, 1869), V, 134-135.

40. Cf. James Cornford, "The Transformation of Conservatism in the Late Nineteenth Century," *Victorian Studies,* VII, No. 1 (September 1963), 35-66.

41. Ruth Glass, "Urban Sociology in Great Britain: A Trend Report," *Current Sociology,* IV, No. 4 (1955), 5-19. This monograph suggests that the author shares, from her neo-Marxist stance, something of the anti-urban sentiment she so analyzes. "Throughout the 19th century,"

she writes, "the towns . . . became more hideous and more unhealthy—physically and socially....
Throughout the 19th century" (the phrase is repeated), there was an "increasing separation of
the social classes within cities." To put it no stronger, neither statement is above reasonable
challenge. A harsher critic might assert that both are nonsense.

42. Legouis, "Wordsworth."

43. Levin L. Schucking, *The Sociology of Literary Taste* (New York: Oxford, 1944), p. 20.

44. The reader may not remember the events that occasioned the writing of this tract. As part
of its pressure for an extension of the suffrage, a London mob intent on holding a rally pushed
over the railings of what was then a middle-class park. Carlyle's remark about the country was
shooting the rapids to "anarchy" seems to have suggested the title of the book, which appeared
from the press only a month before the new Parliament, based on extended suffrage, began its
sessions.

45. See Edward Shils, "Daydreams and Nightmares: Reflections on the Criticism of Mass Culture," *Sewanee Review,* LXV (Autumn 1957), 597-608. Another interesting example of this
genre is Hoggart, who finds that "most working-people are in almost all respects better off, have
better living conditions, better health, a larger share of consumer goods, fuller educational opportunities and so on." The "and so on" even includes a richer use of literacy among an "earnest minority." But for the majority there has been an alleged degeneration from the heights
of a reconstructed "oral tradition," or the best of the popular books that have survived from
the last century to the trash typical of today, which is exemplified in great detail and characterized as "anti-life." Richard Hoggart, *The Uses of Literacy: Aspects of Working-Class Life,
with Special References to Publications and Entertainments* (London: Chatto and Windus,
1959).

46. E. L. Woodward, *The Age of Reform, 1815-1870* (Oxford: Clarendon, 1939); Elie Halévy,
Triumph of Reform, 1830-1841 (New York: Barnes & Noble, 1961); David Roberts, *Victorian
Origins of the British Welfare State* (New Haven: Yale University Press, 1960).

47. C. F. G. Masterman, *The Condition of England* (London: Methuen, 1910), p. 5.

48. Jerome Hamilton Buckley, " 'Victorianism,' " ed. Austin Wright, *Victorian Literature:
Modern Essays in Criticism* (New York: Oxford-Galaxy, 1961), pp. 3-15.

49. Briggs, p. 32.

50. John Saville, *Rural Depopulation in England and Wales, 1851-1951* (London: Routledge
& Kegan Paul, 1957), p. 36

51. Cited in W. J. Reader, *Life in Victorian England* (London: Batsford, 1964), p. 49.

52. From the beginning to the end of the nineteenth century, the population of England and
Wales increased in round numbers from 9.2 to 32.5 million. In 1800 of all urban places only
London County had as many as 100,000 inhabitants; by 1837, when Victoria came to the
throne, there were five cities of at least this size, and in 1900 the number had grown to 31. See
Brian Mitchell, *Abstract of British Historical Statistics* (Cambridge: University Press, 1962),
pp. 20-27.

53. Donald L. Foley, "British Town Planning: One Ideology or Three?" *British Journal of
Sociology,* XI, No. 3 (September 1960), 211-231.

54. Peter Self, *Cities in Flood: The Problems of Urban Growth* (London: Faber and Faber
[1957]), p. 174.

CITY AND COUNTRY: MARRIAGE PROPOSALS

Town and country *must be married,* and out of this joyous union will spring a new hope, a new life, a new civilization.

—*Ebenezer Howard,* 1898

David Riesman, in his essay "The Suburban Sadness," acknowledges that he writes as "one who loves city and country, but not the suburbs." [1] Riesman's position is not at all unusual. Most social commentators regard today's suburbs more with loathing than with love, finding them homogeneous, conformist, adjustment-oriented, conservative, dull, child centered, female dominated, anti-individualist, —in a word, impossible—places to live. It was not always thus, with intellectuals.

For one thing, the American intellectual has not, until recently (until, in fact, the suburb came along as a scapegoat to replace the city) been willing to confess any affection for the city. For another, as the epigraph from Howard suggests, there was a time when the suburb was thought of as the hope of civilization, as the happy, healthy offspring of the marriage of town and country. [2] Howard's Garden Cities represented the apotheosis of the suburban dream, places which were at once *real* communities, collections of people who would work and live together in civic and social harmony, and at the same time totally self-sufficient units, made up of discrete individuals able and willing to pursue their own private goals. Indeed, if hopes had not once been so high for suburbia, it surely would not have fallen so low in critical estimation at the midpoint of the twentieth century. For Howard was by no means the only theorist to envision the suburb as the product of a happy marriage between town and country, a union to resolve one of the most troublesome paradoxes of American civilization.

The paradox is, of course, the continuing worship of rural, countrified life in a nation where the pull of progress has created an unmistakably urban civilization. The roots of the agrarian myth stretch back to the beginnings of Western culture and the paradisiacal garden. But the most powerful expressions of the myth came with the new nation and the Enlightenment, in the voices of such men as Hector St. John de Crevecoeur and Thomas Jefferson. Jefferson's fondness for the farm and dislike of the city are legendary, and Crevecoeur located his ideal Americans on the farms of the "middle settlements," midway between sea and wilderness, where the simple cultivation of the earth would purify them. These men expressed beliefs which have demonstrated amazing staying power. Their persistence can hardly be denied in a land where the Supreme Court must step in to assure city and suburb dwellers of fair legislative representation, where farmers are subsidized not to grow crops, where it is still expedient for a politician to claim a rural heritage. And the beliefs persist despite their obvious lack of relevance to reality. Men mouth agrarian sentiments, but go to the cities, where the money is to be made. The American thinker, almost since the first days of the Republic, has been confronted with this paradox, and as time proceeded American thought arrived at a potential solution. It would be the suburb which would represent the best of both worlds, which would preserve rural values in an urbanizing world, which would enable the individual to pursue wealth while retaining the amenities of country life.

After the Civil War and owing to the development of the railroads, the first American suburbs were developed around New York, Boston, and Philadelphia. From the beginning, these suburbs were regarded as ideal places to live, representing a rather wealthy middle landscape between crowded, unhealthy city life and the coarse and brutal frontier.[3] "So long as men are forced to dwell in log huts and follow the hunter's life," Alexander Jackson Downing wrote, "we must not be surprised at lynch law and the use of the bowie knife. But, when smiling lawns and tasteful cottages begin to embellish a country, we know that order and culture are established."[4] Downing had in mind rural villages full of tasteful "cottages" of real elegance, like those going up at Newport, Rhode Island.

Efforts soon began to scale down the lavish Newport cottage to the pocketbooks of the middle classes. Suburban homes and lots served as promotional bait in a 1876 *Harper's Weekly* advertisement aimed at attracting readers to "the Fourth of July Centennial Demonstration at the Third Avenue Theater." Two two-story cottages and ten $100 lots in Garden City Park, on Long Island, would be raffled off at the demonstration, the advertisement announced, as well as 100 silver watches and 388 one-dollar greenbacks.[5] Later in the same year, this magazine celebrated the joys of suburban life with a cover picture and article on "Summer in the Country." The picture, which shows a young boy and girl "walking side by side in the sweet summer fields," was designed to remind readers, "by contrast, of the sad lot of poor city children, who rarely have the opportunity to breathe the pure air of the country, and refresh their eyes with the sight of flowers and grass."[6] The "flowers and grass" make it clear that the "country" *Harper's Weekly* finds so desirable is somewhat nearer at hand than the Iowa corn fields. If such country was inaccessible to most readers of the magazine, as it probably was in 1876, it still represented a popular goal. Then as now, the place to bring up children was out in the open air, far from noise and smoke.

Three years later, in 1879, the radical Henry George proposed in *Progress and Poverty* that his single tax on land would have the effect of creating a sort of ideal middle landscape. Such a single tax, George maintained, would do away with wholesale speculation in real estate, and:

The destruction of speculative land values would tend to diffuse population where it is too dense and to concentrate it where it is too sparse; to substitute for the tenement house, homes surrounded by gardens, and to fully settle agricultural districts before people were driven far from neighbors to look for land. The people of the cities would thus get more of the pure air and sunshine of the country, the people of the country more of the economics and social life of the city. . . .[7]

Certainly most Americans agreed with this urban politician in an emotional preference for country over city; certainly most desired above all that union of country and city, sunshine and social life, he envisioned as a consequence of the single tax.

It remained for Ebenezer Howard, the London court reporter, to propose specific arrangements for this marriage of city and country in his influential 1898 book, *Garden Cities of Tomorrow*. Howard's proposals were welcomed on both sides of the Atlantic, and they remain today the guiding principles of so important an American critic and theorist as Lewis Mumford. Clearly, the proposals are motivated by agrarian sentiments: "It is well-nigh universally agreed by men of all parties, not only in England, but all over Europe and America and our colonies, that it is deeply to be deplored that the people should continue to stream into the already overcrowded cities, and should thus further deplete the country districts. . . ." How should we go about restoring people to the garden, "that beautiful land of ours, with its canopy of sky, the air that blows upon it, the sun that warms it, and rain and dew that moisten it—the very embodiment of Divine love for man?" The restoration can be accomplished, Howard wrote, only if we reject two-valued, black and white thinking, and consider instead a third alternative.

"There are in reality not only . . . two alternatives—town life and country life—but a third alternative, in which all the advantages of the most energetic and active town life, with all the beauty and delight of the country, may be secured in perfect combination. . . ." To illustrate the point, Howard constructed the metaphor of the magnets. Each person may be regarded as a needle, attracted by magnets. Until now, he wrote, the town has had the most powerful magnet, and so it has pulled citizen-needles from the no longer all-powerful magnetic "bosom of our kindly mother earth." To remedy the situation, "nothing short of the discovery of a method of constructing magnets of yet greater power than our cities possess can be effective for redistributing the population in a spontaneous and healthy manner. . . ." Howard set about to construct this more powerful magnet, which would combine the best of both town and country. There was social opportunity in town, but it was balanced by a "closing out of nature"; there was beauty of nature in the country, but it was measured against "lack of society." The town-country magnet would merge the country's beauty of nature with the town's social opportunity. In economic terms, the town's magnetism resulted at least partly from the high wages paid, but rents were high in town as well. In the country, rents were low, but so were wages. In the new town-country land, however, the citizen would make high wages and pay low rents—he would have his cake and eat it, too.

The town-country magnet became, in Howard's theory, the Garden City, which was to be economically self-sufficient while still at peace with nature. Population would be restricted to a workable size in the Garden City, and jobs, including industrial jobs, provided for all inhabitants. Homes would be surrounded with greenery; the presence of nature was never to be lost sight of in a pell-mell drive for the dollar. In his conception of the Garden City, Howard constructed a new version of the middle landscape, closer to town than Crevecoeur's. In Crevecoeur's version, the middle settlements were located halfway between the city seaports and the wild woods; Howard had moved his middle landscape so that it was now placed between the city and those rural settlements which had served as Crevecoeur's ideal. The ideal middle landscape, in short, was coming closer and closer to suburbia. It would be more explicitly located by intellectuals in the early decades of the twentieth century.

This movement of the middle landscape closer to the city reflected a growing awareness, already obvious in the negative features of Howard's country magnet, that rural life left something to be desired. The farm could never be subject to the vilification the muckrakers brought to bear on the American city, but the agrarian life was not all milk and honey, either. The Country Life Commission appointed by President Theodore Roosevelt in 1908 reported that drudgery, barrenness, and heavy drinking characterized rural regions.[8] The town boy did not have to visit Paris to pack up and leave; the question was rather, "How you gonna keep 'em down on the farm," after they've seen the farm? Young people continued to desert farming for the city, but the standard rhetoric of all Americans, whether they were urban or rural by birth, continued to praise and celebrate the virtues of life on the land. In their hearts, Americans knew that the good life was agrarian; but they listened to their heads, which told them to seek their future in the city.

Somewhat in the manner of Al Smith, who believed that the ills of democracy could be cured by more democracy, Teddy Roosevelt's Country Life Commission recommended a revival of rural civilization as a solution to its apparent degeneration. This revived rural life was to be different, however. In the words of the Commission chairman, Dean Liberty Hyde Bailey of the Cornell Agricultural School, it would be a "working out of the desire to make rural civilization . . . a world-motive to even up society as between country and city." [9] The scales were over-balanced in favor of the city. Something was needed to give more weight to the country's side of the contest. That something, several turn-of-the-century observers were convinced, was represented by the suburb.

Adna Weber, writing in 1900, surveyed suburban growth, then scarcely beginning, and pronounced it the happiest of social movements:

The 'rise of the suburbs' it is, which furnishes the solid basis of a hope that the evils of city life, so far as they result from overcrowding, may be in large part removed. . . . It will realize the wish and prediction of Kingsley, 'a complete interpenetration of city and country, a complete fusion of their different modes of life and a combination of the advantages of both, such as no country in the world has ever seen.' [10]

Court reporter Howard had located his town-country magnet in carefully planned Garden Cities of the future. Weber was more optimistic: mere dispersal of population to the suburbs, a trend already going its merry, unplanned way, would accomplish the modern utopia.

Frederic C. Howe, in his 1905 book, *The City: The Hope of Democracy,* qualified the title's message by suggesting that suburbanization, not urbanization, represented the democratic hope of the future:

The open fields about the city are inviting occupancy, and there the homes of the future will surely be. The city proper will not remain the permanent home of the people. Population must be dispersed. The great cities of Australia are spread out into the suburbs in a splendid way. For miles about are broad roads, with small houses, gardens, and an opportunity for touch with the freer, sweeter life which the country offers.[11]

Avowedly pro-urbanite, Howe could not resist, at least rhetorically, the charms of the countryside. These, he thought, could be made available to every man in the suburbs of the future.

Two eminent Harvard philosophers took much the same view as Weber and Howe, though they did not advocate suburbanization by name. Josiah Royce, who deplored the excessive mobility, the homogenizing tendencies, and the "mob spirit" of city life, maintained that the individual was swallowed up by the city, and could avoid this fate only by fleeing to the provinces. In the "provinces" (what he seems to have meant by this term might be designated "rural villages") were located the small social groups in which freedom 'was to be found. The individual could best exercise his individualism in a socio-economic-political community of limited size: the message, basically, of Thomas Jefferson, restated in twentieth century terms by the leading idealist of the age. George Santayana blended a strong strain of the bucolic with his urbane philosophy. Describing his boyhood town of Avila, Spain, he "expressed his admiration of situations that he described by the phrases *rus in urbs, oppidum in agris,* or *urbs ruri,* some combination of city and country." [12]

The search for the ideal middle landscape persisted along with the belief that city life was stifling to the soul. Louis Sullivan, in his *Autobiography of an Idea,* tells of the sinister effects of being taken to Boston as a young lad. "As one might move a flourishing plant from the open to a dark cellar, and imprison it there, so the miasma of the big city poisoned a small boy acutely sensitive to his surroundings. He mildewed; and the leaves and buds of ambition fell from him." He would surely have run away, the architect recollects without tranquillity, had it not been for his father's wise excursions with him to the suburbs, "on long walks to Roxbury, to Dorchester, even to Brookline, where the boy might see a bit of green and an opening-up of things. . . ." [13]

Perhaps the worst thing about the twentieth century city, as such observers as Robert Park and John Dewey examined it, was its very bigness. In the urban maelstrom, the individual lost the identity that had been so assuredly his on the farm, in the village. The primary group tended to dissolve in the city, Park wrote in 1916, and people lost sight of the values of the local community in a search for excitement. "Cities," he wrote, "have been proverbially and very properly described as 'wicked.'" It is both ironic and appropriate that Park, the nation's first great urban sociologist, should have revealed a nostalgic preference for the secure values of an agrarian civilization, of the family on the farm.[14] Dewey, like Park, noted the frenetic quest for excitement in cities and suggested that it might be simply "the expression of [a] frantic search for something to fill the void caused by the loosening of the bonds which hold persons together in [an] immediate community of experience." As Morton and Lucia White point out in their valuable survey, *The Intellectual versus the City*, Dewey and Park were both playing modern variants on an old theme of Jefferson's, "divide the counties into wards." Like Jefferson, these public philosophers of the twentieth century regarded the small local community as the fit habitation of democratic men.[15]

In 1917, John R. McMahon published a remarkable book entitled *Success in the Suburbs*. He agreed with Park and Dewey that the city failed to provide man with a healthy environment. By some mystical process, nature refused to function inside the city limits, as O. S. Morgan of Columbia University's Department of Agriculture wrote in the foreword: "Soil somehow has ceased here to function normally on root systems, has become dirt and dust. Tonic sunshine has ceased to function in chlorophyll bodies in the leaf, has become an unrevered model after which to pattern an enervating midnight glare." The elect of the city, if they followed the good advice of author McMahon, would throw off this city spell. The advice was simplicity personified. Take yourself to the suburbs, he told his readers, where you can find true success. What was meant by success? Simply "an independent home establishment in a fairly countrified suburb; a household that is self-supporting as to fruits, vegetables, eggs, broilers, and such-like, produced for home use and chiefly by the efforts of the family itself. . . ." Such a successful life means not only health and happiness; it also means financial independence. There will be no *cash* dividends, but in terms of food produced and economies effected above the cost of living in the city, suburban life "returns an annual profit on the investment of something like twenty-five percent." In the suburbs, then, a man and his family can enjoy the moral and physical benefits of contact with the soil, and they can make a pretty penny as well.[16]

McMahon's was a "how to" book, as the subtitle makes clear. To achieve *Success in the Suburbs,* one must know "How to Locate, Buy, and Build; Garden and Grow Fruit; Keep Fowls and Animals." McMahon provides the answers. For him, clearly, "suburbs" seem to connote little value until they are transformed into farms. But as the future site of a nation of subsistence farmers, providing economic as well as spiritual gain, the suburbs would represent the Jeffersonian paradise regained. This paradise is within your grasp, Mc-Mahon told his readers; simply follow my suggestions.

Every spring, he wrote, "city folks yawn and have a hungry look in the eyes. They are restless and discontented, peeved and out of kilter. . . . they are bitten by the bacillicus countrycus, [which] is beneficent to those who live in the country, but . . . torments those who are prisoned in offices and flats." Urbanites should divorce their city jobs and residences to form a more perfect union. Like Howard, McMahon adopts the marriage metaphor. "My argument is that all city folks who can, should marry nature and settle down with her." You don't have to be rich to escape to suburban wedlock, he counsels. All that is needed is "a snug little home in the nearby country and a piece of ground large enough to grow eggs, fruits, and vegetables."

It is amazing how the family will thrive in its new arrangement.

Pale cheeks will grow rosy. Members of the family will get acquainted with one another, finding with relief that they are not "all monotonous Henry James characters" after all. There will be economic rewards as well. The family will raise its own crops for consumption, and avoid paying into the middlemen's profits. In town, the family had lived up to its income and could save little or nothing; on the suburban farm, they "live better and are able to stow away a few hundred dollars annually without feeling it." In bestowing advice, McMahon seasons his overt agrarianism with good, hard, dollar sense.

The first problem is to find a site, and beauty deserves some, but not final, consideration. "Scenery sticks around your habitation a long time and it is wise to pick out a brand that is pleasing and wears well," he writes. "At the same time scenery is not edible and butters no parsnips." [17] The dollar watcher and the philosophical agrarian come together in the same paragraph; the author speaks at once with the voice of Thomas Jefferson, and with that of Benjamin Franklin. Like Franklin, McMahon keeps his eye on the main chance; he is nothing if not practical.

It is the availability of modern tools and materials, in fact, which has made a utopian life on the suburban farm possible. You can achieve your individualism, and be comfortable about it as well. "On a country place you can attain much of the old frontiersman's independence while having comforts and a fullness of life of which he did not dream." There is not even any real risk involved. "Farming," he acknowledges, "is a gamble; suburban gardening should be a lead-pipe cinch." Marry nature and you live happily ever after; spurn her charms and you reject paradise. Attainment of health, happiness, and wealth was easy. It took only a move to the "real up-to-date suburbs, of uncrowded and unfettered Nature, [which] have become the promised land for the city man with limited means but a fair endowment of vim and enterprise. . . ." [18] The world of Thomas Jefferson was not lost. Every man could find agrarian peace and plenty, every man could achieve success on the suburban farm. A rural paradise waited for Americans, just around the corner.

Motivated by this same kind of thinking, Franklin K. Lane, Secretary of the Interior at the end of World War I, backed legislation to return soldiers to health and prosperity on the farm. The solution, once again, was a marriage of town and country, "a new rural life with all the urban advantages." Each family should have enough land to provide for its own needs, Lane believed, but there should also be a central, John Dewey-style local community "having the telephone, and good roads, and the telegraph and the post office, and the good school, and the bank, and the good store all close together, so that the women can talk across the back fence and the man can meet his neighbors." Several soldier settlement bills designed to finance this latest version of the ideal middle landscape were introduced into Congress, but only one, appropriating $200,000 for a preliminary investigation of the public lands available for settlement, was ever passed.[19]

The bills were opposed by the farm lobby, which figured there were enough of nature's noblemen already working the soil. The farmers' position was understandable, especially after the depression of 1921 drove millions out of work and back to the land. By that time, Ralph Borsodi had moved his family out to a subsistence farm, and while others tramped city streets looking for work, the Borsodis cut hay, gathered fruit, made gallons of cider, and "began to enjoy the feeling of plenty which the city dweller never experiences." Borsodi stressed the economic advantages of such a life, particularly if the family produced only for its own consumption. His wife, he concluded, could produce a can of tomatoes "between 20 percent and 30 percent" cheaper than the Campbell Soup Company by eliminating all middlemen. This kind of saving enabled them to be secure in times of economic stress. The farmer was once selfsufficient, producing his own food and clothing, building his own shelter, chopping wood for his own fuel. Borsodi's message was that those days were *not* gone forever; the farm family could still be self-sufficient.[20]

Like McMahon, Borsodi emphasized the part modern machinery played in making his adventure in homesteading a success. But Borsodi viewed success almost exclusively in economic terms. The healthfulness and virtue of country life he may have taken for granted; he did not make much of these beneficial effects in recounting his financial success story. For a century and more, the city had lured people with the promise of economic gain; the country suburb, its adherents now claimed, held even greater promise. An early advertisement for Waleswood, a 220-acre suburban tract outside Minneapolis, paid only token homage to the agrarian myth before hammering home its selling message:

Instead of buying a quart of blue milk a day, take two gallons of rich milk a day from a cow for practically nothing.

Instead of paying 19 to 90 cents or more of hardearned money for a dozen eggs only once in a while, pick up dozens of eggs every day laid for you for almost nothing by generous hens.

Instead of buying one golden egg, buy the goose that laid it for the same money.

Not only was the land fruitful and its creatures generous, but a lot purchased now would be a sound investment for the future. Quite accurately, prospective buyers were reminded that "as the city grows, the value of your property grows. Opportunity knocks but once at every man's door. This is your call." [21] Jefferson would hardly have recognized his agrarian utopia. Base motives threatened to sully the virgin land.

Most intellectuals, however, remained faithful to the Jeffersonian ideal. Twelve southerners, for example, took a famous stand for agrarianism in 1930: the South, they wrote, could—and must—throw off the yoke of industrialism and restore men to cultivation of the soil, "the best and most sensitive of vocations." In a joint opening statement, John Crowe Ransom and Robert Penn Warren and Andrew Nelson Lytle and Allen Tate and the others agreed that to "think that this cannot be done is pusillanimous. And if the whole community, section, race, or age thinks it cannot be done, then it has simply lost its political genius and doomed itself to impotence." Lytle himself took a stand against emphasis on the economic advantages of rural life. Do not industrialize the farm, he advised; ignore those modern tools and methods urged on you by such preachers of the gospel of success as McMahon and Borsodi. "A farm is not a place to grow wealthy; it is a place to grow corn." [22]

The American public generally, despite the dollar appeal of "how to" books and advertisements about generous hens, and despite the inspiring rhetoric of the agrarian ideal, continued to flock to the cities. Then, in the 1920s, suburbanization became a demographic process of magnitude for the first time. (Compared to the flight from the cities after World War II, however, the exodus of the 1920s represented only a minor trend.) Few who migrated to the suburbs were industrious enough to succeed in McMahon's agrarian terms. There was nothing particularly visionary about these new suburbs; they were built to make money for developers. Still, the high hopes inherent in Howard's conception of the town-country magnet and in McMahon's successful suburb-farm refused to fade. In 1925, H. Paul Douglass concluded that a "crowded world must be either suburban or savage." [23] The planners would make sure that it turned out to be suburban. Clarence Stein and Henry Wright, under the financial sponsorship of Alexander Bing, started plans in 1927 for Radburn, New Jersey, which preceded the greenbelt towns of the New Deal as the nation's closest approximation of a Garden City. Other experiments were to follow.

The melodrama of American thought persisted, well into the twentieth century, in assigning the role of the villain to the city slicker. Confronted with his scheming, legalistic ways, the poor farm girl faced Hobson's choice: either sign over the beloved farm or face a fate worse than death. It was the most natural thing in the world, of course, for the American intellectual of the 1920s and 1930s to regard the city with a jaundiced eye; urbanization was steadily destroying the agrarian ideal. In desperation, he turned to the suburbs as the hope of the future, just as the New Deal planners did. That hope, too, ultimately came crashing to earth; when the suburbs turned out to be more citified than countrified, the intellectual of the 1950s relieved his frustrations with a spate of embittered attacks. Suburbia replaced the city as the villain in the rural-urban melodrama. In the mid-1950s it was almost inconceivable to imagine that the suburb, in the dim days before World War II, had been regarded as the *hero* of the piece, the one to rescue the farmer's daughter from the clutches of the city villain. The record of New Deal legislation, however, makes it unmistakably clear that this was the case.

One of the more interesting and ambitious New Deal programs involved the construction of new communities. The 100 communities begun by the federal government in the 1930s, historian Paul K. Conkin points out, "remain vivid reminders of a time, not so long past, when Americans still could dream of a better, more perfect world and could so believe in that dream that they dared set forth to realize it, unashamed of their zeal." [24] Almost all of the 100 communities were made up of subsistence homesteads.

With the backing of President Roosevelt and Congress, $25 million was appropriated in 1933 to establish and put into working order the Division of Subsistence Homesteads, under Harold L. Ickes and his Department of the Interior. Ickes chose M. L. Wilson to take charge of the program. Wilson did not have his head buried in the land: he earnestly hoped to restore "certain moral and spiritual values . . . coming from . . . contact with the soil" by making use of more and more technology and efficiency. The public response to the subsistence homesteads appropriation was immediate and overwhelming. Wilson's division had $25 million to spend; by February 1934, requests for loans amounted to more than $4.5 *billion*. Wilson had a real problem in deciding how best to spend his appropriation, but he had made his basic decisions late in 1933. The typical community would contain "from 25 to 100 families living on individual homesteads of from one to five acres, which would accommodate an orchard, a vegetable garden, poultry, a pig, and, in some cases, a cow. Eventual ownership was promised for most colonists. . . ." Representative Ernest W. Marland of Oklahoma described the individual family's homestead somewhat more romantically:

A small farm with a wood lot for fuel, a pasture for cows, an orchard with hives of bees, a dozen acres or so of plow land, and a garden for berries and annual vegetable crops.

There is always plenty on a farm such as this.

In winter a fat hog hangs in the smokehouse and from the cellar come jellies and jams and preserves, canned fruits, and dried vegetables. In the summer there is a succession of fresh fruits from the orchard and fresh vegetables from the garden.

Heaven, indeed, was to be the destination of subsistence farmers. But dissension within Wilson's division kept the program from growing, and as the economy turned upward, the back-to-the-land movement, which "had been motivated largely by the hopelessness and despair of the depression," began to lose its appeal.[25]

The subsistence homesteads program faded into insignificance, but the community building program of the New Deal was far from dead. Rexford Tugwell spearheaded the second, final, and most significant phase of the program. Tugwell, whose enormous ability was matched by his self-confidence, set about "rearranging the physical face of America." He spurned the emotional attractions of the family homestead, and thought instead in terms of the planning process. For example, he saw that farmers trying and failing to eke out a living on submarginal land would have to be resettled on better land. But there was not enough good land to go around, and the surplus farm population would find its way to the cities, where millions were already trapped in slums. The solution to both problems, "the inevitable movement from farm to city" and the barren poverty of urban slum dwellers, Tugwell found in the suburban town or garden city, in a middle landscape planned in hard, cold, pragmatic terms by the hardest, coldest, most pragmatic of planners. Surplus farm families could resettle in these suburban garden cities, and so could slum families. The federal government, in the person of Rexford Tugwell, set about in 1934 to plan and build these modern "middle settlements."

As head of the Resettlement Administration, Tugwell had originally sketched out a program for twenty-five communities. But the courts and the reluctance of Congress to finance projects that the

Republican National Committee soon characterized as "communist farms" limited the number of such communities. Only three were actually constructed: Greenbelt, Maryland, near Washington, D.C., the most famous; Greenhills, Ohio, near Cincinnati; and Greendale, Wisconsin, outside Milwaukee. Consciously working on behalf of collectivist goals, Tugwell's Resettlement Administration was chewed up in the meat grinder of American politics. By June 1937, the agency was no more.

In the greenbelt towns, however, Tugwell had created the "three largest, most ambitious, and most significant communities of the New Deal." As Conkin comments, they "represented, and still do represent, the most daring, original, and ambitious experiments in public housing in the history of the United States." The three communities relocated low-income families, both from farm and from city, in a suburban environment which combined the advantages of country and city life. The suburbs, clearly, were the hope of the future for Tugwell, who believed there should be 3,000 greenbelt cities, not three. In suburbia, still a relatively unexploited frontier in the mid-1930s, was to be found "the best chance ever offered for the governmental planning of a favorable working and living environment. Past opportunities for federal planning had been ignored, with urban slums and rural poverty the results. This new area offered a last chance." The city had turned out badly, and so had the farm. The suburb was the last possible place to plan for a viable environment, and Tugwell, his idealism showing beneath the pragmatic exterior, was determined not to let the chance go by.

The greenbelt city, as he conceived it, was to be a complete community, with its area and population strictly limited in size, surrounded by a greenbelt of farms. There was to be plenty of light, air, and space, with safety assured for the children, many gardens, and good schools and playgrounds. Jobs were either to be available within the community or close at hand, and the town and its utilities were to be owned collectively, not individually. Planning for the three greenbelt towns began in 1935, and construction was underway during the following three years. When completed the three projects contained 2,267 family units and complete community facilities. In many respects, the towns were successful: residents flocked to occupy the comfortable single- and multiple-family dwellings in all three communities, and visitors from overseas were lavish in their praise. But the greenbelt towns never worked out economically. At the low rents charged, it would have taken over 300 years for Greenbelt, Maryland to pay for itself. In 1949, Congress authorized the administration to sell the greenbelt towns at negotiated sale. By 1954, all three cities had been liquidated for $19.5 million, just over half the total cost to the federal government of $36 million, not taking interest or the devaluation of the dollar into account.[26]

However impractical they may have been in terms of dollars and cents, the greenbelt towns demonstrated what federal planning could accomplish in providing suburban housing for low-income families. Today, of course, the suburbs contain people of all social classes, from the very wealthy to the nearly indigent. But the working class suburb of the 1960s, conceived for profit and constructed in the same spirit, lacks many of the amenities of the greenbelt towns. Those who looked to the suburbs with stars in their eyes in the 1930s may be excused for being disillusioned with the results of unplanned growth. Given enough money and time and the right political climate, Rexford Tugwell might have built a modern utopia in the suburbs of the United States. But there was not enough money or time, and the political climate, with its worship of individualism, was decidedly unfriendly. Tugwell's dream, like most, did not come true.

After World War II, of course, came the deluge. The boys came marching home in 1945 and 1946, produced babies, and looked for homes to house their families. Instant suburbs, thrown up by developers, without professional planning or architectural assistance, supplied the homes, and the GI's moved in. To most of them, the new suburban homes, small and neat, seemed entirely adequate. But those intellectuals who, like Tugwell, saw in suburbia the last chance to create an ideal living environment were saddened. There were not enough playgrounds, not enough walkways, not enough trees—

in short, not enough nature. In their disillusionment the intellectuals turned on the suburbs with a vengeance. Where once they had attacked the city for robbing America of its agrarian dream, now they zeroed in on the suburb, which had betrayed their fondest hopes for a twentieth century restoration of the Jeffersonian ideal.

As the target of abuse shifted from downtown to the fringes of town, the city gained a respectability, a dignity, which it had never before enjoyed. Jane Jacobs, in her urban rhapsody, *The Death and Life of Great American Cities*, perceptively assesses the sentimentalization of nature as a major cause for "the bog of intellectual misconceptions about cities in which orthodox reformers and planners have mired themselves. . . ." Cities are just as natural as countryside, she maintains. Are not human beings part of nature? Are not cities the products of one form of nature, "as are the colonies of prairie dogs or the beds of oysters?" Of course they are, but Americans are not sentimental about cities. They are sentimental about the countryside, but they systematically destroy it in building on it. Each day, the bulldozers flatten out the hills and tear up the trees; each day, acres of Grade I agricultural land are covered with pavement; each day, suburbanites kill "the thing they thought they came to find." Worst of all, it did not have to work out the way it has. There was no need for suburbs at all. Miss Jacobs would do away with the middle landscape, leaving only city and country: "Big cities need real countryside close by. And countryside—from man's point of view—needs big cities, with all their diverse opportunities and productivity, so human beings can be in a position to appreciate the rest of the natural world instead of to curse it." [27]

There is general critical agreement that suburbanization is systematically destroying America's priceless natural heritage. "These dormitory or bedroom communities displace the forests, the fruit orchards, and the fields of waving grain which up until a few years ago covered the countryside," a religious commentator writes.[28] This accusation makes up only half of the indictment, though. For the suburbs are not only killing off the country; they are also doing away with the city. Nathan Glazer argues, for example, that suburbia is invading the city, not vice versa,[29] and political scientists complain that outlying communities are siphoning off the life blood of the city.

The suburbs, in short, have come to be regarded as combining the worst, not the best, of city and country. The dream of an ideal middle landscape has been transformed into the nightmare of a no man's land between two ideal extremes. In their suburbs, Americans have "succeeded in averaging down both the city and the [rural] village." [30]

The flight from the city was entirely predictable in the light of the dominant mythology of American agrarianism. As two sociologists have remarked:

What Suburbia means, then, is a question that can be answered by viewing it more as a continuation of the older values that still exist rather than as a new phenomenon that has somehow taken the worst of all features of American life and encapsulated them within a split-level housing development. Perhaps the fact that Americans are moving in such numbers from the unplanned city to the poorly planned suburb is symbolic that really nothing much has changed except the time and the place.[31]

Nothing much, really, *has* changed. As much as ever, and despite the bitter lessons of history, America remains caught up in the Jeffersonian ideal, in the myth of the sturdy yeoman farmer plowing his own acres in self-sufficient independence, yet somehow part of a rural community. Conrad Knickerbocker has isolated the motivation which continues to produce the exodus to suburbia. The back-to-nature fixation, he writes, "has driven much . . . of the nation into street upon street of meaningless, tiny symbolic 'farms' stretching coast to coast." But these are farms with 60-foot frontages of crab grass, and no front porch on which to simply sit and fan yourself. Robert C. Wood, as Under Secretary of the Department of Housing and Urban Development, also blames "a rustic culture" for creating a decentralized governmental mess around our cities. "The need," he says, "is to develop a metropolitan conscience which demands something more than a rural shopkeeper's values." [32]

It would be reasonable to suppose, from the heat of the tirade against the suburbs, that the concept of an ideal landscape had disappeared from American thinking. But such a supposition underestimates the continuing pull of the country on the imagination of the urban intellectual. New Deal attempts to plan and construct the perfect community ended, if not in failure, at least in financial embarrassment. But the movers and shakers of the Great Society determined to try once more, feeling again that there must be some way of happily marrying country and city. Following this goal, the Johnson administration threw its support behind the New Towns movement.

New Towns, of course, are really only another name for Garden Cities or greenbelt cities. Nevertheless, there are some differences between them. The New Towns are being constructed by private developers (often with government loans). And the New Towns will make a greater effort than was made in the cases of Greenbelt, Greendale, and Greenhills to attract industry. As Wolf von Eckardt writes, the greenbelt program was abandoned "partly because . . . these towns could [not] attract sufficient employment so people could stay put." The success of the New Towns, he maintains, will depend largely on "whether they can actually attract employers." [33] For one goal of the New Towns, like that of Ebenezer Howard's Garden Cities, is to bring enough jobs out into the middle landscape so that the tedious commuting from suburb to city can be eliminated. To the extent that they realize this goal, the communities will be able to keep "closely accessible the recreative values of Nature." (The capitalization is not Ralph Waldo Emerson's, but that of the *Architectural Record*, April 1964.) It is Henry Ford's idea all over again: men can and should be industrial workers eight hours a day and nature's noblemen the rest of the time. The New Towns are not to have any standard population, which can vary from 50,000 to several hundred thousand, but the limit will be predetermined by planning. Surrounding land will be purchased and kept essentially open, to serve as a natural greenbelt.[34]

Perhaps the best known of some 75 American New Towns is Reston, Virginia, a 10-square-mile site 17 miles from Washington, D.C., which is planned for a community of 75,000 persons. Robert E.

Simon, Jr., the original developer, was frankly enamored of outdoor life, and instructed his planners to be certain that the growth of Reston did not "destroy the very rural amenities that its residents would seek." As a consequence, apartments and town houses were built to cluster population and preserve more open land.[35]

New Town planners hope that their middle landscape, once created, will be hospitable to all: "We hope to create a community that is economically and racially integrated—that is, contains a substantial range of income and occupation, and a substantial number of non-white families." But they lack confidence that such heterogeneous towns can be built, so long as private developers stay in charge. The developer must not only be willing to admit minority families; he must actively seek them, since they are not likely to apply in serious numbers. Besides, if housing is not subsidized, it is unlikely that many minority families could afford to move. The solution, as Albert Mayer and Clarence Stein see it, is to put the government back in the real estate business, a business it was supposed to have given up with the sale of the greenbelt cities twenty years ago. So long as there is a possibility of speculative profit, they state, "large-scale logically related development is not going to take place." What is needed is a philosophy of long-range disinterested planning by a powerful New Town Committee or Commission.[36]

Stein, one of the developers of Radburn, New Jersey, is back where he and Rexford Tugwell and the other planners of the twenties and thirties always were—on the side of centralized government direction and control of new American utopias. Ada Louise Huxtable, the architecture critic for *The New York Times*, is less insistent on federal control as well as less Panglossian:

Inevitably [she writes], New Towns may fall short of their objectives, and even share some of suburbia's sins. But only through professional community planning can the chaos of the country's growth be turned into order. Concern with the total community is a heartening sign of sanity, order, rationality and realism in the American approach to the problem of urban expansion. There may still be hope for the suburban dream.[37]

Serious, intelligent planning, serious, intelligent concern with the total community bodes well for the future. Planning is not going to cure all the ills of our cities and suburbs, Huxtable realizes, whether it is done privately or through government channels. The intellectual must realize, with Huxtable, that New Towns and other ideal utopias will inevitably fall short of their objectives. It is not going to be possible to restore rural America: "The wilderness, the isolated farm, the plantation, the self-contained New England town, the detached neighborhood are things of the American past. All the world's a city now and there is no escaping urbanization, not even in outer space."[38] To the very considerable extent that the modern ideal of the middle landscape looks backward to the Jeffersonian ideal for direction, it is doomed to failure, and its adherents to disillusionment. In any marriage between city and country today the city is going to be the dominant partner.

NOTES

1. David Riesman, "The Suburban Sadness," in Dobriner, *Community*, p. 375.

2. Ebenezer Howard, *Garden Cities of Tomorrow* (London, 1965), p. 48. Italics his.

3. The term "middle landscape" is borrowed from Leo Marx, *The Machine in the Garden* (New York, 1964). Marx applied the concept of the middle landscape primarily to literature, not to intellectual history, but it has relevance to both disciplines. Note, for example, its application to Crevecoeur's "middle settlements" in J. Hector St. John de Crevecoeur, *Letters from an American Farmer* (London, 1926), pp. 44–45.

4. Alexander Jackson Downing, in John Burchard and Albert Bush-Brown, *The Architecture of America* (Boston, 1961), p. 101.

5. *Harper's Weekly*, Vol. XX, No. 1006 (April 8, 1876), p. 294.

6. *Harper's Weekly*, Vol. XX, No. 1027 (September 5, 1876), p. 709.

7. Henry George, *Progress and Poverty* (New York, 1884), p. 405.

8. Carl N. Degler, *Out of Our Past* (New York and Evanston, 1959), p. 327.

9. In A. Whitney Griswold, *Farming and Democracy* (New Haven, 1952), pp. 179–80.

10. Adna F. Weber, *The Growth of Cities in the Nineteenth Century* (Ithaca, New York, 1963), p. 475.

11. Frederic C. Howe, *The City: The Hope of Democracy* (New York, 1905), p. 204.

12. Josiah Royce, *Race Questions, Provincialism and Other American Problems* (New York, 1908), pp. 97–98, and George Santayana, *The Background of My Life* (New York, 1944), p. 298.

13. Louis Sullivan, *The Autobiography of an Idea* (New York, 1922), pp. 98–99.

14. Robert Ezra Park, *Human Communities: The City and Human Ecology* (Glencoe, 1952), pp. 34, 140.

15. John Dewey, *The Public and Its Problems* (New York, 1927), pp. 211, 214. See also Morton and Lucia White, *The Intellectual versus the City* (New York, 1964), pp. 177–79. The Whites maintain that the attitude of the intellectual toward the American city underwent a change in the late nineteenth century, from an attitude of basic hostility to one of belief in the potentiality of the city, once it was reformed. But the reformers seemed almost invariably to want to change the city back into the rural village.

16. John R. McMahon, *Success in the Suburbs* (New York and London, 1917), pp. x–xi.

17. McMahon, *Success*, pp. 16, 24, 193–94.

18. *Ibid.*, vii, 173, 201.

19. Paul K. Conkin, *Tomorrow a New World* (Ithaca, New York, 1959), pp. 51–53.

20. Ralph Borsodi, *Flight from the City: The Story of a New Way to Family Security* (New York, 1933), pp. 1–19.

21. Newspaper advertisement, undated, in files of Bloomington Historical Society, Bloomington, Minnesota.

22. Twelve Southerners, "I'll Take My Stand" (New York, 1930), *City and Country in America*, ed. David R. Weimer (New York, 1962), pp. 121–22.

23. Harlan Paul Douglass, *The Suburban Trend* (New York, 1925), p. 327.

24. Conkin, *New World,* pp. 6–7. In reviewing the community building programs of the New Deal, this essay relies heavily on Conkin's excellent book.

25. Conkin, *New World,* pp. 87–130.

26. Conkin, *New World,* pp. 153–325.

27. Jane Jacobs, *The Death and Life of Great American Cities* (New York, 1961), pp. 444–47.

28. Frederick A. Shippey, *Protestantism in Suburban Life* (New York and Nashville, 1964), p. 117.

29. Quoted in Anselm Strauss, "The Changing Imagery of American City and Suburb," *Sociological Quarterly,* Vol. I, No. 1 (January 1960), p. 21.

30. Burchard and Bush-Brown, *The Architecture of America,* p. 121.

31. Thomas Ktsanes and Leonard Reissman, "Suburbia—New Homes for Old Values," *Social Problems,* Vol. VII, No. 3 (Winter, 1959–60), p. 195.

32. *Life,* Vol. LIX, No. 26 (December 24, 1965), pp. 37, 139.

33. Wolf von Eckardt, "New Towns in America," *New Republic,* Vol. CXLIX, No. 17 (October 26, 1963), p. 17.

34. Albert Mayer in consultation with Clarence Stein, "New Towns: and Fresh In-City Communities," *Architectural Record,* Vol. CXXXVI, No. 2 (August 1964), pp. 131–32.

35. "Reston," *Architectural Record,* Vol. CXXXVI, No. 1 (July 1964), p. 120.

36. Mayer and Stein, "New Towns," pp. 134–36.

37. Ada Louise Huxtable, " 'Clusters' Instead of 'Slurbs,' " *New York Times Magazine* (February 9, 1964), p. 44.

38. Morton and Lucia White, *The Intellectual versus the City* (New York, 1964), p. 238.

SYLVIA F. FAVA

THE POP SOCIOLOGY OF SUBURBS AND NEW TOWNS

The mid-twentieth century is a sociologizing age, as the early twentieth was a psychologizing period, and still earlier periods were dominated by biological and mechanical frames of reference. We hear sociologizing at cocktail parties and kaffeeklatsches, in corporate boardrooms and in laundry rooms—and sometimes even in sociology classrooms. The household words and themes of pop sociology include *anomie,* alienation, the Protestant Ethnic, intergroup relations, the "empty nest stage" of family life, mass society, the generation gap, participatory democracy, the "other directed type," conflict, the role of women, the "power elite" and the "establishment" and, of course, the urban crisis.

In many ways the world is now viewed in sociological images—groups, affiliations, social class and social mobility, deviance and control, the processes of change, the structure of institutions, demographic and ecological balance. We have now reached the point where few college freshmen have to be taught that socialization has another meaning than the nationalization of steel and coal production. Sociological thinking has become part of what John Kenneth Galbraith called "the conventional wisdom—the structure of ideas that is based on acceptability."[1]

Much of the sociology we find around us is pop sociology. The overriding characteristic of pop sociology is that it involves no suspension of judgment or assessment of evidence and is therefore stereotyped and unscientific. Pop sociology's second major feature—the ideological, moral or evaluative tenor of its statements—is linked to its stereotyped approach and, in fact, often explains why such an approach was applied. These two defining traits of pop sociology lead to a host of subsidiary characteristics. Pop sociology is "instant"—it never fails of an answer because judgment is seldom suspended. It is simple and clear. Indeed it is oversimplified, for it has few definitions or delineations of statements; pop sociology is relatively untested. It is also all-encompassing; it applies sociological approaches broadly to all areas and topics. Pop sociology is

American Studies, Vol. 14 (Spring, 1973) 121-133. Copyright © 1973 by Midcontinent American Studies Association, Reprinted by permission of the author and publisher.

often geared to a wide audience in response to a social "crisis." In sum, pop sociology may be provocative but it is also superficial, often to the point of inaccuracy or confusion. Pop sociology is not new; it is deep-seated and probably as old as sociology. What is new is the widespread currency of pop sociology.

As indicated above, the most important characteristic of pop sociology is its lack of rigor or systematic thought. Pop sociology is seldom empirical or "factual" but that is not its crucial lack; whether empirical or speculative it fails in giving a reasoned base and thorough search. These very failings give pop sociology its virtues. Precisely because it is free-flowing and unfettered by a broad conceptual apparatus, pop sociology may provide useful insights. One of the uses of pop sociology lies in providing hypotheses for new research. Unfortunately this is not typically the course of pop sociology; rather it is offered, without *caveats*, to a wide public as "answers" and conclusions.

Although usually presented in simple language, pop sociology must be distinguished from the attempts to "translate" technical sociological concepts, language and findings into layman's terms. Such "translation" is the aim of the project, Sociological Resources for the Social Studies, sponsored by the American Sociological Association and supported by the National Science Foundation. The volume on urban sociology is a notably successful attempt at clearing out the underbrush and presenting the major contributions in a responsible, interesting and lucid way.[2]

Several illustrations may clarify the nature of pop sociology. The youth rebellion, particularly on campuses, is the focus of pop sociology that we are probably most familiar with at the present time. The explanations include affluence and poverty, each of which is used to "explain" disregard of property and propriety; permissive parents who don't keep their offspring in line and restrictive parents who have to be rebelled against; rebellious youth is characterized as still struggling to find itself via identity crises and is also characterized as exceptionally mature and clearthinking.[3] A year or so ago the major focus of pop sociology was the "culture of poverty" in which the concepts of culture and subculture were bandied about so loosely as to be almost shapeless, particularly when they were applied to discussion of the lower-class black family.

Pop sociology is widespread in the mass media and practiced by the "man in the street." But it is also often found among professional social scientists themselves, particularly when they are pressed into making quick analyses of profound issues for a waiting public. Thus, an issue of the *New York Times Magazine*[4] featured a symposium, "Is America by Nature a Violent Society?" in which the following analyses were made:

> However repulsive and shocking H. Rap Brown's quip may seem—"Violence is as American as cherry pie"—his motive for saying it must not obscure the fact that he was telling it like it is.
>
> The American white-collar set have so little direct experience with violence that it is difficult for them to conceive of it as an ever-present reality—or possibility—in a person's daily life, although they know that the Indians were herded onto the reservations by force, that violence was used both to keep Negroes in slavery and to free them, and that assault and battery, rape and murder occur every now and then. The older people in the labor movement know something

of the historic confrontations between trade unionists and the forces of law and order, though young workers know almost nothing of the great labor struggles of the past. Negroes understand the reality of violence better than most Americans, for most of them have witnessed it in varied forms, even if they have not experienced it. But all Americans need to face the fact that American society—as compared with some others in the world—is a very violent society. Self-delusion is self-defeating. We can never lower the level of violence unless we admit that it is omnipresent and understand the forces that generate it. (St. Clair Drake)

The next participant in the symposium says:

In a period which has seen the German massacre of the Jews, the communal horrors of Indian partition, the convulsive destructiveness of the last days of L'Algerie Francaise, the mass executions accompanying the Indonesian change of regime, the terrible civil wars in Nigeria and the Congo, and the wild riots in Sharpesville, it is difficult for the hardiest celebrant of the American Way of Life to claim for his country any special gift for violence. We are, it turns out, a people like any other. There is nothing particularly distinctive about the ways we destroy one another.

The notion that "violence is as American as cherry pie" is one more cliche which we invoke to prevent our seeing our situation for what it is . . . . (Clifford Geertz)

Why should we take pop sociology seriously? Perhaps for somewhat the same reasons that caused pop sociology to become prominent now: the predominantly *social* nature of many of the problems around us today: civil rights, family interaction, the aged, population growth and redistribution; the emergence of large-scale organization and bureaucracy in virtually every phase of life including the school, religion, and leisure; and the very rapid social change on a scale without precedent in human history. The pervading nature of these pressures leads to a sense of urgency in understanding and in finding solutions.

The urgency of our concern often produces elements of pop in the many attempts to .apply social science, especially sociology, to policies and programs on specific current issues. Since so many of these current issues are urban-located or urban-related, approaches to urban phenomena are often infected with pop. The pressure on sociology and other social sciences for "answers" to the urban enigma are widespread. The pop approach and reform may often be related, as sociologically unsound or half-baked programs are put into effect based on *convictions* rather than evidence. Thus, a *belief* in participatory democracy—or in the stultifying impact of suburban life—may lead to projects or to individual and group actions which are not well-supported by data or logic. All action programs tend to be "arts" rather than "sciences," as administrators know. Yet even a brief look at the community action field—whether the war on poverty, community control of schools, decentralization of government, advocacy planning, or other instances that might be cited—suggests that action programs often have in addition some pop qualities, pseudo-expertise and ideological bias, compounded by urgency, concern and widespread interest.

How is suburbia a manifestation of pop sociology? Suburbia has a legitimate claim as the first of the major social changes that attracted broad public attention and was widely disseminated through the mass media.[5] The "teenager" syndrome and the early Kinsey reports on sexual behavior are, I believe, the other two major examples of pop sociology in the immediate post-war period.

Suburbia entered the public awareness about the time World War II ended, when the building-boom in outlying areas became a visible signal of something new on the horizon. Sociologists had been studying and writing about metropolitan development, of which suburban development is a part, for several decades before then; United States suburbs themselves date at least into the latter part of the nineteenth century and had become widespread by 1920. It is neither the time lag between professional and public awareness nor the popularity of the topic which makes suburbia "pop," however, although these do enhance the process. It is the spurious accuracy and partisanship which make pop sociology of many public, and some professional, presentations of suburbia. The result is a debased public currency of suburbia.

The pop image of suburbia revolves around the related themes of a contrast between the central city and the suburb, and stultifying, homogeneous conformity. Thus, the suburbs are presented as bedroom communities, residential outposts of the white, educated, affluent middle class for which Scarsdale has become the national byword. The central cities are the home of the blacks, the poor, and the locales of the problems besetting American society. This stereotypical central city-suburban contrast has long since been shown false in the professional literature.

There is no one kind of suburb (neither is there one kind of city), hence there is no one central city-suburb contrast. It follows there are no uniquely urban or suburban problems. The sociologist Leo Schnore, has been working for at least a decade on detailing the various types of central city/suburban contrast and seeking the dynamics explaining the formation of types of metropolitan area.[6] Using education as an index of socio-economic status, he delineated six different patterns of variation between central city and suburb. Only one of these exemplified the pattern reflected in the pop conception of suburbs, in which the lowest classes are overrepresented in the central city and the higher the educational status the more suburbanized the population.[7] The New York metropolis exhibits this classic pattern, while Los Angeles exemplifies another and Tucson and Albuquerque still other patterns. The classic pattern appears to be associated with the larger metropolitan areas and those which are "older," that is, which reached large size relatively early. In the "newer" and smaller metropolitan areas suburbanization may not be so far advanced toward the classic pattern, or population may actually be redistributing in accord with newer, different industrial and transport processes.

On the basis of the professional literature, then, a simple contrast between high status suburbs and low status cities is at best only partly true. Similarly, if we turn to the pop picture of the stultifying and conformist nature of suburban life we find that professional sociology has shattered this image. At least as long ago as Bennett Berger's 1960 study,[8] there have been data available to show that suburbanites are not miraculously reborn in the suburban setting. Politics and voting behavior, religion, family life, personality formation, educational goals and practices, leisure pursuits, interactive patterns in the neighborhood and participation in voluntary organizations have all been put under the microscope in literally dozens of studies. They show there is no single way of suburban life nor any uniform effect of the suburban experience on those who live in suburbs.

The reality of the suburban impact on individuals' lives and thought is far more complex than pop sociology would lead us to believe. One study dealt with the question of whether there are distinctive suburban psychological characteristics, particularly the assertion that suburban residence fosters anti-intellectual attitudes.[9] The data included questionnaire responses from over 33,000 college seniors graduating in 1961 from 135 colleges in the United States. Initial comparisons showed no significant differences in intellectual attitudes between college seniors who had been raised in cities and those who had been raised in suburbs.

However, further analysis showed that there *is* a relationship between suburban residence and anti-intellectualism, but that it is more complex than commonly supposed. When the items measuring anti-intellectualism were cross-tabulated with the kind of communities students said they *wished* to live in rather than by the communities the students had grown up in, then the suburb-oriented students differed significantly from the urban-oriented students in anti-intellectualism. That is, those who indicated a *desire* to live in the suburbs were less likely to be concerned with access to cultural activities and less likely to think of themselves as intellectuals. The final analysis suggests that anti-intellectualism in suburbia is partly a result of family-cycle (more married students prefer suburbs and they are likely to have less time for intellectual activities), partly a result of selectivity (the students expressing a preference for suburban living are more anti-intellectual) and partly a result of the influence of community of origin (regardless of their marital status and intellectual attitudes, students who were brought up in suburbs more often expressed a desire to live in suburbs than those who had been raised in the city).

The vision of a homogeneous and conformist suburbia has been negated by sociological research, yet the pop version remains and continues to be spread by the mass media. Why? The answer, I think, lies in the ideological aspect of popness. The pop sociology of the suburbs is not only inaccurate, it is inaccurate for a reason. (In saying this, I do not mean that there exists a conscious plot to make it inaccurate.)

The ideological aspect of pop suburbia has two main components. The first relates to the persistence of the myth of homogeneity. According to one sociologist, the belief that suburbs are homogeneous operates to sustain a belief in the "American dream" of equals cooperating in a democratic society. The American dream is undermined by the realities of long-standing economic and ethnic differentiation and by our fundamental ambivalence toward melting-pot as opposed to pluralist development. In view of the flaws in the American dream it becomes important to reaffirm it in the major new setting of American life, the suburbs. Thus, the myth of the homogeneous, classless suburbia persists.[10]

Although the foregoing observations were based on impressionistic data they are lent some substance by Herbert Gans' study of Levittown, New Jersey, in which he concludes, after several years of participant-observation and close study that one of the shortcomings that Levittown shares with other American communities is an

> inability to deal with pluralism. People have not recognized the diversity of American society, and they are not able to

accept other life styles. Indeed, they cannot handle conflict because they cannot accept pluralism. Adults are unwilling to tolerate adolescent culture, and vice versa. Lower middle class people oppose the ways of the working class and upper middle class, and each of these groups is hostile to the other two. Perhaps the inability to cope with pluralism is greater in Levittown than elsewhere because it is a community of young families who are raising children. Children are essentially asocial and unacculturated beings, easily influenced by new ideas. As a result, their parents feel an intense need to defend familial values; to make sure that their children grow up according to parental norms and not by those of their playmates from another class. The need to shield the children from what are considered harmful influences begins on the block, but it is translated into the conflict over the school, the definitional struggles within voluntary associations whose programs affect the socialization of children, and, ultimately into political conflicts. Each group wants to put its stamp on the organizations and institutions that are the community, for otherwise the family and its culture are not safe.[11]

The second ideological component of pop suburbs relates to the allegedly conformist, anti-intellectual features of suburban life. Most likely this evaluation is a function of the fact that most writers on suburbs are upper middle class intellectuals who are projecting onto the suburbs their dissatisfaction with the "bourgeois" and to them debased standards in lower middle class suburbs. Most recently this tendency has been revealed in the characterization of Spiro T. Agnew. One newspaper columnist, under the title, "The Sterile Paradise of Suburban Man," says:

Agnew's biography sounds like Warren Harding's might if Harding had been a character in a novel by Sinclair Lewis and Lewis had been writing in the 1960s. He [Agnew] is so typical of the new suburban man that he almost seems to parody his class. . . . The people to whom he speaks are at least as afraid of losing what they already possess as they are eager to acquire more. For every daydream of personal success they have two nightmares of armed, marauding Negroes who will burn down their communities. They do not want to nationalize the giant corporations . . . they only want the great businessmen they've been raised to respect . . . to protect them and stop encouraging their enemies, the black and the student dissenters. . . . And his audiences seem eager to live in the sterile paradise his speeches promise. As far as many of America's new suburbanites are concerned, Agnew, son of a poor Greek immigrant, the luckiest Horatio Alger in this country's history, is describing the enchanted, protected land their parents and grandparents came all this way to find.[12]

Another author says: ". . . Agnew the Vice President is no more than the commonplace made exceptional, the conventional made controversial, instinct promoted into intellect and suburbia made sublime."[13] This kind of bias would account for the lingering tendency of even professional sociologists to write condescendingly of suburbs. To the upper middle class professional the "city" is the place where civilization resides.[14]

In the broadest sense it appears that the suburban myth of harmony, greenery and cultural kitsch is the contemporary staging ground for the long-standing American preference for rural life. In the modern age, when, through the sheer lack of farm experience on the part of the vast majority of the population, agrarianism has lost its force as a normative standard, the familiar dialogue between ruralism and urbanism may peter out. In place of the nineteenth-century discussions of whether the city or the country is more "civilized," we may have discussions of whether urban or suburban life is more "cultured." In place of the city versus the country debate we may have the city versus the suburb. This does not necessarily mean that suburbs are replacing the country in the sense of being rural; it does mean that the suburbs, like all community forms, have the power to arouse emotion and partisanship. As new community forms arise, they become invested with symbolic meaning and enter the arena of public opinion.

After studying the political structure of suburbs, Robert Wood, a political scientist, concluded that it represented a renaissance of the small-town and village ideal.[15] Suburban governments, according to Wood, are typically small, ineffective and expensive, unsuitable for coping with metropolitan area problems. Yet suburbanites stubbornly resist efforts at a consolidation into larger governmental jurisdictions, and small-scale suburban governments are, in fact, proliferating. Wood points out that the attachment to suburban government is ideological, stemming from a belief that the small community produces the best life, and the best government.

> Suburbia, defined as an ideology, a faith in communities of limited size and a belief in the conditions of intimacy, is quite real. The dominance of the old values explains more about the people and politics of the suburbs than any other interpretation. Fundamentally, it explains the nature of the American metropolis. . . . If these values were not dominant it would be quite possible to conceive of a single gigantic metropolitan region under one government and socially conscious of itself as one community. The new social ethic, the rise of the large organization, would lead us to expect this development as a natural one. The automobile, the subway, the telephone, the power line certainly make it technically possible; they even push us in this direction.
>
> But the American metropolis is not constructed in such a way; it sets its face directly against modernity. Those who wish to rebuild the American city, who protest the shapeless urban sprawl, who find some value in the organizational skills of modern society, must recognize the potency of the ideology. Until these beliefs have been accommodated reform will not come in the metropolitan areas nor will men buckle down to the task of directing, in a manner consonant with freedom, the great political and social organizations on which the nation's strength depends.[16]

It has become increasingly difficult to maintain the simple pop sociology view of suburbs as evidence mounts, from the 1970 census and other sources, of the diversity of suburbs and the increasing resemblance of older suburbs to cities, in terms of structure and problems. Crime and delinquency rates have been rising rapidly in many suburbs, as has the drug problem; welfare, pollution, traffic congestion and unbalanced budgets have emerged as major issues; office decentralization has accelerated in many large metropolitan areas and some shopping centers have become miniature downtowns in the range and variety of goods and services offered—and as locales for vandalism and burglary, as congregating places for "undesirables." "Black suburbs" have become increasingly important, although this trend does not appear to be accompanied by racial or economic integration, despite the mounting attack on suburban exclusionary zoning. Both the professional literature and the mass media have begun to reflect this new view of suburbia.[17]

Suburbs are now being succeeded by a new community focus of pop sociology, New Towns, the large planned communities of which Reston, Virginia, and Columbia, Maryland, are often cited as examples.[18] Suburbs were the focus of community pop sociology in the period of public awareness of metropolitan emergence; New Towns are the expression of community pop sociology in the era of the mature metropolis.

New Towns represent a new policy for the same set of needs expressed earlier in the image of suburbia. There is the same anti-urbanism, the fear and distrust of the city, expressed now in the desire to control and manage urban growth and density by carefully pre-cast new communities. As with suburbs there is also the same concern with diversity, the containment of conflict and the maintenance of outward harmony and equality. There are, however, two important ways in which New Towns contrast markedly with suburbs. First, New Towns, usually called New Communities in this context, have become a legislatively-enacted goal of the federal government. Although it has been argued that home mortgage legislation, subsidies for highway construction and other governmental policies indirectly fostered suburban expansion,[19] there was never specific suburban legislation.

The official support of the federal government for New Towns dates to the passage of the Demonstration Cities and Metropolitan Development Act of 1966. This Act expanded FHA mortgage coverage, through the Department of Housing and Urban Development, to include privately financed New Communities. However, these provisions were hedged with so many restrictions that the New Communities provisions were not put to effective use. Many of these restrictions were removed by the Housing and Urban Development Act of 1968, legislation which has been called the urban equivalent of the Homestead Act of 1862. Title IV of the 1968 Act, entitled "New Communities," expanded the financial backing of New Communities and this prompted a large number of applications to HUD by private developers.[20] By 1971 five New Communities had received federal financial guarantees. The Housing and Urban Development Act of 1970, under Title VII, "Urban Growth and New Community Development," carries federal support of New Towns several important steps further,[21] and has attracted widespread interest from private and public developers.[22] By Spring 1973 fifteen New Communities had received federal guarantees of the specified financial obligations.

The second major way in which New Towns in the United States contrast with suburbs is in the explicit concern in the New Towns with social issues. Thus, Title IV of the 1968 Act includes as one of the conditions of eligibility that the New Community include the "proper balance" of housing units for families of low and moderate income. The

1970 Act lists among the ten reasons for developing new communities that "continuation of established patterns of urban development . . . will result in . . . (1) unduly limited options for many of our people as to where they may live, and the types of housing and environment in which they live; . . . (2) further lessening of employment and business opportunities for the residents of central cities and of the ability of such cities to retain a tax base adequate to support vital services for all their citizens, particularly the poor and disadvantaged; (3) further separation of people within metropolitan areas by income and by race."[23] Each New Community proposal presented by HUD must contain a special social plan indicating how it proposes to implement the stated goals.

In understanding the social concerns of the New Communities legislation one must recognize that the New Towns movement in the United States gathered momentum in the 1960's in the wake of the "urban crisis." Important milestones in the mounting urban concerns of that period include the first message on cities to Congress by any President, President Johnson's March 1965 message on "Problems and Future of the Central City and Its Suburbs," and his February 1968 message, "The Crisis of Our Cities"; a series of comprehensive reports[24] documenting in staggering detail a group of urban problems: poverty, unparalleled growth, gross housing inadequacy, racial segregation, crime and violence; and the piecemeal recognition of the changing nature of the American city as metropolitan development entered a new phase heralded by suburban dominance.[25]

New Towns are clearly a matter of public policy. How does our public and professional view of them partake of pop sociology? Essentially because New Towns are seen as a solution to many urban and indeed national ills for which critical evidence on specific social questions involved is lacking or ambiguous. Ideology has taken the place of evidence; matters of belief have become accepted as matters of fact.

Such socially-relevant terms as "participation," "balance," "diversity" and "optimum size" have seldom even been defined in the context of New Towns discussion. New Towns involve assumptions regarding the nature and desirability of neighborhood interaction; high-rise and multi-family vs. low-rise and single-family homes; the impact of density and community size on the human psyche; the importance of propinquity as a catalyst for meaningful contact; the merits of community self-sufficiency; the benefits of diversity and balance; the manner in which housing choices are made; the virtues of local participation and decentralization.

An overview of the published work on New Towns indicates the pop nature of public and much professional thinking on the social goals of New Towns. There is a Niagara of material: for example, at least seven bibliographies on New Towns in the United States.[26] Allowing for duplication there are several thousand separate published books, articles and reports. They come from a broad spectrum of national circulation magazines (*Harper's, U.S. News and World Report, Saturday Review*) and from the professionals journals, house organs and publications of sociologists, planners, architects, builders, large corporations, housers and public officials. The literature is overwhelmingly pro-New Town, indicating a broad dissemination and acceptance of the New Town idea, which is underscored by the passage of the 1970 Housing and Urban Development Act and by the testimony in its favor from witnesses representing a wide variety of groups.

Only a relatively small proportion of the published work deals with the social aspects of New Towns in the United States; most treats architecture, design, finance, management and legislation. This emphasis seems significant in view of the importance of social goals both in the federal legislation and in many of the privately financed New Towns.

For the purpose of pop sociology, there are two significant characteristics of the existing socially-relevant material. First, the empirical material is typically fragmentary, low-level description with little possibility of generalizability. In this, the literature on the New Towns resembles the pop sociology of suburbia. The two are also alike in that definitional problems compound the difficulty of generalizing. One man's New Town is another's satellite city and still another's "large development." Second, much of the material has no empirical base at all, but is hortatory—it merely advises and states the desirability of New Towns to achieve social goals and policies. Given these two characteristics it follows that the "how" of achieving the social goals of New Towns is not often specified.

Behind the pop treatment of suburbia lay a backlog of professional research which needed popularization; for the New Towns, there was no such backlog. The central issue of racial and economic integration in New Towns is a case in point.[27] While this situation offers opportunity for well-focused research on major public policy implications of New Towns, it also warns against unexamined acceptance of the pop sociology view of New Towns as the brake halting the movement toward "two societies." There are only two investigations of any depth related to this matter; neither is conclusive. In one study a multiple-choice questionnaire which had been developed from long depth interviews, was administered to almost 800 residents of New Towns in two different metropolitan areas of California.[28] The results indicated that a major reason for buying in New Towns was the belief that "planning" protected the community against the intrusion of economic and racial diversity.

The other study examined a matched sample of ten new communities differing in location, age and degree of planning. It concluded that degree of residential satisfaction with the community as a whole was positively associated with degree of planning.[29] The analysis of reasons for satisfaction with the immediate neighborhood was less clear, although dwelling unit density, the condition of the neighborhood (whether it is "well kept up") and compatibility of neighborhood residents were important features. The authors stress the difficulties in measuring compatibility, which they found related to attitudes rather than to the expected socio-economic and demographic homogeneity. "For people in our sample it appears that shared attitudes and evaluations concerning the neighborhood and community were most salient in defining neighbors as both 'friendly' and 'similar.' . . . In other words, when consensus (homogeneity) exists among neighbors about qualities of the residential environment, the neighbors themselves tend to be more positively evaluated."[30]

The matter of operationalizing the concept of "homogeneity" (and, of course, "heterogeneity" and "balance") remains, although both New Towns studies above indicate the importance of some kind of local homogeneity, as do studies in such diverse New Town settings as Britain[31] and Israel.[32] The burden of these studies is not to discourage policy planners from aiming at racial and economic integration and "balance" in New Towns. On the contrary, it should point up the necessity of going beyond the labeling of pop sociology which simply defines "balance" as a goal.

The pop sociology of New Towns offers a current opportunity to utilize the immediacy and provocativeness of the pop approach in generating wide interest, while avoiding the instant "solutions" of pop. If sociology is to be useful in dealing with vital issues such as the form of future urban growth then action must be taken. However, the public and the government must recognize more fully the need for experimental approaches which permit tests of the validity of unproved assumptions. As we have indicated, the pop sociology of suburbs and New Towns provides many such assumptions. What has been lacking is the spelling out of assumptions and the attendant hidden hypotheses with which pop sociology abounds and the systematic testing out of these hypotheses in a variety of simulated or actual suburbs or New Town contexts. The result would give us knowledge about the social processes at work and the limits of such knowledge. We would have laid the basis for improved decision-making in selecting the goals for further community development. More broadly we would have substituted sociology—warts and all—for the silicone curves of pop sociology.

NOTES

1. *The Affluent Society* (Boston, 1958), 18.
2. Helen MacGill Hughes, compiler and editor, *Cities and City Life* (Boston, 1970). It is most instructive for an understanding of pop sociology to compare the Hughes book with even a superior, relatively well-balanced treatment of urban phenomena in the pop genre: Vance Packard's *A Nation of Strangers* (New York, 1972).
3. In contrast to the pop treatment of youth, see Philip C. Altbach and Robert S. Laufer, eds., *The New Pilgrims: Youth Protest in Transition* (New York, 1972). This reader includes historical and cross-cultural materials and relates youth protest to the strucure of society as an aspect of generational conflict, social class and radical movements; an appended bibliography by Kenneth Keniston contains several hundred items reviewing research and further indicates how youth movements are imbedded in the overall social system.
4. April 28, 1968.
5. For example in such works as: Frederick Allen, "The Big Change in Suburbia," *Harper's*, CCVIII, 1249 (June, 1954); Hal Burton, "Trouble in the Suburbs," *Saturday Evening Post*, CCVIII, 12-14 (September 17, 24; October 1, 1955); R. Gordon, K. Gordon, and M. Gunther, *The Split Level Trap* (New York, 1961); Sidonie Gruenberg, "The Homogenized Children of the New Suburbia," *New York Times Magazine* (September 19, 1954); Harry Henderson, "The Mass Produced Suburbs," *Harper's*, CCVII, 1242-1243 (November-December, 1953); T. James, "Crackups in the Suburbs," *Cosmopolitan*, CLI, 4 (October, 1961): John Keats, *The Crack in the Picture Window* (Boston, 1956); Alice Miel, *The Shortchanged Children of Suburbia* (New York, 1968); A. C. Spectorsky, *The Exurbanites* (Philadelphia, 1955); William H. Whyte, *The Organization Man* (New York, 1956); Peter Wyden, *Suburbia's Coddled Kids* (Garden City, 1960).
6. See for example, the articles collected in Parts II and IV of Leo F. Schnore, *The Urban Scene* (New York, 1965); also his "Measuring City-Suburban Status Differences," *Urban Affairs Quarterly*, III, 1 (September, 1967) and Schnore and Pinkerton, "Residential Redistribution of Socioeconomic Strata in Metropolitan Areas," *Demography*, III, 2 (1966). For a different approach which also supports the diversity of the central city-suburban contrast see, Advisory Commission on Intergovernmental Relations, *Metropolitan Social and Economic Disparities* (Washington, D.C., 1965) and Advisory Commission on Intergovernmental Relations, *Metropolitan Fiscal Disparities*, vol. 2 of *Fiscal Balance in the American Federal System* (Washington, D.C., 1967).
7. "Urban Structure and Suburban Selectivity," in Schnore, *The Urban Scene*.
8. *Working-Class Suburb* (Berkeley, 1960).
9. Joseph Zelan, "Does Suburbia Make a Difference," in S. F. Fava, ed., *Urbanism in World Perspective* (New York, 1968).
10. Bennett Berger, "Suburbia and the American Dream," in Fava, *Urbanism in World Perspective*.
11. Herbert J. Gans, *The Levittowners* (New York, 1967), 414.
12. Paul Cowan in *The Village Voice* (New York) October 10, 1968.
13. Peter Jenkins, "Agnew is the Common Man Made Exceptional," *New York Times Magazine* (October 29, 1972), 94.

14. The reviews of Gans' *The Levittowners* have already noted that it is the first major sociological work on suburbs which does not condescend to the new middle classes. Gans "does not find them comic or menacing, barbarians to be subdued or living corpses to be exhumed," says Marvin Bressler in his review of Gans' book in *The Public Interest* (1968), 102.

15. Robert C. Wood, *Suburbia, Its People and Their Politics* (Boston, 1958), chapter 1.

16. *Ibid.*, 18-19.

17. John B. Orr and F. Patrick Michelson, *The Radical Suburb* (Philadelphia, 1970); Scott Donaldson, *The Suburban Myth* (New York, 1969); "The Suburbs: Frontier of the '70's," special issue of *City*, V (January-February, 1971); "Suburbia: A Myth Challenged," cover story in *Time*, XCVII, 11 (March 15, 1971); "The Outer City: U.S. in Suburban Turmoil," series of five articles in the *New York Times* (May 30-June 3, 1971).

18. A useful definition of New Towns in the United States is that they are ". . . *large-scale developments* [1,000 acres or more] *constructed under single or unified management, following a fairly precise, inclusive plan and including different types of housing, commercial and cultural facilities, and amenities sufficient to serve the residents of the community. They may provide land for industry, offer other types of employment opportunities, and may eventually achieve a considerable measure of self-sufficiency. With few exceptions, new communities under development today are within commuting distance of existing employment centers.*" Advisory Commission on Intergovernmental Relations, *Urban and Rural America: Policies for Future Growth* (Washington, D.C., 1968), 64. HUD has estimated that in 1947-1969 there were 63 new communities built or under construction in the U.S. which met such a definition. Virtually all were built under private financing since they predated the federal supports for New Towns. "HUD Survey and Analysis of Large Developments and New Communities," *Urban Land.* XXIX (January, 1970), 11-12.

19. See for example, B. Weissbourd, "Segregation, Subsidies, and Megalopolis," in Fava, ed., *Urbanism in World Perspective.*

20. The 1966 Act had required developers to obtain funds from private lenders and was restricted to mortgages on land; the 1968 Act authorized HUD to guarantee the bonds and other obligations issued by developers of New Communities to finance land acquisition and its development for building.

21. Major new provisions: (1) the federal government will assume responsibility for formulating a national urban growth policy which includes the encouragement of a variety of planned new communities; (2) the Domestic Council in the Office of the President will send to Congress every two years, beginning in 1972, a Report on Urban Growth covering the preceding ten years; (3) the creation within HUD of a Community Development Corporation working with public bodies and private developers to spur new community development through a system of loans, guarantees, and technical assistance to provide for planning, land acquisition, development, public facilities and services; (4) loans for new communities totaling $240 million are authorized ($20 million limit per community) as are $500 million in guarantees of obligations of private *and* public developers ($50 million limit per community).

22. For example, see Eleanore Carruth, "The Big Move to New Towns," Fortune, LXXXIV, 3 (September, 1971).

23. Housing and Urban Development Act of 1970, Part B, Sec. 710 (b).

24. An incomplete list would include: National Commission on Urban Problems (the "Douglas Commission"); President's Commission on Urban Housing (the "Kaiser Commission"); National Advisory Commission on Civil Disorder (the "Kerner Commission"); Advisory Commission on Intergovernmental Relations, *Urban and Rural America: Policies for Future Growth.*

25. The 1970 census showed, for example, that in only 7 of the 25 metropolitan areas with over a million in population, did the central city population outnumber that of the suburban areas surrounding it; in 1960 central city population outnumbered suburban in 15 of the same 25 metropolitan areas.

26. Joy Akin, *The Feasibility and Actuality of Modern New Towns for the Poor in the United States* (Monticello, Ill., 1970); James A. Clapp, *The New Town Concept: Private Trends and Public Response* (Monticello, Ill., 1970); HUD, *New Communities: A Bibliography* (Washington, D.C., 1969); T. C. Peng and N. S. Verna, *New Towns Planning, Design and Development: Comprehensive Reference Materials* (Lincoln, Neb., 1971); Melvin C. Branch, "New Towns," in his *Comprehensive Urban Planning* (Beverly Hills, Calif., 1970); Housing and Home Finance Agency, *New Communities: A Selected Annotated Reading List* (Washington, D.C., 1965); *Minnesota Experimental City Progress Reports*, 2nd edition, Appendix A, "A Compendium of Publications relating to Socio-Cultural Aspects," and Appendix D, "Bibliography" (Minneapolis, 1969).

27. The question has been examined in detail elsewhere. See Sylvia F. Fava, "The Sociology of New Towns in the U.S.: 'Balance' of Racial and Economic Groups" (paper delivered at the American Institute of Planners Conference, Minneapolis-St. Paul, October 1970).

28. Carl Werthman, Jerry S. Mandel and Ted Dienstfrey, *Planning and the Purchase Decision. Why People Buy in Planned Communities* (Berkeley, 1965).

29. John B. Lansing, Robert W. Marans and Robert B. Zehner, *Planned Residential Environments* (Ann Arbor, 1971).

30. *Ibid.*, 125.

31. B. J. Heraud, "Social Class and the New Towns," *Urban Studies*, V (February, 1968); and Heraud, "New Towns: The End of a Planner's Dream," *New Society*, XII, 302 (July 11, 1968).

32. Judith Shuval, "Relations between Ethnic Groups," Appendix A to "The Integral Habitational Unit at Kiryat-Gat," *Ministry of Housing Quarterly* (Israel), III (December, 1967), 92-98.

PART THREE
SUBURBANIZATION AND NEW TOWNS AS IDEOLOGICAL MOVEMENTS

WILLIAM M. DOBRINER

THE SUBURBAN EVANGEL

There is probably nothing in modern social science for which so many explanations have been advanced to explain and interpret a phenomenon, with such inconclusive results, as the forces which have given rise to the contemporary suburb. Suburbs are significant in the structure of American community organization, but no one has really discovered why they have grown so large and so fast. The questions relating to suburban development are deceptively simple. What are the factors behind suburban growth? Why are cities losing population? How big will the suburbs get? Will the growth stop? Some of the problems are purely demographic, and reasonable projections of suburban growth for the future can be made. The questions, however, which touch upon the "forces" behind suburban growth—the motivations of suburbanites, the shifting institutional structure of metropolitan areas and changing ideologies—are another matter. These factors are indeed complex, and they are all somehow involved in the Suburban Evangel, the multidimensional force of urban decentralization—but no one knows quite how.

Almost every writer who essays to conquer the suburbs conceptually devotes some time to the reason behind suburban growth. There have been attempts to reduce suburban growth to psychological variables. In this regard, suburbanites are alleged to be a type who have needs different from those of city dwellers. Suburban growth has been explained in terms of certain overriding values which the suburbanite purportedly holds and hopes to achieve by living in the suburbs.

The value-orientation approach has two sides: the values may be found in the suburbs, or some negative factor may reside in cities. As David Riesman suggests, suburban growth may be viewed as flight from something terrible in the city, or search for something wonderful in the suburbs. Is it a push of negative forces which drives people out of cities, or a pull of positive expectations which attracts them to the suburbs?

Another tradition takes a more structural and formally analytic view of the matter. Economic factors and technology are singled out for particular mention. The suburban revolution is "explained" in terms of electric motors, automobiles, commuter trains, and expressways. Closely linked to the technological factors are the structural forces of the national economy. Suburbs grow because city land is expensive and suburban land is cheap. Consequently, pent-up city populations flow out into the economic and geographic areas of least resistance.

The fourth explanatory model poses a series of hypotheses which view suburban growth as a major social movement. Unlike the value approach, which stresses consciously held negative or positive values of city and suburban life, the social-movements approach views suburban growth as a solution unconsciously arrived at, to some deep and pervasive modern social pathology. A suburban migrant may articulate a whole series of reasons for his move to suburbia, but the social-movements approach probes beneath the surface of socially approved responses. Suburbia thus viewed is a deep-seated quest for community, an escape from industrialism, or the search for grass roots democracy.

The four explanatory models of suburban growth—the social-psychological study of suburban personality structure; the value-orientation view; the social-movements approach; and the technological-economic view—are by no means mutually exclusive. Often two or more emerge with one and the same explanation of suburban growth. However, if we are to unlock the mystery of suburban growth, we must look at all four in some detail.

The Psychology of the Suburbs

The "psychology" of the suburbanite may be set forth in fairly simple terms. The suburbs constitute a dimension of the metropolitan community which attracts certain types of individuals. A distinct sociopsychological selection process dispatches those types to the suburbs, and retains others within the central city core. Harlan Douglas was the first to formally advance a theory of suburban personality.[1] "The people of the residential suburbs," Douglas wrote, ". . . live where they do by reason of natural selection based on a peculiar psychology and motivation." The suburban type, as Douglas saw it, is the kind of person who finds the congestion, noise, and organization of city life at odds with his needs'for independence and the comparative openness and quiet of the suburbs. Surbanites, reasoned Douglas, are characterized by an "aesthetic affinity" for open living. They are a "chosen people separated from their fellow city-men by the strength of a particular group of inner attributes."

Nine years after Douglas advanced the case for psychological selection as a factor in suburban migration, Lundberg and his colleagues picked up the theme.[2] They argued that "certain selective influences are at work in determining the inhabitants of a suburb." "We must assume," they wrote, "that those who choose to live in the suburbs, have, on the whole, certain tastes and preferences which distinguish them from otherwise similar people in the city." Lundberg and his associates isolate two basic character traits of the suburbanite: "A greater sensitivity to nature and the outdoor life . . . the rural heritage is a little more recent and vivid in this type"; "The suburbanite's comparatively deep attachment to neighborhood and domestic life and the traditional family pattern. . . ."

Even a cursory examination reveals that the "psychological" characteristics are not psychological at all. The one or two traits which constitute the key dimension of "suburban" personality—"privacy," "neighboring," "independence," "sensitivity to nature and the outdoor life"—are hardly grounds for building an entire "suburban" personality syndrome. These "characteristics," perhaps with the exception of the "privacy" and "independent" categories, are not particularly reducible to social class characteristics. Even their empirical foundations are suspect. I do not know of any study which has attempted to measure the extent of these characteristics in an urban or suburban population. To be sure, Fava has put the neighboring hypothesis to the test; however, the visibility principle may be the major force behind the suburban informal relationships rather than a psychological predisposition. Indeed, this entire line of inquiry is largely ignored today in favor of other approaches to suburban growth. This does not necessarily mean that such an approach is fruitless; rather, that if it is to be undertaken seriously, it must wait upon the development of a sophisticated conceptual statement of the suburban personality syndrome (if such exists) and the proper empirical techniques and procedures to test it.

FLIGHT AND SEARCH IN THE SUBURBS

Conscious evaluation as a force in suburban migration presupposes the negative images of the city (flight) and positive values which encourage people to seek a new life in the suburbs (search).[3] There has been no systematic study of what is "wrong" with cities, as perceived by suburban émigrés, but the literature is rich with judgments of what suburbanites *might*, or should, say. The city has long been the center of alien ethnic groups, crime, and violence. Cities are becoming increasingly concentrated with the nonwhite races, and urban school systems are reflecting that concentration. Flight to the suburbs may be a polite assertion of the principle of white supremacy. However, in the rhetoric of conventional social democracy, the suburban migrant would rather say he moved to the suburbs for the positive values that everyone approves of. On a questionnaire he might indicate he moved because it was "better for the children," rather than to admit, "We wanted to get away from the Puerto Ricans."

The flight factors are submerged in the studies of suburban migration, but the search values receive a great deal of attention. Indeed, most empirical approaches to suburban migration reveal that positive search thinking has triumphed over negative flight thinking. Dewey, for example, surveyed 12 thousand families in the unincorporated areas of Milwaukee County, Wisconsin. The first three reasons given for moving to the suburban areas were: Better for children (over 30 per cent), Less congested (over 17 per cent), Cleaner (about 16 per cent).[4] Anderson's study of the Ithaca, N.Y., fringe area indicated the following: Prefer living in the open, away from crowding (18 per cent), Prefer residence near place of work (11 per cent), Better for children (9 per cent).[5] Martin's studies of the Eugene-Springfield, Oregon, rural-urban fringe reported the following: Less congested (21 per cent), Better for children (17 per cent), Could not get a place in town (12 per cent).[6] These three studies show a clear preference for the suburbs over cities for two reasons—suburbs are better for children and less congested than cities.

The better-for-children theme is perhaps the most popular of all the positive attractions of suburban life. Bell recently incorporated an entire complex of themes such as a high evaluation on family living, early marriage, a short childless time span after marriage, and other associated characteristics as indications of familism.[7] In a study of two Chicago suburbs, Bell classified the dominant themes underlying reasons given for moving to the suburbs. Upward vertical mobility or career orientation were not significant reasons. But Bell classified 31 per cent of the sample as exemplifying pure familism in their choice of suburban residence, and a "familistic orientation" affected decisions to move to the suburbs in a total of 83 per cent of the cases studied. The better-for-children reason was given by 81 per cent of the respondents. In addition, values such as the opportunity to garden and to enjoy the immediate outdoors seem to play some role. Patio cookouts and the like strengthen family solidarity and cohesion. The search for suburbia seems to focus on the good life, for the family. Quantitative approaches which rely heavily on the reasons for suburban migration given by the émigrés are characterized by a major flaw: they rely *exclusively* on the verbalized reasons. People characteristically give socially approved responses; chiefly, "We did it for the children."

To my knowledge, there has been no intensive *qualitative* study of suburban migration. Bell probed below the better-for-children category to get specific reasons why the suburbs were thought to be better for children, socially and physically. But I suspect that some of this data may be in significant degree preconceived by the questionnaire or interview schedule, and not an accurate reflection of basic motivations for suburban migration. An illustration might be useful here. A few years ago I did a series of pilot interviews in two Long Island communities on reasons for suburban migration. I had developed a check-off type of interview schedule, listing a series of reasons based upon the literature of similar studies. I had gone to about twelve houses in one community (upper-middle class and predominantly Protestant), and the responses were overwhelmingly familistic—"better for the children"; "good schools." At the twelfth house I decided to put the formal schedule aside and do a little probing. After the usual "good schools" response, I suggested that there were a number of communities on Long Island with excellent schools and then mentioned the names of a few localities with high Jewish populations. My respondent shifted uneasily in his chair and looked at me quizzically for a moment. Then he said,

> Well, yes, I know they have good schools, but after all you do like to live with people who are your own kind. Now those two other places, you know, are Jewish. Now don't get me wrong—I'm no anti-Semite, but if I have to live anywhere where there is a concentration of people of one kind, I might as well be among my own.

I interviewed six other respondents in that community and probed each in depth in a similar way on the religious and ethnic question. In three others I found that ethnic and religious variables figured importantly in their decision to settle where they did.

The following week I selected a Jewish neighborhood on Long Island and interviewed eleven housewives. Eight of them initially gave a better-schools or better-for-the-children response. When I asked why they had not settled in some of the villages which have excellent schools but not particularly large Jewish populations 5 of the 8 brought up the religious and ethnic question. One respondent put it this way:

> When we decided to move to the suburbs we looked Long Island over for about a year. We spoke to many of our friends, too. But you like to live in a neighborhood where you are comfortable, where you are wanted and everyone gets along. We picked this village and this particular neighborhood because it has the kind of people who we can get along with.

Another young college-educated (psychology major) mother nailed the matter down:

> Look, we're Jewish. There are some places around here where Jews aren't welcome. So why go there? The kids might have bad experiences. I know it's homogeneous around here but the children get off to a good start. No fears or uncertainties. Everyone gets along with each other pretty well. I'll tell you something interesting. The family next door has a fourteen-year-old girl. Her mother was telling me the other day that her daughter is just beginning to realize that Jews are a minority in the United States! Now there's something that sociologists should be able to do something with!

It is impossible to adduce a major social trend on the basis of less than 25 interviews, but the consistency with which ethnic and religious factors plainly underlay the better-for-the-children reply was significant in point of uniformity of the response and in point of the fact that people give socially approved answers couched in generalities. However, the unique New York City environment may intensify the response. Protestants in the New York metropolitan area are a minority, only 16 per cent of the population. Roman Catholics constitute 30 per cent and Jews 18 per cent of the population. (*The New York Times*, January 4, 1959.) Thirty-four per cent of the population indicated "no religious affiliation." This city pattern may be extending into the New York suburbs. There are certainly Jewish, Protestant, and Catholic suburban areas around the city. However, there are no available data to indicate if such suburbs are increasing in number or remaining constant. Historically, the New York suburbs are Protestant upper and middle class. But with the rise of large numbers of Jews and Catholics into the middle class along with the suburbanization of blue collar groups, this characteristic is changing.

The search for an ethnic and religious community may only occur when a family can afford it. These are "luxurious" factors. It is problematic if the blue collar family looking for the $14,000 house in Levittown is much concerned with a religious or ethnic "consciousness of kind." Levittown is quite hetergeneous in this regard. But when a Levittown family advances economically, wants a larger house, and starts looking around for it, religious, ethnic, and status factors may emerge. The materials introduced here suggest that ethnic and religious variables along with familism may play an important part as factors in suburban migration.

Suburbia as a Social Movement

Movement to the suburbs proceeds in some sort of expectation of what suburban life will be. The potential suburbanite arms himself with reasons for the move. The move must seem rational to him within his framework of goals, means, and values. But the fanciful reasons he gives for the move may have "meaning" to the "actor" within the context of popular ideology; they give him a sense of rationality in the structure of his own system of action, but obscure fundamental societal and cultural forces which are behind the surface imagery of suburbanization. Massive and latent forces in the social process give rise to the attitudes and motivations and validations for the move to the suburbs. Suburbanization may therefore be conceived of as a social movement the real impellers of which are blurred to and lost from the eyes of the actual participants.

Many years ago, W. I. Thomas coined the phrase "definition of the situation." Although the term has come to have many meanings, generally it refers to the interpretation an individual or group attaches to a social situation. For example, on the level of the group, is a situation formal or informal? On the level of the person, is it pleasant or unpleasant, demanding or not? We make judgments, predictions, and expectations of all social situations. If we are of a basically suspicious psychological predisposition, we define many situations as suspicious. Another person, more easygoing and trusting, would perceive social situations with less suspicion and more trust. Psychological makeup thus modulates our perceptions and definitions of situations. All is not left to the individual, however—society defines situations. To Thomas, one of the major problems in socializing the child is resolution of the conflict between the personal definition of a situation ("I want to punch Johnny in the nose!") and the social definition of it ("Little children must never hit or hurt each other.").

One of the most critical affectors of human relationships is social definition. In the course of his socialization the child internalizes socially approved definitions of situations. By the time he reaches maturity, society and culture have performed a wonderful alchemy on the mind. The socially sanctioned ideologies of justification, the standard definitions of reality, are now "reasons"—a fundamental component of personality. Whether Catholics, Communists, or capitalists are heroes or villains depends largely upon the culture one is born into. In a similar manner, you want to go suburban because "it is better for the kids," or "the city was getting too crowded and we wanted more living space." The "reasons" men advance for their behavior are only verbalizations, the actor's need to explain his own course of action to himself, and there is not always a high correlation between the manner in which men perceive a social situation and the reality of that situation. The majority of people may believe that there are no social classes in the United States, but that does not make the United States objectively classless. Because men say they move to the suburbs to escape city congestion, we need not accept that as the objective sociological definition of the situation. The point is this: What men "think" about a social situation or their own actions is sociologically significant even though the thought be objectively spurious.

In what manner is the suburban revolution the manifestation of a contemporary social movement? Riesman says, "I see the suburbs today as signifying, in their familism and search for community, a tacit revolt against the industrial order." [8] The demands of industrialism, argues Riesman, of skill, professional ability, and foresight have now been met—the challenge of great industrial growth is over and we have produced a marvelously productive engine. We are rich enough to afford waste, and the old values of hard work and thrift no longer make sense. A man no longer prides himself as much on his ability to produce as he does on his ability to consume. In short, productive relationships have lost their significance. In turn, consumption practices and style of life have entered a new era. As Riesman sees it, with the decline of traditional work values, job and factory no longer have any real significance in a society which is consumption oriented. According to Riesman, face-to-face relationships and a "domestic togetherness which gives meaning to life" prevail in the suburbs. The flight from the city is an escape from industrial rationality, urban violence, and ethnic and racial heterogeneity. The simple pastoral images of suburban life—green fields, small community, the establishment of identity around the primacy of family relationships—suggest a glorious renaissance of "basic" values. To eyes bewildered by too much city complexity, too much drive, too many emotional demands, too much anxiety, too much bureaucracy, too many risks, too many buildings, and too much to lose, the suburbs seem oases in a desert of urban-industrial duplicity. According to Riesman:

> . . . the city has come to stand in our minds for the market, for impersonality, for great ambitions and risks and great failures and losses —for that boom and bust world, hectic and driving, that still is very much the American picture in the rest of the world, but on which we ourselves . . . are increasingly soured.[9]

Flight from the city, then, is flight from the consequences of a society that has outgrown its value system and has not had time to replace it with something "better." This is essentially Whyte's position, and it is not a great deal at odds from the Riesman view.[10] Whyte begins with the Protestant Ethic as outlined by Weber, who had argued that a causal relationship existed between modern capitalism with its rational organization of labor, the pursuit of profit, and religious ideology. It was Weber who suggested that the rise of mature capitalism was critically affected by Protestant (particularly Calvinist) ethics and theology. Mature capitalism, Weber contended, is not based simply on the drive to acquire property and wealth but is founded on a rationalistic emphasis on order, discipline, and organization. Acquisition of worldly goods, in the Protestant view, was a sign of grace and an augury of salvation, for mankind's purpose on earth is to increase the bounty of God's universe. The elect were those who had increased the abundance of the earth; the damned were those who did not produce, hence added nothing, and who took rather than gave. Those of wealth and property were looked upon as having done God's work. In this manner, Weber reasoned, the religious "calling" of Protestantism was fused to rational economic behavior. A man could save his soul by getting rich. It was, therefore, this incredible fusion of religious justification to acquisitive behavior which gave rise to the intense industrial and economic growth in capitalist-Protestant nations.

Whyte looks back on the era of the Protestant Ethic in the United States and the hard values men lived by. The guideposts of thrift, intense economic competition, hard work, self-denial, and moderation have been washed away in the tides of the Social Ethic—i.e., the Suburban Ethic. Like Riesman, who is more overtly anti-suburban, Whyte finds the suburbs a soft retreat from the demanding values of the eighteenth and nineteenth centuries. The themes of the suburban ethic are *not* themes of production. One senses in the works of Riesman and Whyte some identity with the rigors of the Protestant Ethic. They admire the city; it seems to them forever restless, exciting, productive, and moving. To them, the suburbs seem to be something of a tragedy, full of foolish ritual, decadence, superficiality, and a quavering nostalgia. But what happens to a society that never takes the risks, that seeks to avoid anxiety, that measures a man by the size of his car's tail fins and feeds off an industrial carcass produced by a hardier breed of men in a former time? Riesman and Whyte see in the suburbs a fleshy social movement dedicated to the moment, the now. The Social Ethic has sucked the fire out of the nineteenth century's spirit of drive, energy, personal denial, thrift, and movement, leaving as ashes the vacuous, static, delusory, uniform, hedonistic, and self-destructive values of today. In their view, nowhere do these trends find fuller and more visible expression than in the suburbs.

Robert Wood takes a less polemic position.[11] He views the search for suburbia as the search for community, roots, and the political purity of the small village. Part of the flight to the suburbs is an escape from big city politics, machine government, and graft. A precept widespread in America, Wood suggests, posits that which is socially little to be good and that which is socially big to be evil: the bigger the government, the worse it is. Cities are enormous, hence they must be incredibly corrupt. According to Wood,

> If a belief in small government and small society helps to explain why the modern suburb exists in an age of bigness, the suburban renaissance should not be surprising. The conviction that provincial life is best has been with us for a long time and it has endured in the face of greater attacks than the ones contemporary America presents. We show our instinctive commitment to the ideology by the fact that we rarely examine its assumptions critically. We show our conscious allegiance by the oratorical homage we pay to the ideal of small neighborhoods, single homes, and political jurisdictions of limited size.[12]

The suburbs are not only politically small, they promise political visibility and local control. Unlike the amorphous big city political machine, the suburbs are paradigms of political simplicity and uncorruptibility.

> In the suburb, according to the folklore, the school board is likely to be composed of neighbors or friends . . . Its members do not come from another part of a larger city; they are available and accessible. So are the mayor, the county clerk, the commissioners, the councilmen, and selectmen. So are the chief of police, the water superintendent, the plumbing inspector, and health officials. In this way, elected officials, bureaucrats, party leaders—the entire apparatus of democratic politics—are exposed to view.[13]

In Wood's view, the movement to the suburbs is a quest for some degree of personal involvement with, participation in, and control over the governmental structure. In some cases the visibility principle does operate, permitting the suburbanite to have greater insight and involvement in local matters. Local control of public education, and the issues surrounding it, might be a case in point. However, in governmental structures and jurisdictions, the suburbs have achieved a level of political complexity and obscurity which puts the big city to shame. In point of proliferation and reproduction of governmental units, suburbs are the rabbits of the political world. There were about 16,000 local political units in 192 standard metropolitan areas of the United States. About 40 per cent of these are school districts, one in six is a special single-function district such as soil conservation, drainage, fire protection and the like. The remainder consist of municipalities, incorporated villages, townships, and counties. These units are steadily increasing. The Chicago metropolitan area, for example, had 55 units in 1890; 109 in 1920; 960 in 1954. The New York metropolitan area consisted of 1071 separate jurisdictions by 1954; Philadelphia, 702; and St. Louis, 420.

What happens to political visibility when the suburbanite finds himself bound into a murky structure of overlapping, submerged, and superimposed election districts, school districts, sanitation districts, fire districts, police jurisdictions, postal areas, incorporated and unincorporated villages, towns, and cities? If the quest for political simplicity is a factor which sends thousands into suburbia each month, there is doubt they will find what they are looking for.

If it is the search for the American "miniature" which is partially responsible for suburban growth, one wonders what makes cities so unattractive to so many. It is argued that the city, with its alleged compartmentalizing of human relationships, its population density, its crass formalisms and rationalization of human affairs, has become antithetical to the needs of human nature and society itself. Industrialism may have been the force which compacted millions in the dark, dense, steamy cities of the nineteenth century, but crime, slums, institutional fragmentation, heterogeneity, and social atomization are splitting twentieth century cities apart. The flight to the suburbs, accordingly, is seen as modern man's flight to find himself again, and to re-establish a form of community in which he can enjoy technological progress but also social stability, community, and identity. For many, including Wood, the rise of suburbia and the nostalgic image of the small and good community, of sunlight and space, of stable and integrated families, of good neighbors and honest politicians, is a quest for community and a return to grass roots living. For Riesman and Whyte, the flight from the city and its alleged abuses leads to a social environment which in the long run is more destructive to the national society than are the pathological conditions of city life. Nevertheless, the suburban migration continues, and the rural ideal for the common man may yet prevail over the urban.

The rural ideal is clearly invoked by the very labels given to suburban developments: "Country Village," "Woodbury Knolls," "The Ridge," "Pinewood," "Sayre Woods South," "Skyline Village," "Colonial Village," "Point-O-Woods," "Sweet Hollow," "Peppermill Village," "Wenwood at Brookville," "Smoke Rise," "Green Mansion," "Victorian Woods," "Stonebridge-At-The-Lake," "Country Ridge," "The Gates." . . . What frustrated hungers can feed here? What inner needs are served in the marvelous imagery?

There are at least two promises that the names of suburban developments make to the city dweller—nature and community. Cities conjure terrible visions of dirt, fumes, and listless settlements of foreigners in the ever present slums. But in suburbia there is nature: hills, woodland retreats, verdant hollows, rounded knolls—clean, green, and sweet. "Five Oaks," are straight, tested, tall and true. You can trust a tree, a hill, if not a city. The names of suburbia say, "Come back!" Come back to the *real* things—the green mansions, the sylvan hollows, and sun-sprayed meadows, the private small and uncorrupted little green places. Come back to the permanent, immutable, and trusted forms of nature. All else is suspect— bosses, cities, Miami Beach, management, Puerto Ricans, big business, the Russians, the Teamsters, the market—come back through "The Gates" to another world. Return to "Country Village" and colonial America. No great heaving city this, no paranoid bureaucracy, just a simple untroubled rural village where there is a family and "roots" and friends. Everything is in order, and a man can see all the forces which shape his life. "Peppermill Village" physically transports the suburbanite back in time 150 years. The Cape Cods and saltboxes, the "colonial farmhouses," the antique lanterns and split-rail fences on one-acre "estates" are just a few of the artifacts of yesteryear. For $38,000 a Madison Avenue account executive can become Tom Sawyer for a few blessed hours each weekend.

A. C. Spectorsky framed the suburban movement in a somewhat different manner.[14] He conceived "exurbia" as a "Limited Dream," the compromise with the "Unlimited Dream." The Unlimited Dream is every man's dream of escape and creation. The Unlimited

Dream would take the Madison Avenue advertising man to the South Seas to write the novel or play that has always been there waiting to be born, but circumstances—the job, the children, the mother-in-law, the "gang," money—always somehow got in the way. If two years in Spain are not within the reach of possibility, a two-acre retreat in Fairfield or Rockland County is. The Limited Dream is an adjustment to reality, but it is nonetheless an escape from the city and its pressures. Headlong they pour into the suburban (i.e., exurban) hinterlands to find, among the "Country Villages" and the steadying artifacts of the Protestant Ethic, succor from the rat race.

Spectorsky's Limited Dream of exurbia emerges as the physical expression of retreat from the many hurts inflicted by twentieth century urban society. For Riesman, the suburbs and their growth constitute a repudiation of the industrial order. For Whyte, that growth is the rise of the Social Ethic and a society whose fundamental aim is the headlong pursuit of fun and games. For Wood, it is the search for grass roots democracy. How can one assess the efficacy of these themes? They plunge beneath the imagery of surface justifications and reach into a dimension of causation that touches upon the psychology of unconscious motivation and the shifting sub-currents of basic institutions. Before attempting some kind of assessment of the value of the social movements view of suburban growth, let us take a look at one more approach.

THE ECONOMICS AND TECHNOLOGY OF SUBURBANIZATION

If suburbia grows because men hold values they hope to realize there, it also grows because of certain structural characteristics of the American economy, of governmental policy and basic changes in technology. There couldn't have been a significant suburbanization of population in the nineteenth century because of simple technological reasons. There were no efficient means of mass transportation 100 years ago. The nation was still essentially rural in outlook; cities were regarded as centers of sin and corruption. Urban populations were pressed in upon each other. The results were concentrated, dense, ugly cities. City planners did not exist in that glorious time of boundless private enterprise. Planning was an automatic response to the magic laws of supply and demand. It was a time of great urban growth, but it was also a time when the rural ideal, rugged independence, Protestantism, and the simple village triumphed over urban machine politics, foreigners, poverty, and dependency. But rural ideal or not, jobs and economic opportunity were in the cities. So they grew, but it was not until the twentieth century that technology made it possible to seize the best of both worlds, to live in the country yet work in the city.

The mass-produced automobile and the interurban railway provided the technological base for the decentralization of urban populations. As the standard of living increased, more urban people found their way to the suburbs. But there was no compromise of rural and urban forms. The suburbanites carried the spirit of the city to rural areas, and, in the long run, very little of rural America remained once suburbanization invaded the rural countryside. Harlan Douglas put it wonderfully when he wrote in 1925:

> Out toward the fringes and margins of cities comes a region where they begin to be less themselves than they are at the center, a place where the city looks countryward. No sharp boundary line defines it; there is, rather, a gradual tapering off from the urban type of civilization toward the rural type. It is the city thinned out . . . It is the country thickened up . . . It straddles the arbitrary line which statistics draw between the urban and rural spheres; but in reality it is the push of the city outward. It makes physical compromises with country ways but few compromises of spirit. It is the city trying to escape the consequences of being a city. . . .[15]

Technology liberated men from the physical city, but other factors played a significant part in the suburban explosion following World War II. Leo Schnore approaches the postwar suburban boom, not from the viewpoint of psychology or value orientations, but from the perspective of economic forces.[16] He points out that city growth is usually explained in terms of "the push and pull of economic opportunities." The entire sociohistoric movement of population away from rural into urban areas has been due, he says, to the rise of job opportunities in cities and relative economic decline of rural areas. This has produced a "multiplier" effect: increase in economic opportunities causes urban population growth, and thus more employment opportunities, and so on.

The phenomenal increase in the residential suburbs following World War II cannot be stated in the traditional terms of "economic" opportunities which underlie city growth. Schnore points out, however, that the typical city is now going through a conversion of land uses. Before the suburban exodus, the city was the principal residential location of its own labor force. Now, cities are putting formerly residential land to industrial, commercial, recreational, and transportation uses.

Why are "housing opportunities" shifting from the cities to the suburbs? Schnore answers by pointing out that central cities have exhausted the land areas left for residential construction. Land costs are simply too high and zoning regulations are prohibitive; commercial properties earn more money than residential, and great expanses of relatively cheap suburban land are available to the mass-production builder. But there is a more fundamental, sociological force at work, according to Schnore:

> It appears that the location of the dominant units in the community set the broad pattern of land use for smaller and less powerful units, such as households. In one sense, this is nothing more than another expression of the relationships . . . between (1) "basic" industries, (2) residential population, and (3) "non-basic" industries. Basic industries locate at particular sites, with the residential population taking up positions with reference to these centers of production and employment. The distribution of residential population, in turn, is the prime determinant of the location of such non-basic activities as retail trade and service.[17]

Schnore's view of suburban growth is not concerned with motivations, ideals, or psychology. His approach is basically sociological in that he deals with variables within the framework of the social structure. According to Schnore, the dominant forces of suburbanization are economic. It was economic opportunity that made cities grow, and it is now a shift in the economics of land uses within the central city core that underlies the suburban transformation. Central city land areas are simply too costly and scarce to continue to serve as the principal location of the area's labor force. As city land increasingly goes over to the "dominant units" of the community— economic uses—the urban population must find residential sites elsewhere. The need, therefore, is for housing, and builders answer the need by constructing large-scale tract and development housing on relatively cheap land in the suburban areas. Increasingly concentrated suburban populations create "non-basic" economic opportunities. Such non-basic industries as retailing, service, and light manufacturing industries follow their markets into the suburbs.

The role of economic factors, however, has not been ignored by other students of suburban growth. In his study of suburbanization in Canada, S. D. Clark argues that the movement is essentially "non-selective" in terms of the "kind of people involved." [18] Clark relies heavily on the role of economic factors in suburban migration. City populations spill into the Canadian countryside, according to Clark, for basically one reason: "the great house-hungry population of the city . . . can find space for itself only by spreading beyond the limits of the urban community." Latent, in Clark's view, is the less-congestion theme. However, he emphasizes that:

> What they seek is only a house, and they move where they do only because it is there they can find a house they can afford. . . . The individual choice that is made is on the basis simply of capacity to pay. What is being bought is a house and not a social environment and it is this which gives the housing market which grows up under conditions of large-scale residential development the character of a mass market.

For Clark, the suburban movement basically stems from city congestion and the inadequacy of urban housing—the suburbs constitute the geographic/economic area where shelter can be secured within the family's means. Clark discounts the themes of sociopsychological selectivity and the quest for a particular environment.

There are other structural factors which have been cited as forces underlying the growth of suburbs. The general increase in population within the past decades have left cities with even greater congestion. This population pressure, low housing production in the Depression years, plus the austerity of the war years left the nation with intensified housing needs that could not be quickly met in cities, but could in suburbs. In addition, Federal financial support in the form of FHA and G.I. mortgages made it easy for the veteran to secure the housing he wanted. Thus, for many newly married veterans the move to the suburbs had little to do with values, the suburban vision, or flight from some alien force in the city. The suburbs were the only place he could take his family. A house in Levittown could be had merely by proving one had a job, was indeed a veteran, and could wait six months for his section to go up.

Suburbia, in this case, was simply survival and had very little to do with psychological selection or the pursuit of a conscious value.

The postwar years were prosperous years. With the government underwriting mortgages and with plenty of jobs around, the suburbs flourished. Part of their growth, therefore, is a reflection of the prosperity and the rising standard of living reaching well down into the working class. At one time, home ownership was a middle- and upper-class characteristic. The working class was constantly harassed by economic insecurity and relatively low income. During the postwar years, however, production was high and working class incomes steadily mounted. With government money to support mortgages, the working class began their migration to the suburban areas.

THE HIERARCHY OF DETERMINANTS

I have attempted to organize the many factors behind suburban growth into four basic views. We can discount the present utility of the character structure approach to suburban migration for reasons already mentioned. We have left, then, the value orientation, the social movements, and the technological-economic hypotheses of suburban migration.

The *value orientation* approach deals with conscious evaluations made by the migrant in terms of his values and goals. Suburban migration entails rational acts, about which empirical questions can be posed to reveal the expectations, reasons, and motives of the migrants, the responses classified into categories of "familism," "status-seeking," and "ethnic-religious predispositions." The value orientation approach can yield much valuable information about how people interpret suburbia and why they want to live there.

The *social-movements* approach focuses on the problems of latent and emergent ideology, and the strains, ambivalences, and frustrations in urban-metropolitan society. People "feel" the consequences of massive shifts in the institutional framework of society, but they don't understand them—complex forces are too submerged to be visible to them. They express disquietude, unease, and *anomie* when they say they moved from the city because it was too congested or impersonal, or say "I had to get away from the rat race, at least for a little while." Such expressions are the verbal symbols of a more fundamental process. Men constantly redefine their image of the ideal community in response to ideological conflicts buried deep in the social structure. The social-movements approach, while it deals with the strains modern man encounters within his social order, is not very specific about or systematic in the analysis of the sources of those strains. The approach is characterized by the use of intuitive and impressionistic proofs. The emphasis, in the main, is on the strain-producing characteristics of modern society and only in the broadest outlines suggestive of the institutional foundations of the strain.

The *technological-economic* approach, unlike the *social-movements* is not interested in the felt and unfelt hurts of the migrant or the ideological search and flight of modern man, it attempts rather, to isolate and define the critical institutional processes which are involved primarily in the ecological processes of metropolitan areas. The question, at this analytic level, is in the formal analysis of structural, institutional change, and relationships per se. In short, the *technological-economic* approach gets into actual structural dynamics of modern society and at the very point where the social movements analysis becomes vague and impressionistic. For example, in Schnore's economic analysis of suburban growth the causes were traced to housing opportunities in the suburbs coupled with a decline of housing opportunities in the central city. These forces are purely institutional and they are related to the basic procedures and practices of American society. Finally, the *social-movements* approach, while attempting to deal with the sociohistorical factors leading to the rise of cities and their eventual "explosion" treats with variables that are not easily adapted to statistical or quantitative analysis. How does one measure a "yearning for grass roots living," or a "revolt against industrialism." One suspects, however, that a more systematic use of concepts and history, along Weberian lines, might be fruitful here.

In the final reckoning, *conscious evaluations, social movements,* and *technological-economic* forces constitute a hierarchy of the determinants involved in suburban growth. The migrant must have "reasons" and a "definition of the situation." The source of his strains, needs, and hopes lies, at least in part, in the ideologies of modern society. But the development of new "definitions of the situation," of new ideologies, rests in some significant degree upon the structural dynamics of institutions within the total societal matrix.

These three approaches are essentially complementary; and together they can throw considerable light on the complex processes of metropolitan ecology.

NOTES

1. Harlan P. Douglas, *The Suburban Trend* (New York: The Century Co., 1925), p. 34.
2. George A. Lundberg, *et al., op. cit.,* pp. 42-50, *passim.*
3. David Riesman first used these terms in a talk—"Flight and Search in the New Suburbs"—at Smith College, April 16, 1959.
4. Richard Dewey, "Peripheral Expansion in Milwaukee County," *American Journal of Sociology* LIV (September, 1948), pp. 118-125.
5. W. A. Anderson, *Social Change and an Urban Fringe Area:* Cornell University Agricultural Experiment Station, Rural Sociology Publication 35, (February, 1953).
6. Walter T. Martin, *The Rural-Urban Fringe* (Eugene, Ore.: University of Oregon Press, 1953), p. 37.
7. Wendell Bell, "Social Choice, Life Styles, and Suburban Residence," in Dobriner, *op. cit.,* pp. 225-47.
8. David Riesman, "The Suburban Sadness," in Dobriner, *op. cit.,* p. 375.
9. David Riesman, "Flight and Search in the New Suburbs," a talk delivered at Smith College, April 16, 1959 (mimeographed), p. 12.
10. William H. Whyte, Jr., *The Organization Man* (New York: Doubleday & Co., 1956).
11. Robert C. Wood, *Suburbia* (Boston: Houghton Mifflin Co., 1958).
12. *Ibid.,* p. 20.
13. *Ibid.,* p. 12.
14. A. C. Spectorsky, *The Exurbanites* (Philadelphia: J. B. Lippincott Co., 1955).
15. Harlan P. Douglas, *op. cit.,* p. 4.
16. Leo F. Schnore, "The Growth of Metropolitan Suburbs," *American Sociological Review,* Vol. 22 (April, 1957), 165-73. Reprinted in Dobriner, *op. cit.,* pp. 26-44.
17. *Ibid.* (Dobriner), pp. 38-39.
18. S. D. Clark, *The Suburban Community,* unpublished paper (mimeo).

LEONARD REISSMAN

THE VISIONARY PLANNER FOR
URBAN UTOPIA

TO THE visionary the city is a problem environment, one that
has developed without plan and one more sensitive to the narrow
economic demands of the moment than to the lasting moral
and social needs of individuals. He sees in the industrial city
what the practitioner has seen: congestion, slums, blight, inefficiency, and all the other consequences of civic irresponsi-
bility. Although both types are impressed by the same urban
realities, they differ markedly in the interpretations they give to
them. For the practitioner, congestion, blight and the rest of
the shoddy inventory are the problems; for the visionary they
are but the symptoms. The basic problem is the ethos and organization of industrial society itself. This difference separates the
visionary from the practitioner. Because of it they are oriented
differently in their study of and solutions for urban problems.
The practitioner, as earlier described, is committed by his job
to piecemeal solutions that can be enforced quickly, such as

The Urban Process (New York: The Free Press, 1964), Chapter 3. Copyright © 1964
by the Free Press of Glencoe, a Division of the Macmillan Company. Reprinted by
permission of Mrs. Ethel Reissman and the publisher.

widening streets, zoning, partial urban renewal, or streamlining some phase of governmental organization. The visionary is a vehement opponent of these temporary measures. Rather, he insists that radical surgery is the only way to save the patient. The point is sharply made by Mumford who establishes the visionary's perspective in this respect. "Much recent housing and city planning has been handicapped because those who have undertaken the work have had no clear notion of the social functions of the city. . . . And they did not, apparently, suspect that there might be gross deficiencies, misdirected efforts, mistaken expenditures, here that would not be set straight by merely building sanitary tenements or widening narrow streets." [1]

The visionary concentrates, then, on practical problems but is concerned with long term qualitative considerations and social needs, and approaches these problems through a social ideology and an aesthetic philosophy. In brief, an urban problem for the visionary includes anything that violates his high standards of morality and aesthetics. His solution is usually nothing short of a massive reconstruction of metropolitan society. Standards of such a high order, after all, should not be compromised. The practitioner is committed to a job; the visionary is dedicated to an ideal.

The visionary's ideals are contained in The Plan: a blueprint, more or less detailed, for building into reality those forms, those values, and those qualities which he believes the city must contain. Sometimes, he even takes the trouble to indicate how we can reach that goal. In its fullest form, the blueprint includes not only plans for buildings, homes, and the general physical format of the city, but also definitions of what urban social institutions are to be included, and even the new psychology of the urbanite that is to emerge from all this. This is no picayune puttering with street plans or building facades or zoning regulations. It is a manifesto for an urban revolution.

The ideological roots that sustain the visionary go back to the middle of the nineteenth century and the protest, predominantly by socially conscious intellectuals, against the evils of industrialism. The protest centered on the effects of industrialism rather than on industrialism per se. It was more in opposition to the social system than to the machine. The benefits of industrial technology for human progress were more or less conceded. The argument, however, was with the social system that subordinated man to the machine and to the profit motive. The answer lay not in wrecking the machine but in controlling its social and ecological consequences. These indictments probably reached their highest pitch in the writings of Marx, in Engels' description of English factory life, and in Booth's classic studies of life and labor in London. These writings described with care the human consequences of industrialism: the effects of poverty, child labor, the erosion of the human spirit, and the senseless lives of the mass of people caught up by the factory and the city. It was in this period that dehumanization or alienation were understood in their crudest sense: depriving the individual of the barest essentials of humanity. By our own time of affluence, they are much more subtly and sophisticatedly defined.

What added fire to the intellectual's protests, aside from the real misery they saw, were the intolerable social discrepancies created by industrial society and above all else, the differences between rich and poor. For the intellectuals the discrepancy was a betrayal of a promise. About one hundred years before, with the onset of the industrial revolution, society had been dedicated to a new social philosophy that emphasized human dignity, the rule of law, the triumph of reason, and freedom. These new values were to replace the aristocratic rigidity, religious dogmatism, and monarchical absolutism condoned by the medieval philosophy of society. What the intellectuals had not seen was that the new ideology was meant to apply only to a small segment of society, not to all of it. By the middle of the last century, the intellectuals apparently were shocked into reality and they saw a social nightmare instead of the promised dream. Mandeville's *Fable of the Bees*, an allegory that argued that society as a whole benefited even as individuals suffered from the laissez-faire economic activity of its citizens, became a fairy story not even accurate for activity in the hive. The rule of law became a codified disregard of social responsibility. The new ideology became based more on the unassailable primacy of the natural order, of which the social order was conceived to be a part, than on the ability of man to shape his social order. In short, the gap between the promise of industrialism and its reality, especially in the city, became too wide to be ignored.

The disenchantment with industrial society emerged in one of three ways, depending upon the value placed on industrialism and the social change thought to be needed. (1) Reaction against it all by which industrialism was entirely, if naively, discredited. The machine, the factory, and the city were considered to be beyond salvation in that they could not add anything worthwhile to society. In a reaction against industrialism the tightly comforting security of medievalism was sought through its image of a rediscovered rural utopia. This philosophy has continued, in one form or another, up to the present, where it has become centered around the small community as the alternative to the metropolis. (2) Reform of some features of industrial society to keep such advantages as labor-saving machinery, release from monotonous tasks, and the comforts that machines could fashion. The reformers championed what Mannheim has called a "spatial wish," the projection of utopia into space.[2] By controlling industrialism for the benefit of all in a new social environment, the reformer argued, man could once again progress. Applied to the city, this view became the basis for the "Garden City" and its variations. (3) Revolt was yet a third alternative. The revolutionary accepted industrialism as a necessary historical phase; history neither could be set back to some earlier epoch nor could it be stopped. Industrial society could not be preserved as it was, nor could it be remodeled, even in part. Instead, a massive reconstitution was required, by which all existing institutions, values, and social mechanisms would be replaced by a new social order forging into reality the unfulfilled promises of industrialism. Mannheim, once again, has called these wish fulfillments "chiliasms," projections of dreams into time, the social utopias.

The visionary at one time or another has been identified with all three of these disenchanted responses to industrialism. Ebenezer Howard set forth one such spatial utopia in some detail. Later visionaries, such as Frank Lloyd Wright, perceived that tampering with the urban pattern necessarily involved changing economic mechanisms, political administration, and social philosophy. And throughout much of the writing by visionaries, the simple desire to return to a rural civilization is obvious again and again.

§ Planning as a Social Movement

The above description of the visionary, of his reactions to the industrial city, and of the manner he chose to enforce his values, all imply the elements of a social movement. A "social movement" is used here in its sociological meaning, to identify a concerted response by a group in support of a set of values. It need not involve organization, although the town planning movement did have organization. It does not require that the participants know they are part of a movement, although such was the case here. Social movements, in other words, are not always conscious, explicit, or fully organized. It is possible, within the meaning intended here, for individuals separately to promulgate an idea or a cause, either without steps to attain the end or without consciousness of having company in their endeavor.

I have used this conception of a social movement to avoid the implication that the visionaries were tightly organized behind a single set of beliefs. Quite the contrary, for the visionaries were too individualistic to be led, too authoritarian to be politicians in a democracy, and, in some cases, too egomaniacal to compromise their beliefs in order to move further toward their ultimate goals.

To add perspective to the analysis of the visionary's plans, therefore, let me cast him explicitly into that framework, into the role of leader of a social movement.

Planning, as understood by the visionary, should be kept clear from what is usually understood by that term today. For the visionary, planning expresses an ideology of urban reform and revolt. It goes beyond the piecemeal planning of the practitioner, for one thing. For another, it has a facade of rationality that is characteristic of most planning, but in the case of the visionary there is less reason and more emotion behind the facade.

Four criteria can be used to establish the visionaries and

their plans as part of a social movement. First, the plans contained a set of propositions that could unify belief, even though these propositions were differently enunciated by different people. Most visionaries agreed that the city had deteriorated, that the industrial city was inhumane, and that the need for change was great. Although they disagreed about how to effect urban changes, there was no argument about the need for change.

Second, the movement had a history. Its point of origin, as earlier noted, was in the general protest against the effects of industrialism. The continued growth of technology, of science, of a factory society and a machine culture, added more substance to the visionary's argument and new examples of how inhuman industrial cities could become. The expansion of the industrial city, coupled with a prevailing philosophy more attuned to economic demands than to social needs, assured the visionary planners of a cause and identified an enemy—land owners, industrialists, and the like. The perseverance of these problems helped give the movement relevance, over time, and time in which to develop a sense of tradition and continuity. Social movements sparked into being by a topical issue, no matter how vital, dissolve once the issue has disappeared or else try to stay alive by moving on to other causes. In the case of town planning, the movement was able to capitalize on existing protests against industrialism, and it had sufficient time to mobilize some of those sentiments in its own behalf.

Third, the movement created a following. The followers, then as now, have been intellectuals predominantly, because they were the first to recognize the discrepancies between what was promised and what was attained by industrialism. The visionaries never seemed to be wise in the ways of mass politics, or didn't want to be, so the movement never spread. Mass protest movements properly led stay close to the ground to pick up a following, but utopian movements fly too high to be pursued by the masses. In certain cases, the visionaries were snobs by temperament, more entranced by their own ideals than dedicated to recruiting a following. The planning movement did find followers, however, although intellectuals predominated among it. What is more, the movement gained sufficient political strength to put some of its plans into effect: Howard's two garden cities, Letchworth and Welwyn, the Greenbelt towns of the New Deal era in the United States, and the British New Towns Act in 1946. The fact that there were followers, then, did give the movement some political reality. The importance of city planning and town planning today is further proof that we are considering more than the wishful dreams of a handful of politically ineffectual intellectuals.

Finally, the town planning movement had an organizing myth which did much to make it cohesive. The function of the planning myth was to condense a complicated intellectual message into shorthand which could readily be translated into action. The myth pointed to the existing evils and devised an overall answer to erase them. The shorthand of the myth avoided any reference to practical difficulties that might complicate the simple question and answer. The myth thereby became an appealing part-truth, attractive for its simplicity, as are most myths.

The myth put forth by visionaries was based on urban characteristics that were certainly real. The evils within the industrial city at the turn of the century were plentiful and easily described. The reason for the degraded urban situation, the explanation went on, was that the city had been allowed to grow without plan, or at least without reference to human values. Economic competition had been elevated to the status of a natural law, rationality was measured primarily by profit, and self-interest was considered the primary instinct of man. Moral values and civic responsibility were twisted to serve economic values. Little wonder the industrial city developed as it did. However, argued the planners, man is rational. He can plan and thereby create a better, more harmonious, and more humane environment for himself. The economic forces and scientific knowledge that produced the industrial city could be mobilized to build anew the planned city.

The plan does not necessarily prescribe social revolution. Rather, existing social forces can simply be directed into other channels in order to realize the full potentials of an industrial society. Howard, for example, was careful to point out that his plan for the garden city was neither socialistic nor communistic.[3]

The plan, then, stated the conditions and the means for attaining a new environment. It seemed on the surface desirable, feasible, and necessary. The myth that it contained was a naïve view of human motivation and of political structure: that reason is enough to change society from what it is to what we would like it to be. Above all, the visionary made the tacit assumption that his values were shared by most other people. This assumption proved to be the fatal flaw of most such plans.

Perhaps the best way to understand the visionary's contribution to an urban sociology is to look at some examples. Three have been chosen, each one because it is representative of a particular type. (1) Ebenezer Howard, the father of city planning and creator of the "garden city," a term that Osborn[4] notes has become part of all modern languages: *Cité-Jardin, Gartenstadt, Cuidad-jardin, Tuinstad;* (2) Frank Lloyd Wright for the brash plan; (3) Lewis Mumford for an approach that is sociologically informed. Many others, such as Saarinen, Le Corbusier, Gropius, Neutra, Sitte, the Goodmans, and Gallion are not included. They are important in their own ways, but a detailed analysis would not have added greatly to the fulfillment of the main intent of this discussion, to present a range of sociologically relevant ideas. After all, the main purpose is not to assess the relative merits of lineal cities, ribbon developments, super-blocks and the *ville radieuse,* but to consider the nature of urban society.

§ Ebenezer Howard: The Garden City

Howard's book, *Tomorrow: A Peaceful Path to Real Reform,* was first published in 1898, and with slight revisions reappeared in 1902 under the title *Garden Cities of To-Morrow.* The book placed Howard among the intellectuals of the protest movement of the last century. Apparently his protest was independently arrived at, for Howard did not pore over books or steep himself in the literature, at least according to F. J. Osborn's evaluation of him.[5]

Though not a scholar, Howard did know something of the intellectuals' protest of his time. He was a reader not only of the daily press but also of Edward Bellamy's *Looking Backward* and Henry George's *Progress and Poverty*. In any case, Howard tasted the flavor of protest that filled the period.

In a singular example of the organizing myth at work, Howard began by identifying the problem in a way calculated to win agreement from different quarters. It was

a question in regards to which one can scarcely find any difference of opinion. It is well nigh universally agreed by men of all parties . . . that it is deeply to be deplored that the people should continue to stream into the already over-crowded cities, and should thus further deplete the country districts.[6]

He took a short step to the solution.

All, then, are agreed on the pressing nature of this problem, . . . and though it would doubtless be quite Utopian to expect a similar agreement as to the value of any remedy that may be proposed, it is at least of immense importance that . . . we have such a consensus of opinion at the outset. . . . Yes, the key to the problem how to restore the people to the land—that beautiful land of ours, with its canopy of sky, the air that blows upon it, the sun that warms it, the rain and dew that moisten it . . . will be seen to pour a flood of light on the problems of intemperance, of excessive toil, of restless anxiety, of grinding poverty. . . .[7]

Howard's complaint was not only against urban congestion, but against the values of the industrial system that produced the city. It is worth quoting his remarks here in some detail, for in them Howard clearly showed the basis of his protest.

These crowded cities have done their work; they were the best which a society largely based on *selfishness* and *rapacity* could construct, but they are in the nature of things entirely unadapted for a society in which the *social side* of our nature is demanding a larger share of recognition. . . . The large cities of today are scarcely better adapted for the expression of the fraternal spirit than would a work on astronomy which taught that the earth was the centre of the universe be capable of adaptation for use in our schools. Each generation should build to suit its own needs; and it is no more in the nature of things that men should continue to live in old areas because their ancestors lived in them, than it is that they should cherish the old beliefs which a wider faith and a more enlarged understanding have outgrown. . . . The simple issue to be faced, and faced resolutely, is: Can better results be obtained by starting on a bold plan on comparatively virgin soil than by attempting to adapt our old cities to our *newer* and *higher* needs? Thus fairly faced, the question can only be answered in one way; and when that simple fact is well grasped, the *social revolution* will speedily commence.[8] [Italics added.]

These bold statements can be considered the garden city manifesto, and like the manifesto of Marx and Engels it identifies the evil, pinpoints the causes, and suggests the solution.

The crowded, industrial cities house the evils of our civilization. These evils have developed because the qualities of selfishness and rapacity have been valued long beyond their usefulness to society. They are now clearly out of tune with the social demands of a more developed, industrial society. In society, as in science, man must abandon outmoded methods and create new ones to meet current demands. Man is not, in Howard's view, at the mercy of uncontrollable social and natural forces. If the seventeenth and eighteenth centuries increased man's ability to control nature, then the task of the nineteenth century was to mobilize man's ability to control society. It was to this belief that Howard was dedicated, and it was to this conviction that his appeal was aimed.

To simplify his argument, Howard devised a now classic image: three magnets labeled "town," "country," and "town-country" are grouped around a rectangle labeled "The People: Where Will They Go?" The town and country each contained advantages (the positive pole) and disadvantages (the negative pole). Only the third, the town-country, was free of disadvantages, taking the best from the other two. The town magnet has the attractions of high wages, employment opportunities, amusements, edifices, and well-lit streets. However, it repels because of high rents and prices, excessive hours of toil, distance from work, foul air, slums, and gin palaces. The country magnet has the attractions of nature, sunshine, woods, and low rents; it repels because of lack of sociability, low wages, lack of amusement, deserted villages, and the lack of public spirit. It is only a clerical task to list the advantages of both as part of the town-country magnet: nature, opportunity, low rents and low prices, high wages, pure air and water, no smoke, no slums, bright homes, freedom, and cooperation. There are no disadvantages to the town-country, or garden city, life.

This was nature's way, Howard maintained in his argument, and it drew upon science, reason, and natural law. In the images and structure of his arguments and the facile way he led the argument to a determined conclusion, Howard exhibited the utopian mentality. He was sincere, convinced, and dedicated. His main objectives, W. A. Eden has observed, went well "with the ordinary aspiration of the class to which Howard belonged, the somewhat earnest, chapel going or chapel emancipated lower middle class which had lately acquired political power and was destined to inaugurate a revolution by returning the Liberal Party with its high majority at the General Election of 1906." [9]

Howard's plan was to purchase about 6,000 acres of open country and in the center, on 1,000 acres, to construct Garden City, for a population of 30,000. A green belt, i.e. countryside, was to surround the city with a natural wall much the same as the wall of the medieval city. The purpose of the barrier for the garden city, as for the medieval city, was to protect it against invasion and encroachment, not from the barbarians but from London's overflow population. At the same time, the green belt would also restrict urban growth from within. Much of his discussion of the plan concerned the financing of the venture: providing balance sheets which proved the plan to be economically sound and the Garden City to be a self-sufficient proposition. The sizes of building lots, street widths and locations, the location of public parks, factories, and agriculture were specified, although Howard emphasized that his description was meant to be suggestive, not final. A hypothetical budget was drawn up for roads, bridges, schools, a library and museum, parks and ornamentation, sewerage disposal, and for a sinking fund. From a reading of this description today, Howard emerges as a colonial clerk neatly setting down the row of figures on the balance sheet. Howard must have known intimately the Victorian mentality that he wanted to persuade, and probably shared it.

Howard's brief inventory of the obstacles to his plan was hardly complete, nor did he even spend much time arguing over the few he did choose to identify. Human nature, as it was then conceived, was a major obstacle. After all, people are selfish and not given to altruism. Howard's answer, such as it was, maintained that these qualities could not be allowed to make any difference. The garden city was economically feasible and socially necessary. If it failed, we were only inviting catastrophe, for cities would continue to grow unplanned and make us their victims. On the other hand, Howard held, once the Garden City was built and its feasibility proven, similar cities could be started and, as a result, a new day would dawn for England and eventually for mankind. Man would no longer be the victim of his industrial creation, but its master. He would discover that his real wealth lay in the land rather than in the marketplace or factory.

Most utopias remain dreams, and their authors die convinced that they held a secret to which the world unfortunately would not listen. Still other utopias, put to the tests of reality, failed because they were poorly conceived, with insufficient attention paid to the complex reality they sought to reform. So too did Howard taste the bitter fruit of reality. He lived to see two garden cities begun, and to see both flounder. He saw enough to show him, if not to convince him, that there were more obstacles to the realization of his plan than he had imagined. Still, there were some benefits, finally proven by the permanence of the experiments and by the financial value of the bonds of the garden cities, although many years after his death in 1928. The plan failed ostensibly for financial reasons, but more important, its failure could be traced to the revolutionary character of its ideas. For better or worse, Howard advocated an ideology of government ownership or control. To Victorians raised in the philosophy of laissez faire, the truth of which seemed self-evident, Howard was advocating no less than revolution. Neither his explicit denial of sympathy with communism and socialism, then active on the Continent, nor his bookkeeper's account sheet could disguise the revolutionary consequences of his ideas. Those who followed Howard were also to learn that their leader was talking of more than architectural reforms alone. Yet, Howard's intent was not to be revolutionary, but simply to pursue his assumptions to a realistic conclusion. Any plan or urban change such as he had in mind must challenge existing social mechanisms because those very mechanisms produced the evil he complained of.

Five years after the publication of Howard's book, a company was formed to build Letchworth, the first garden city.[10] The book became a best seller. A sizable amount of money was raised, although not enough. Of the authorized capital of £300,000, only £100,000 of shares were subscribed beyond the £40,000 pledged by the directors of the newly formed company. Heavy interest charges were incurred for the additional mortgages that were needed and a heavy financial burden was thus placed in the venture from the beginning. Money remained a problem, along with the inevitable dissension between the business and ideological leaders of the project. Nor were matters helped by the fact that Letchworth was a bad site, having few natural attractions. Public interest in the project quickly dissipated. After forty-three years, all of the accumulated dividends were finally repaid. "It was . . . indefatigable faith," wrote Rodwin, "which made Letchworth survive, despite all the difficulties, neglect, and derision."

With the cavalier attitude, obstinacy, and unquenchable optimism that are so characteristic of dedicated egomaniacs, Howard took an option on another piece of land in 1920, Letchworth's marked lack of success notwithstanding. Welwyn Garden City was located twenty miles northwest of London, on the same highway and railroad as Letchworth. Money, once again, was a problem, but this time the financing was more complicated by the economic depression of that period and the competition from the Letchworth venture. Tight money meant higher interest rates, and consequently the financial burden was heavier than it had been for Letchworth. The government advanced some funds, but these loans were sporadic, grudgingly given, and carried with them a right to participate in the management. Again, as in Letchworth, dissension was ever present between the lenders worried for their money and the planners worried for their ideals. After two major reorganizations, in 1931 and in 1934, a large part of the share capital was written off and restrictions on dividends were removed. Howard had died in 1928. Welwyn remained, although its development did not proceed fully according to plan.

Aside from lack of funds and dissension, the garden cities encountered less obvious but equally damaging obstacles. These were due to a naïveté about sociological factors, which, by the way, even later planners did not avoid. Rodwin has noted these in his evaluation of Howard.[11] First, Howard wanted to create a politically independent city. This requirement opened the door to a whole set of new problems concerning revenue and jurisdiction, besides further complicating the already complex administrative relationships between cities. By insisting on independence, Howard overlooked the nexus that existed, and continues to exist, between urban centers in an industrial nation.

Second, the direction of population movement did not fulfill Howard's prediction. Instead of people moving constantly into the large cities, as Howard had predicted for London, such migration leveled off and was redirected into the region around the large central city. *Urban* congestion, therefore, did not remain the key problem; *metropolitan* congestion was to complicate the problem even more. Third, the automobile and mass transportation significantly altered the urban journey from what it had been in Howard's time. He thought that people should walk to work, as one way of being close to nature. The automobile, as fact and as symbol, changed the urbanite's outlook; he would not remain a pedestrian. Urban traffic thereby became a major problem. Whether or not the garden city would have solved or would have exacerbated that problem is hard to say, even though it is a question contemporary planners take into account. Finally, Howard apparently gave little thought to human motivation; how to entice people to move into the garden city. His assumptions concerning human nature and human motivations were primitive and naïve. It is an ideological disease of visionaries, Howard included, that they assume their values to be the best for all. Do people in fact, want to live close to nature? Do they want to exchange concrete for meadows? The answer obviously must be that some do and some do not. It is the human variety that the utopian planner so frequently overlooks. He makes the unwarranted assumption either that people are alike or that they can be molded, shaped, and moved to conform to design, very much as buildings can. Rodwin concluded:

Unawareness of many of the pitfalls, coupled with the extraordinary loyalty to the idea of garden cities, ranks high among the factors which account for the survival of the two towns. Whatever judgment one may form of the experiment, the fact is that the leaders succeeded in their initial objective. [Only, it must be added, if that objective is very narrowly defined.]. . . . In the process of development, the towns also pioneered some significant planning innovations, including use and density zoning, a form of ward or neighborhood planning, employment of an agricultural greenbelt to control urban size, and unified urban land ownership for the purpose of capturing rising land values for the benefit of the residents.[12]

Welwyn and Letchworth were not the end of the garden city movement nor of its importance to the present discussion. During the Second World War, government officials in London foresaw the need for postwar housing and, to their credit, the necessity for directing some of the population out of London itself. Several Town and Country Planning Acts were passed and a Town and Country Planning Ministry created, all before 1945. In 1946, the New Towns Act was passed and "the building of cities for the first time in contemporary Western history became a concern of long-term national policy." [13] These developments are best shown in the story of Stevenage, one of the towns built under the national act, whose problems have been so excellently assessed by Harold Orlans.[14] Stevenage gives us a more recent perspective on the consequences of Howard's ideas and, at the same time, conveniently displays the principle limitations of sociological understanding of the visionaries.

Stevenage in 1945, immediately prior to its selection as a site under the New Towns Act, was in its development and location somewhere between a village and a town. It was within London's metropolitan influence, being a dormitory suburb for clerks and businessmen who commuted to London. However, it still valued its local traditions and agricultural activity. The project called for building a garden city in Stevenage to house a population of 30,000, and one proposal forecasted a population double that size within ten years. The partners in this venture were the Stevenage Urban Council and the Ministry of Town and Country Planning. Although a spirit of cooperation was present at the initial discussions about the project, it was not long before dissension, the ever-present threat in social planning, broke out between the partners. The local authorities resented the manner in which the Ministry pushed ahead with its plans without local consultation. The Ministry, apparently intent on making this project a national model, neglected its public relations in the local community.

Local residents organized themselves into the Residents' Protection Association to protest the Ministry's "tyranny of the acquisition of houses and lands, and the tyranny of control from Whitehall over homes." [15] The residents took legal action against the Ministry, and even though they lost the case, they did succeed in stopping any development during the time, so that only twenty-eight houses were built in the four and one-half years after the project started, instead of over 300 that were to have been completed, A key to the conflict, Orlans believed, was the ideological split between the rural conservatism of Stevanage residents and the public-welfare ideals of the Ministry. What the residents of Stevenage soon came to realize was that the garden city development meant the effective end to their tradition of local independence by the shift to greater public ownership and control. Relations had improved by 1950, after the court action, but the Residents' Protection Association remained for the "exploitation of opportunities to obstruct the progre-s of the New Town and to secure all possible concessions for property owners and ratepayers." Such was the stormy history of the garden city plan in Stevenage.

This brief history of the Stevenage project is meant to highlight certain sociological features, principally the kinds of objections that can develop when the visionary's urban ideals are concretized. I leave out the obvious economic and political problems that are raised and look at what are presumably picayune matters. Orlans' analysis is valuable because he has indicated not only the problems of the politicians but also those of the technicians.

One explicit aim of the Stevenage plan, as it is of most town plans, was to create a *balanced* community: "We want to revive that social structure which existed in the old English villages, where the rich lived next door to the not so rich, and everyone knew everybody." [16] The economic bases for this idea are perhaps reasonable, especially the attempt to achieve some economic stability by having more than one industry or business located in the town. As the above quotation shows, however, behind the desire for balance is frequently the unconscious wish for the norm, for what Orlans has called "the golden mean in which all the parts of a community and all citizens would work together harmoniously and without friction." [17]

Not all town planners, of course, agreé on the desirability of social balance. Even among those at Stevenage, a counter argument was advanced in support of a *homogeneous,* not a mixed community, on the grounds that a deliberate mixture of social classes would hamper the spirit of neighborliness. It is hard to say which argument is more naïve. Both are based on private values more than on social wisdom. There is only the narrowest factual basis upon which to make a choice of population, and this basis is the social consequences that would follow from each alternative. The choice actually made, however, depends heavily on the values the individual planner chooses to hold. Howard, for example, wished to move the working man out of an unhealthy city into the middle class atmosphere of the garden city, where he might spend his time in the "healthy and fascinating pursuit of gardening." [18] Other planners envisioned a new city with all social strata transformed by a mystical, architectural osmosis into an equalitarian society. The troubles with this kind of social engineering are manifold: Whose values are to guide the plan; once enforced, who controls society and how does he make it go in the proper direction?

One illuminating instance of the planner's naïveté concerning Stevenage centered on the "Reilly Green," or common, which took its name from a plan devised by Sir Charles Reilly. The arguments supporting a common, around which small neighborhood units would be constructed, claimed that it would remedy such defects as "loneliness, juvenile deliquency, parental cruelty, poor health, declining birth-rate, late marriage, ignorance, property-possessiveness, etc." [19] More judicious planners, undoubtedly, would not care to make so broad a claim. But the essence of most plans is to restructure social life according to some ideal, and to do it primarily through the manipulation of buildings and space and only secondarily, perhaps, through the manipulation of the people themselves. As one of the architects in the national ministry reported: "We do not claim that a sensible physical arrangement of houses and other buildings normal to a good residential negihborhood will automatically produce a friendly and neighborly spirit. But we do claim that it will give considerable initial advantage to the development of a healthy social life." [20]

This statement illustrates a common misconception among town planners: that architectural forms can alter social forms. Some planners, like Frank Lloyd Wright, go even further, contending that architectural change is the *sine qua non* of social change. It is a narrow assumption, similar to the misconception that slums cause criminal behavior and delinquency. We know now that complex behavior and motives cannot be explained merely by simple physical facts. Tenements do not make criminals any more than mansions make law-abiding citizens. Social contacts in the family, school, and church, as well as other broader social phenomena, and many individual aspects of the personality shape the human product. The visionary, nevertheless, seems to insist on his belief that the individual who is put in a magic house, in a magic setting, and surrounded with what are essentially the trappings of middle class life, will emerge a stolid, socially acceptable human product in the middle class tradition. It is a highly doubtful assumption. Even granting its truth, one might ask: Why establish middle class traditions as the epitome of the good life?

Another aim of the visionaries is to reconstruct social life and this aim is frequently expressed in the "planned neighborhood." The planners of Stevenage were no exception. Arguments may develop over the optimum size of the neighborhood, whether the cul-de-sac is a way to achieve neighborhood social contacts or where to place the community center to maximize intended neighborhood relationships. There is little disagreement, however, about the desirability of creating a neighborhood to begin with. The neighborhood seems to be the *sine qua non* of every planner's dream. It is a primary element in his ideology, and in the neighborhood, he believes, is the basis of social control to effect wanted social changes. Planners believe, as Orlans concluded the New Town planners believed, "that sociability [the planned neighborhood] and community activity could be organized or, at least, encouraged by a congenial physical environment and genuine social reform which would counteract the consequences of industrialism, occupational specializations, and class segregation and conflict." [21] But, as Ruth Glass has correctly stated: "the return to the small self-contained urban [neighborhood] unit appears to be a forlorn hope. The existing trend is for a progressive division of labour and of interests. . . . This trend can be controlled but it cannot be cancelled." [22]

The visionary, like Howard, raised in a milieu of protest against the evils of industrialism, stands fair to be disappointed. His cause may be just, his vision bright, his side that of the angels. Morally and intellectually impelled to transmogrify industrial, urban man into a middle class, provincial, conforming, garden-city species, the visionary claims too much and knows too little. The Plan has him hypnotized into believing that this all is really feasible. But the dream cannot withstand reality, which he seems imperfectly to appreciate. He has, unfortunately, come to believe that massive social forces, with the impetus of centuries behind them, can be contained and redirected toward nirvana by an exquisitely designed community and a neatly planned neighborhood.

"Must utopia, realized, always disappoint?" Orlans asks, and answers:

To be persuasive and practical (to persuade different kinds of people and to be practiced in different times and places) a utopian idea must be relatively simple and generalized. But life is more complicated than any simple idea, and probably than *any* idea or image, one can have of it—"the inexpressible complexity of everything that lives" is how Tolstoy, for all his genius in expressing that complexity, put it. This is the rock upon which utopia, and reason itself, founders.[23]

§ Frank Lloyd Wright: Broadacre City

Wright was more than simply the American counterpart to Ebenezer Howard and his Broadacre City more than just the American version of Garden City.[24] Howard, as a true Victorian, after carefully adding up the economic costs and arguing for the feasibility of the garden city, had accepted much of the prevailing ideology. An overcrowded and congested London was bad business whereas a planned garden city was good business. Wright, on the contrary, never entered the market place to sell his plans. He much preferred to be the prophet on the mount shouting "Doom!" to the multitudes below. Wright felt the city and the industrial civilization that produced it must perish. They were the consequences of diseased values, and to achieve health, new values had to be established in a new environment. Wright was more consciously a social revolutionary than was Howard. He was prepared to recognize social mechanisms and willing to alter them. Howard's aim was to build a few garden cities to prove they were feasible, and by this publicity to have the revolt against the city initiated by society itself. Wright was more impatient. He wanted the wholesale decentralization of cities carried on simultaneously with the creation of Broadacre City. He had no patience with businesslike arguments to support his plan. Perhaps one could not blame him for his impatience and his loftiness, since he was so convinced that human civilization would be strangled by its industrial creation unless decisive and total action was taken. Any less drastic plan would have been hypocritical.

As the citizen stands, powerful modern resources, naturally his own by uses of modern machinery, are (owning to their very nature) turning against him, although the system he lives under is one he himself helped build. Such centralizations of men and capital as he must now serve are no longer wise or humane. Long ago—having done all it could for humanity—the centralization we call the big city became a centripetal force grown beyond our control; agitated by rent to continually additional, vicarious powers.[25]

The city, according to Wright, has perverted our values and has become the environment of false democracy, false individualism, and false capitalism. We have, by our inaction, allowed ourselves to be overwhelmed and dominated by falsity. "The citizen," Wright argued, "is now trained to see life as a cliché." He must be trained to see life as natural for "only then can the democratic spirit of man, individual, rise out of the ground. We are calling that civilization of man and ground . . .

democracy." [26] As for capitalism: "Out of American 'rugged individualism' captained by rugged captains of our rugged industrial enterprises we have gradually evolved a crude, vain power: plutocratic 'Capitalism.' Not true capitalism. I believe this is entirely foreign to our own original idea of Democracy." [27]

The cause of these perversions of our basic social values in the city is industrial civilization, where most of the visionaries locate the blame. Wright's contribution was to specify the causes more precisely. First, among these is *land rent*, and Henry George is resurrected as a guide to salvation. The rent for land has contributed to the "overgrowth of cities, resulting in poverty and unhappiness." Land values are artificial monsters that have taken over the destiny of the city, thereby removing us further from the natural state of mankind. Second, *money*, "a commodity for sale, so made as to come alive as something in itself—to go on continuously working in order to make all work useless. . . . The modern city is its stronghold and chief defender." [28] Here the Puritan and Jeffersonian in Wright emerges, berating man to get back to the land and to honest labor. Third, *profit*. "By the triumph of conscienceless but 'rugged individualism' the machine profits of human ingenuity or inspiration in getting the work of the world done are almost all funneled into pockets of fewer and more 'rugged' captains-of-industry. Only in a small measure . . . are these profits . . . where they belong; that is to say, with the man whose life is actually modified, given, or sacrificed to this new common agency for doing the work of the world. This agency we call 'the machine.' " [29] In these few words, Wright has fairly condensed the Marxian theory of surplus value. Fourth, *government* and *bureaucracy*. "In order to keep the peace and some show of equity between the lower passions so busily begotten in begetting, the complicated forms of super-money-increase-money-making and holding are legitimatized by government. Government, too, thus becomes monstrosity. Again enormous armies of white-collarites arise." [30] These are Wright's beliefs on the state of industrial civilization. The need for revolt is clear; the means are at hand.

Infinite possibilities exist to make of the city a place suitable for the free man in which freedom can thrive and the soul of man grow, a

City of cities that democracy would approve and so desperately needs. . . . Yes, and in that vision of decentralization and reintegration lies our natural twentieth century dawn. Of such is the nature of the democracy free men may honestly call the new freedom." [31]

How emphatically this point of view, so characteristic of the visionary, separates him from the mundane practicality of the practitioner. For Wright, the city in its present form cannot be saved, nor is it worth saving. A new environment must be envisioned and built. It must be one that is developed out of our technology, but one that excises the diseased growth that has infected our basic and still sound values. The plan is Broadacre City, realized by "organic architecture" or "the architecture of democracy."

Broadacre City was a more detailed utopia than Garden City. Wright had drawn not only the ground pattern (one acre to the individual) but also planned homes, buildings, farms, and automobiles. He also clearly specified the activities that would be permitted. Wright held definite views, to say the least, not only about architecture, but music, education, religion, and medicine as well. He was an authoritarian, some would say a messianic figure, as sure of the true and the good and the beautiful as were Christ and the early Christian prophets, along with Lao-tse and Mohammed, whom he sought to emulate.

Wright's plans for the physical setting and social order of Broadacre City were comprehensive. They contained small factories because the newer technology has made the centralized large factory obsolete, wasteful, and constricting. Office buildings housing the financial, professional, distributive and administrative services necessary for business, would be organized as a unit. Professional services would be decentralized and made readily accessible to the clients. Banks, as we know them, would be abolished and in their place there would be a "non-political, non-profit institution in charge of the medium of exchange." Money no longer would have the power it now has; therefore, the need for its "glamorization" would be removed. Markets and shopping centers would be designed as spacious pavilions to make shopping itself a pleasant and aesthetic experience. There would be apartments, motels, and community centers. Radio would carry great music to the people. "The chamber music

concert would *naturally* become a common feature at home."
[My italics.] Churches would be built, but the "old idea" of
religion would be replaced by a more liberal and nonsectarian
religion. There would be less concern with the hereafter, with
superstition, with prejudice, and with deference to authority.
With this new religion man, though still humble, would be made
more understanding of himself and more democratic towards
others.

Wright also had plans for education and the material to be
taught in the schools and university of Broadacre City. He
would replace the specialized, mass product of the universities of
his day with a student who would obtain a deeper understanding of nature's laws governing the human spirit. Education
would be a total and continuous process for the resident of
Broadacre. Aside from the schools, this would be accomplished
by "style centers," and "television and radio, owned by the
people [which would] broadcast cultural programs illustrating
pertinent phases of government, of city life, of art work, and
[would have] programs devoted to landscape study and plant-
ing or the practice of soil and timber conservation; and, as a matter of course, to *town planning* for better houses." [32]

This plan is not utopian, Wright argued, but rather a
description of elemental changes that he saw "existing or surely
coming." Either the vision is realized or society as we know it
is doomed.

This long discourse . . . is a sincere attempt to take apart and show . . .
the radical simplicities of fate to which our own machine skills have
now laid us wide open and [to] try to show how radical eliminations
are now essential to our spiritual health, and to the culture, if not
the countenance, of democratic civilization itself. These are all changes
valid by now if we are to have indigenous culture at all and are not
to remain a bastardized civilization with no culture of our own, going
all the way down the backstairs of time to the usual untimely end
civilizations have hitherto met.[33]

With Frank Lloyd Wright, the visionary's argument found
its most dramatic and radical expression, and its most completely detailed one. Wright magnified Howard's plan and
spelled out more specifically the visionary's discontent and re-

bellion against the industrial city. In Wright's words, the planned utopia became a loud protest against the evils of industrialism. His architectural philosophy was, at the same time, a radical social ideology. Wright recognized this and did not hesitate to make the connection clear. His principle contribution to the study of the city, if one does not care to accept his dream or his philosophy, was in the repeated insistence on the relationship between the city and the society that produced it. The contemporary city, for Wright, was a product of industrial civilization. One could not understand the first without the second, which included understanding all of its institutions: the political system, social stratification and the economic order, religion and education. Wright might be excused for his authoritarianism, for his failure to consider the motivations of individuals, for his brash structuring of existing social relationships into something he wanted. For he did grasp something of the underlying complexity that sustained the city as a social environment. That he refused to consider what others wanted, or what others thought, was- due to his conviction that he was absolutely right. Can the prophet, after all, have any doubts?

§ Lewis Mumford: The New Urban Order

Mumford added greater social realism to the visionaries' argument.[34] He was more aware than most of economic forces and social ideologies and their effect in shaping the city. For that reason, his analysis of the "new urban order" was sociologically informed. He showed little patience with the social engineers and architectural planners who have become so hypnotized by their own goals that they show little understanding of the existing environment from which they must begin.

I have selected Mumford for balance, to exemplify the more realistic dimensions of the visionary type. *The Culture of Cities*, both as urban history and as a sociological analysis of the contemporary city, is exceptional. Mumford, of course, is not alone in possessing realism, but, more than anyone else, he has combined his realism with an understanding of the city, and expressed it in a book that deserves its rank as a classic. Arthur B.

Gallion, for example, in *The Urban Pattern*,[35] has presented an urban history that is as informed and as sociologically realistic as Mumford's, yet in his analysis of the contemporary city Gallion seems to have forgotten the social variables he specified at the beginning, and he assumes the utopian mentality. In somewhat similar fashion, Percival and Paul Goodman, in *Communitas*,[36] have shown an exceptionally keen understanding of the forces of urban society, and they have incorporated that understanding into a standard by which to evaluate the plans of others. Their own plan for the future city tends, however, to fall short when measured against the same standard. This is due, I strongly suspect, to the fact that any plan for a future city must avoid many aspects of social, economic, and psychological relevance. It is impossible, it would seem, to to take all of these factors into account. The Goodmans try to guard against this by insisting upon the flexibility of their plan and upon its suggestiveness rather than its concreteness, as did Howard before them. Even so, it seems that The Plan must raise more problems than it solves.

It is not Mumford's history of urbanism that is my concern, but rather his analysis of what he has called the "social basis of the new urban order." Mumford began with an inventory of the architectural and sociological components that are available today for urban reconstruction. Modern architecture, he argued, has new materials to use and a wide engineering knowledge upon which to depend. Even more important, these new materials as the products of a "collective economy" are meant to be used by all persons; "one's economic position may entitle one to a greater or smaller quantity, but the quality is fixed." [37] "Collective largesse," not niggardliness, is the hallmark of our industrial civilization; what the Goodman's have aptly labeled a "technology of surplus." In short: the materials are available for urban reconstruction and in sufficient quantity and quality. Furthermore, architectural knowledge is also at hand to make use of these materials.

Modern hygiene has given us the knowledge not only to combat disease but to prevent it. The city of the future, unlike the city of the past or of the present, could now be built as a life-supporting environment. What has been learned from the past is that health is a collective responsibility: water and waste disposal, for example, have become the accepted responsibilities of urban governments. More important for the future, however, positive attitudes toward health and hygiene have become dominant, and the life-destructive environment of the city will not be readily tolerated. "The drift to the suburbs," Mumford contended as early as 1938, "which has been one of the most conspicuous features of the growth of cities during the past half century, was one response to the more constant concern with health and education that has characterized the life of the middle classes." [38] Perhaps so, but the wider emphasis upon health is certainly not misplaced.

The prolongation of youth is another value emphasized on the contemporary scene. In the earlier decades of industrialism, youth was cut short by child labor, and life itself was shortened by a studied avoidance of concerns with safety and the basic requirements of health. At present, however, the emphasis has changed; youth is prolonged through education, through sports, and through the medical gains that have prolonged life generally.

Another value that has undergone change has been the open-hearted acceptance of the new, as if for its own sake. It is a quality that Mumford called "the capacity for renewal," a positive willingness to look to the future rather than to the past for our direction. The monument has lost its significance for the contemporary city where men no longer glorify the past or allow themsleves to be chained to it. "Instead of being oriented, then, toward death and fixity, we are oriented to the cycle of life, with its never-ending process of birth and growth and renewal and death." [39]

The rejection of the monuments of the past has been coupled with the rejection of uniformity in man himself. From an interest in caste, we have turned to an interest in the individual personality. Even though occupation, regional background, or other major social categories may direct personalities toward conformity, the individual still retains a uniqueness and a character that has come to be idealized in the present. At the same time, Mumford argued, socialization has been an equally dominant demand; that is, an appreciation for the collectivity and for what it can add to the real meaning of individual liberty. The "dogmas of private property and individual liberty" of a century or more ago overlooked the highly central role that society must play in creating and guaranteeing such liberties.

The effect of these changes and conditions has been to give us the social philosophy, the technology, and the material means to alter our environment. What is more, the city can be altered to benefit more than just the few. The mode of existence that was once thought to be the natural privilege of only the aristocracy is now available to all as their right.

This, then, is the meaning of the change that has been slowly taking place in our civilizaion since the third quarter of the nineteenth century. The increase of collectivism, the rising of municipal and governmental housing, the expansion of co-operative consumers' and producers' associations, the destruction of slums and the building of superior types of community for the workers—all these are signs of the new biotechnic orientation.[40]

The change has been abetted by education, which has become as vital for the modern city as religion was for the medieval city. Through education, the masses can be transformed into intelligent individuals seeking to achieve common ends through cooperation and understanding. The transformation is, of course, still incomplete, primarily because we still treat education as a mass commodity rather than as a more individualized and private experience. The desired conditions for education become "small groups, small classes, small communities; in short, institutions adapted to the human scale."

Mumford has specifically noted that the social forces he has described as "bases of the new urban order" are not all operative. The gap between the present and the future as he foresees it is still there. This kind of recognition has made Mumford unique among the visionaries. When confronted with the fact of the contemporary city, he does not abandon the understanding he has shown in his earlier analysis of urban history. The same complex forces must be assessed in reading change into the future. Mumford has said himself that

social facts are primary, and the physical organization of a city, its industries and its markets, its lines of communication and traffic, must be subservient to its social needs. Whereas in the development of the city during the last century we expanded the physical plan recklessly and treated the essential social nucleus, the organs of government and education and social service, as mere afterthoughts, today we must treat the social nucleus as the essential element in every valid city plan.[41]

The plan for the future city, then, must take account of social relationships and must be cognizant of the functions meant to be served by the planned urban arrangements of the future. The point that most visionaries have consistently overlooked is that their own personal values, no matter how sincere, are simply not legitimate grounds upon which to insist that the city be recreated. Instead, as Mumford was at great pains to explain, the social needs and desires of the urban community must themselves be part of the equation and must provide the grounds for rebuilding. Neither can architectural design be used as the sole, or even primary basis for rebuilding the city. This argument is but a variation on past arguments—justly held in moral contempt—by which the factory and its demands were allowed to dictate the character of the urban environment. The emphasis by architects on, say, the functional home rather than upon the functional needs of a society—whatever they are—is misplaced and just as unfortunate as the tragic, misplaced emphasis in the last century on industrial, as opposed to social, development. Is Wright's design for urban living any more realistic, desirable, or democratic than what has emerged during the past century in a city catering to the demands of industry? Neither the nineteenth century's or Wright's solution has given fair voice to the people and their desires. The means taken to achieve a goal, as John Dewey has emphasized repeatedly, is itself part of that goal and will inevitably determine it. In the present context, then, the visionary's authoritarian insistence upon his plan cannot lead to democratic consequences. It is this kind of error that Mumford has avoided, in large measure, because he has been content to show the needs rather than to draw the plan itself.

§ Conclusions

The visionary has made several contributions to a sociology of the city. Behind the plans he has expounded, behind his sustained note of protest and his prophecies of urban doom—from metropolis to necropolis—there are to be found ideas that are integral to an understanding of the city. Social scientists, uncomfortable perhaps with the artistic language of the visionary and unwilling to understand the nature of his protest, have therefore omitted from consideration an important segment of information about the urban environment.

The visionary has succeeded even better than the social scientists in indicating the multiplicity of factors that, in effect, create the city as we know it. In some cases the visionary has done this explicitly. All three visionaries discussed here, for example, have shown a lively comprehension of the city's industrial roots. That these have not been sufficiently detailed is as much an indication of the limited understanding we all possess as of shortcomings peculiar to the visionary alone. In other instances, the visionary has shown the complexity of the urban environment implicitly, by the naïveté of his plans and by his failure in trying to realize them. Human motivations and human needs have most obviously been overlooked in many of the plans of the visionaries, or else have been seriously oversimplified. That people want to live in small communities and want to get back to nature is by no means an established fact, yet the visionary frequently assumes it to be so. A more proper balance can be provided by the sociologist in this respect from his knowledge of social values and social norms. However, even the sociologist frequently has been naïve in appreciating the urban complexity that he has chosen to study.

Beside the motivations of the individual there must be considered the structure of society itself. Political organizations and allegiances must inevitably become involved in any planned urban change, for the alteration sooner or later calls for a shift in the existing constellations of power. Similarly, the profit motive and the economic structure are implicated. Either the change must show a profit for those willing to support it or it must be convincingly shown that change is necessary for survival. Rarely do the visionary's plans satisfy the former condition, and as of now, they do not satisfy the latter condition, except for an elite group of disciples. What the visionary's failures give the social scientist should be an appreciation for the social mechanisms that he is trying to understand. Even though the scientist's immediate interest may not be in planned change, this evaluation of the visionary should contribute a measure of understanding of the factors involved. The studies of utopias are sociologically relevant not because of an interest in utopias, but because of an interest in the reasons why they fail. A morbid conclusion, perhaps, but true.

One final point: The study of the city carries with it, often implicitly, a social ideology and a social philosophy. The visionary has not run from protest but, on the contrary, has been eager to make his protest evident. Sociologists, on the other hand, disciplined in the need for objectivity, often let such values creep in the back door, as they stand at the front door proclaiming their objectivity. For years, although increasingly less so now, sociologists, nostalgic for a return to a rural way of life, studied the city critically and angrily. Even urban ecologists, as will be shown, made much of the objectivity of their methods. Yet their analysis often overlooked one of their own basic value assumptions: that the city was the result of economic rationality. Objectivity in science is necessary; about that there is little dispute. However, such objectivity is achieved not by hiding one's biases and refusing to look at them, but by recognizing them openly so that they do not clutter one's conclusions.

The industrial city, as the visionaries have shown, is an historical product of values that lie at the core of our civilization. It is inconceivable that any serious study of the city can avoid recognizing those values.

NOTES

1. Lewis Mumford, *op. cit.*, 479.
2. Karl Mannheim, *Ideology and Utopia* (New York: Harcourt, Brace & World, 1946), 185.
3. Ebenezer Howard, *Garden Cities of Tomorrow* (London: Faber & Faber, 1946), 114.
4. F. J. Osborn in the preface to Howard, *op. cit.*, 9.
5. F. J. Osborn, quoted in Lloyd Rodwin, *The British New Towns Policy* (Cambridge: Harvard University Press, 1956), 11.
6. Howard, *op. cit.*, 42.
7. *Ibid.*, 44.
8. *Ibid.*, 146.
9. Quoted in Rodwin, *op. cit.*, 12.
10. The details of the history of Letchworth and Welwyn have been taken from Rodwin, *op. cit.*, 12-15.
11. *Ibid.*, 27-36.
12. *Ibid.*, 15.
13. *Ibid.*, 39.
14. Harold Orlans, *Utopia Ltd.* (New Haven: Yale University Press, 1953).
15. Quoted in Orlans, *op. cit.*, 67.
16. *Ibid.*, 82.
17. *Ibid.*, 87.
18. Note the remark made by Boumphrey, quoted in Orlans, *op. cit.*, 94. "The whole essence of Howard's idea was that by rehousing the working-class man in a garden city, he would be transported into a clean atmosphere and healthy surroundings . . . and instead of wasting his spare time in the gin palace, to the detriment of his health, pocket, and home life, he could spend it in the healthy and fascinating pursuit of gardening."
19. *Ibid.*, 95.
20. Quoted in Orlans, *op. cit.*, 96-7.
21. *Ibid.*, 99-100.
22. Quoted in Orlans, *op. cit.*, 100 f.n.
23. *Ibid.*, 282.
24. The analysis of Frank Lloyd Wright's plan is taken from his *When Democracy Builds* (Chicago: University of Chicago Press, 1945) and *The Living City* (New York: Horizon Press, 1958). The latter is a later edition of the first book. Wright quotes are reprinted by permission of the publisher, Horizon Press, Inc., from *The Living City* by Frank Lloyd Wright. Copyright 1938.
25. Wright, *Living City*, *op. cit.*, 20.
26. *Ibid.*, 25.
27. *Ibid.*, 46.
28. *Ibid.*, 33.
29. *Ibid.*, 33.
30. *Ibid.*, 34.
31. *Ibid.*, 193.
32. *Ibid.*, 193.

172 / LEONARD REISSMAN

33. *Ibid.*, 221-2.
34. Lewis Mumford, *op. cit.* Mumford's recent book, *The City in History* (New York: Harcourt, Brace & World, 1961) appeared after this section was written. The last, however, is substantially the same as the earlier book, as far as this discussion is concerned. If anything, *The City in History* has become more mystical on the relevant points about the future of cities than was *The Culture of Cities*.
35. Arthur B. Gallion, *The Urban Pattern* (New York: D. Van Nostrand Co., 1950).
36. Percival and Paul Goodman, *Communitas: Means of Livelihood & Ways of Life* (Chicago: University of Chicago Press, 1947).
37. Mumford, *op. cit.*, 419.
38. *Ibid.*, 423.
39. *Ibid.*, 435-38.
40. *Ibid.*, 464.
41. *Ibid.*, 482.

PART FOUR
NEW TOWNS CRITICIZED
AS SUBURBIA

WILLIAM ALONSO

THE MIRAGE OF NEW TOWNS

Calling for "new towns" has long been a favorite activity of architects and architectural critics, but in recent years just about everyone seems to have taken up the cry. The list of such advocates now includes giant corporations, real estate developers, the American Institute of Planners, the mass media, the former President, the Urban Affairs Council of the current President, several state legislatures, various cabinet members, congressmen, senators, governors, the National Association of Counties, the National League of Cities, the United States Conference of Mayors, and Urban America.

The reasons for this surge of interest in new towns are elusive. Some of the advocacy is probably self-serving, as in the cases of congressmen or federal bureaucrats seeking to maintain diminishing constituencies, self-aggrandizing professional groups, and of business firms in pursuit of new markets. For many, glimmering images of simpler, future Camelots combine the American nostalgia for the small town with a desire to escape from the biting reality of our complex urban problems. But mostly the idea of new towns has some magic that fires the imagination, stirring some Promethean impulse to create a better place and way of life, a calm and healthy community of crystalline completeness.

These romantic associations make it difficult to analyze the new towns strategy as a rational policy. When a cabinet member speaks of "avoiding chaos," "organic balance," "creative possibilities," "building poems," "communities of tomorrow," and the like, he has adopted the vague rhetoric of architectural and utopian writers. This rhetoric abounds in code words. For instance, one of the most frequently stated reasons for new towns is that they will be *planned* (a term in urban matters that is acceptable to both the political right and left). But in itself, the fact that something is to be planned is of interest only to the professionals who get the work and to later chroniclers. To most people, such planning is merely an input, and

The Public Interest, No. 19 (Spring, 1970), 3–17. Copyright © 1970 by National Affairs, Inc. Reprinted by permission of the author and publisher.

the important question is one of output: what does such planning do to what the new town will do? Some other code words are *balanced, exciting, variety, living environment, choice, human scale.* To make sense of the new towns concept,[1] it is necessary to translate its advocates' rhetoric into clear language, and this in turn requires one to distinguish between purely instrumental objectives and their intended ultimate purposes.

The discussion that follows will focus on proposed policies of directing to new towns only a substantial portion of our future urban growth rather than all. There are two reasons for this. The first is that, with the exceptions of some journalists, nobody seriously proposes to channel *all* further growth to new towns. Second, it is inconceivable that such a policy would work. The British experience is instructive here. As of December 1967, after 20 years of sustained effort, the population of new towns had grown by only 554,373, or only 1 per cent of the national population. During 1967, the population of the new towns grew by 34,577, which is less than 10 per cent of the yearly British population growth.

What are new towns for? I have discovered about two dozen principal objectives, some with several variants, and in the pages that follow, I will examine critically the main purposes new towns advocates have in mind. But let me here summarize briefly my principal conclusions. First, there is little force to the arguments of those who urge a major national commitment of effort and resources to a program for directing a substantial portion of our urbanization into new towns. On the other hand, there may be some sense in the limited use of new towns for the testing and development of technological, physical, and institutional innovations which might be applicable to the expansion and rebuilding of existing cities.

---

1. A comment on nomenclature may be helpful. Some have tried to draw a distinction between *new town* and *new community,* but today the terms are used almost interchangeably. *New community* has a slightly wider meaning and is often applied to subdivisions which would not be called *new towns* by anyone. On the other hand, some rebuilding within existing cities is being called "new towns in town." I shall reserve the terms *new towns* and *new community* to developments that are built at some distance from existing urban areas.

New towns may be either *independent* if they provide for the employment of their residents, or *satellite* if there is to be substantial commuting to existing centers. Most of the well-known new towns in this decade (Reston and Columbia) and of the recent past (Radburn or Forest Hills) have been satellites; but, historically, independent new towns have been quite numerous. In a sense, of course, almost every American city was an independent new town at the time of its founding. But the 19th century saw the intentional creation of a great many company towns (Lawrence, Lowell, Pullman), utopian and religious new settlements and towns developed by the railroads as they spanned the continent. Present day independent new towns are most frequently resort or retirement towns, although there are occasional instances of cities created to provide housing for workers in large isolated projects (Boulder City and the atomic energy towns of Oak Ridge and Los Alamos are examples). My discussion will include both types.

Finally, there are major differences between the new town and the concept of growth center. First, new town proposals are for newly built settlements, while growth centers are usually existing settlements which are to be expanded to the point of self-sustaining growth. Second, new town proposals often stress self-containment as a labor market, while growth center proposals often stress the role of providing jobs for those living in the surrounding region. Third and most important, new towns proposals are based on the idea of steering growth away from urban areas which are regarded as too big, while growth centers are viewed as steering growth toward underemployed populations or some unexploited resources. Although the two ideas somewhat complement each other, I shall concern myself with only new towns.

"Where shall they live?"

It is common to argue that present urban areas cannot cope with the expected growth of urban population. A recent statement of this type was made by the National Committee on Urban Growth Policy. It predicted that from now until the year 2000 United States urban population will grow by 100 million, and recommended that to help accommodate this growth, we build 100 new towns of at least 100,000 population, and 10 new cities of at least 1 million population. The very roundness of these figures suggests their tentativeness and leads one to wonder how the proposals might have differed if men had six fingers on each hand. Nonetheless, even accepting these targets, *the year 2000 would see only 7 per cent of the 300 million population residing in these new settlements,* with 80 per cent of the foreseen growth taking place in existing areas. If the hoped-for replacement of one-third of the existing dwellings is achieved, *almost 90 per cent of new housing would be produced in existing urban areas.* Thus, as radical as the National Committee's proposal seems, it would affect only a small part of our population and an even smaller part of our housing production. A program that marginal in its effect cannot stand very high on the list of national priorities.

Further, given the uncertain state of our knowledge, we cannot say that existing urban centers can absorb 80 million persons but cannot absorb 100 million. *If each of our smallest 200 metropolitan areas took in a half million persons, we could hold the 100 million without any of these areas exceeding 2½ million.* The National Committee's argument is further weakened when we examine the growth assumption: our national rate of population growth has declined steadily for the past 15 years and now stands at 1 per cent. At this rate, by the year 2000 the increase will be only 75 million—or 5 million less than the growth that the Commission allocates *existing* areas.

The argument from efficiency

Less crude than the lack-of-room arguments are those holding that further growth of large urban areas is inefficient. In brief, such arguments state that urban costs per capita rise with increasing urban size, or that marginal costs increase with population. According to this line of reasoning, urban areas grow beyond their "least cost" point because arriving people or firms are not discriminated against but are rather placed on the same footing as everyone else. They pay *average costs* (in taxes, etc.) and these are lower than the *marginal* costs that their arrival imposes. A considerable literature addresses itself to the shape of this cost curve and the location of its bottom, but the question has not been settled of whether costs rise disproportionately to population for a given level of services.

Whether they do or not, when the city is compared to a firm, and the concept of "efficiency" is introduced, an analysis based only on costs is incomplete. The objective of any unit of population is to make money, not to save it. In the case of a city, the point of minimum costs is relevant only if we assume constant product per inhabitant. It appears, however, that product and income per inhabitant rise with increasing population faster than costs, even taking into account differences in cost of living. *Efficiency arguments for diverting growth away from existing urban areas depend upon the assumption that new towns will enjoy a greater difference between marginal product and marginal cost, than is to be found in our cities. In fact, the opposite seems to be the case if we judge by existing cities that are comparable in size to proposed new towns.*

Migratory way-stations

It is often suggested that the new towns would intercept migrants from the rural areas on their way to large cities and would thereby give our large metropolitan areas time to absorb their earlier migrants. This image of a flood of rural immigrants, however, is quite out of date. Migration of farm population to metropolitan areas has dropped to an insignificant trickle, largely because there are so few farmers left; and migration of any sort plays a decreasing part in overall metropolitan growth. Of the 10.9 per cent growth of metropolitan areas during the 1960-66 period, only 22.6 per cent came from immigration as compared to 35 per cent during the 1950-60 period. Moreover, most of the domestic migration came from smaller urban places rather than from farms. Beyond this, the picture is confused. For example, compare the yearly rate of 492,000 migration into metropolitan areas with the rate of 138,000 migration out of nonmetropolitan areas and the rate of 377,000 civilian immigration *into this country* during the 1960-66 period. These figures suggest that nearly *three-fourths of the migratory increase into metropolitan areas is international in origin, and that only 6 per cent of metropolitan growth comes from domestic migratory flows.*

Many metropolitan areas, in fact, are losing population through out-migration. The fastest growing metropolitan areas, and the strongest magnets to migrants in proportion to their size, are those between 200,000 and 2 million, while those over 2 million were attracting only 0.2 migrants per hundred population per year, and those under 200,000 had net out-migration. Nine areas accounted for 81 per cent of all net in-migration, leaving an average of fewer than 500 migrants per year entering each of the others. To put it another way, *28 metropolitan areas in the south, southwest, mountain states, and Pacific coast accounted for 99 per cent of the net in-migration.* Please note: neither New York, nor Philadelphia, nor Chicago is among these twenty-eight.

Black migration to metropolitan areas during the 1960-66 period averaged 145,000 yearly—about 30 per cent of all net migration—down from a 172,000 yearly rate from 1950-60. From 1960-66, such migration accounted for some 34 per cent of the growth of black metropolitan population—*but only 31 per cent of these black migrants were from farms.* The black population is already far more urbanized than the white, and the shifting proportions of blacks among urban areas of diverse sizes indicates that, on the whole, they are moving not from farm to city but upward along the urban-size hierarchy.

Is this flow of migrants so large that we should reorganize our urban system to gain a breathing spell? It would appear not. If we exclude the 28 metropolitan areas in the developing and urbanizing crescent from the south to the Pacific states —and in these areas there is far less talk of an "urban crisis" than elsewhere—the other metropolises are trading either already-urban migrants with each other or are swapping earlier migrants for new immigrants. New back migration from the farms is relatively small and declining, and the other black migration is primarily from small urban places to larger, urbanized areas.

Second, if new towns were developed, would they attract these migrants? Again, it would appear not. New towns or even new cities would of necessity be small, at least in the beginning, and the pattern of migration, especially for blacks, is away from smaller urban places toward bigger ones. Of course it might be that new towns of extraordinary amenity, offering strong inducements, and having a credible guarantee of future size might succeed in attracting people but there is no assurance that these arrivals would be the same migrants that were supposed to be intercepted. Further it may be that the cost of the inducements to effect such a geographic shift might be better used directly for the welfare and acculturation of the intended populations.

Third, if the new towns can attract population, would they do so in time? From the present state of vague discussions and the experience of such programs as urban renewal, one may estimate that ten years from now there may be some small beginnings on the ground, and that it would be another decade before the new towns would involve enough people to affect significantly the migration flows to metropolitan areas. Of course, a determined federal government could act much faster, breaking ground within a year and promoting fast growth by hothouse techniques. But this would make extremely unlikely those elements of amenity, detailed programming, technical and institutional innovation, private-public cooperation, and so forth, that are integral to most new town proposals. The dilemma is that quickly-developed towns would be new but not innovative, and would be a poor magnet for migrants if we are to judge by existing cities of comparable size. On the other hand, innovative new towns would have a long gestation.

A variant of the objective of intercepting migrants for the relief of urbanized areas is the notion that industrial new towns, if established in rural or other areas of declining employment in primary production, could provide enough good jobs to ensure people a permanent alternative to out-migration. This idea was advanced by the Department of Agriculture during the Johnson years under the label "urban-rural balance." The proposals included new towns, "growth centers" based on existing communities, and "new communities" that would encompass several counties in ways which were not clear. Although these proposals were not very specific, they apparently called for new towns that would be quite small, just large enough to absorb the district's surplus population.

It is true that standardized process manufacturing has been leaving the larger metropolitan areas and moving to smaller metropolitan areas, but it is doubtful that enough plants would locate in rural surroundings or in small towns for such a policy to be effective. Also, because the size of a plant typically increases with decreasing urban size, this suggested pattern would lead to a very large number of one company new towns under absentee ownership. Do we want this?

More important, it appears that the rate of out-migration does not vary with local hardship. Migrants leave at a steady rate regardless of local conditions, although such local conditions do affect the rate of *in*-migration. These facts have important policy implications. They suggest that population maintenance and jobs-to-people programs, if successful, may bring new people to depressed areas (which usually have a labor surplus) rather than retain the original residents who are leaving. It is well known that those who leave these areas are younger and better educated than those who stay behind, so that their departure weakens the local economy out of proportion to their number. Unfortunately, it appears that migrants entering depressed areas are more like the stayers than the movers (older, less educated, and less skilled), so that the newcomers do not replace the qualities lost through out-migration.

Preserving the countryside

It is sometimes suggested that new towns are needed to preserve agricultural land. This argument originated in Britain. But in this country, where historically *we have been abandoning agricultural land,* the argument lacks force. To accommodate 100 million people at suburban densities (with homes, factories, and so forth) would take about 14 million acres. This makes up less than 1 per cent of the United States mainland territory, less than 2 per cent of the present area in forests, and less than 5 per cent of the area now in crops. It is also only about one-half *the decrease* in planted crop acreage that occurred during the 1959-64 period. The territory to be occupied by urban growth, in short, is relatively small.

Beyond this one must question whether new towns would take up less space. It is hard to believe that they would. Densities are likely to be low, as the American preference for large lots meets low land prices, and most descriptions of new towns stress the land-consuming amenities that will be found there (such as parks, playing fields and artificial lakes). Some designers advocate very high density towns but it is doubtful that these would prove attractive. Some point out that growth at the margin of existing urban areas overrruns some of the most valuable and productive agricultural land; but the value and productivity of this land derives not from its intrinsic fertility but from the more intensive use of capital, labor, and other inputs on land valued for its adjacency to urban markets. Growth of existing areas would merely slide these rings outward.

Another conservation-of-land argument is based on the sprawl of marginal urban growth. Sprawl is an ill-defined word, referring to a condition characterized by very large lots, or by a ribbon development along major highways, or by the leapfrogging of clustered development that results from speculation. Thus, by thin development or by leaving gaps, sprawl covers more land than continuous compact development. I am unaware of studies showing the extent to which bypassed land is withdrawn from agricultural production; the one study I know of that attempts an economic analysis of how sprawl functions concludes that it may be an effective way of withholding land from premature development at low densities.[2] This depends, of course, on whether growth eventually backtracks to fill in the gaps at higher densities when demand has ripened. My impression is that this does occur. But even if sprawl is dysfunctional it would seem that the effects of redirecting a fraction of urban growth to new towns would be correspondingly small.

A frequent argument for new towns is that sprawl is expensive because of additional utility and street costs. Although the proposition is plausible, studies show these costs to be quite insensitive to alternative forms of development. Even if these costs did vary, they are so small that their marginal changes with urban form would not justify much of anything. For instance, the 1966 per capita expenditures of local governments were $31 for utilities (including debt maintenance and transit) and $22 for streets.

Some economic arguments

It is often suggested that new towns will stimulate the economy, presumably by their contribution to demand. Such an argument is often advanced by the same people who promise that new towns will be cheaper to develop and to run than the corresponding extension of existing urban areas. Such inconsistency aside, if new towns are to be used to stimulate the economy during recessions, their rate of development must conversely be slowed when the economy is working at full capacity. But new towns could not very well be used as a balance wheel for the cyclical control of the economy. Their lead times for decisions and action are far too long, and the success of various aspects of their development depends upon keeping to a time schedule. The heavy front-end investment reassured by new towns presents critical cash flow problems for the private developer, and a slowdown would be disastrous for him. From the public point of view, a slowdown would be extremely costly in terms of the opportunity costs of idle capital.

Most new town proposals stress that they will be as self-contained as possible, providing housing, jobs, schools, and shops for their residents, even if the proposals are for new towns on the edge of existing cities or in central city redevelopment projects. The purpose of this closure, often called "balance," is not altogether clear. It seems to stem in part from a desire to produce a sense of community that combats alienation—this will be discussed later—and in part from the intention of reducing commuting costs and congestion by reducing the distances involved. Two questions may be raised in this respect: (1) Does this make economic sense? and (2) Would it work?

As mentioned earlier, the cost-minimizing strategy makes sense only if productivity is fixed; in fact, income and most other measures of material welfare rise strongly with urban size. This is not the place to present a lengthy discussion of

2. R. O. Harvey and W. A. V. Clark, "The Nature and Economics of Urban Sprawl," *Land Economics* (February, 1965). See also, J. Lessinger, "The Case for Scatteration," *Journal of the American Institute of Planners* (August, 1962).

the reasons for this rise. They have to do with adaptability and innovative power and, in general, with the advantages of high *connectivity* for actual and potential interaction within a large system. In these terms, seeking closure at a small scale may economize on certain inputs (such as those of commuting) but result in lower per capita production (and lower disposable income after accounting for commuting costs) as well as the risks of instability and low adaptability which affect small cities. In small cities, a declining firm can be a local disaster, new firms are less likely to develop because of the sparseness of *linkages,* a dismissed worker has fewer chances for reemployment, a boy has fewer career opportunities, a woman fewer choices for shopping, and so on. In short, trying to save on transport costs may be penny wise and pound foolish.

But could such self-contained new towns be achieved? It seems to be quite hard. Several much admired European new towns, such as Tapiola, have about as many jobs as they have workers; but, in fact, residents work outside and outsiders commute to work inside. The British experience demonstrates how difficult it is to ensure labor market closure. British authorities have had extraordinary power since, in the face of a crushing housing shortage, they made the award of housing in new towns conditional on local employment and vice versa. The British new towns still show about the same number of jobs as workers but, after some years, 7.3 workers enter and leave the town in their daily trip to work for every 10 who live and work in the same new town.

People seem generally unwilling to constrain themselves to a localized and therefore small range of choices; and when feasible, they avail themselves of outside opportunities. It is extremely doubtful that new towns that are near metropolitan or other urban areas could maintain self-contained labor markets, with their residents making only occasional trips to the larger cities for specific services and facilities. Yet, if the new towns are not independent or self-contained, the space that intervenes between them and other opportunities can only lengthen travel and make it more costly. Thus a new town pattern of development might have an effect opposite from that intended, lengthening travel—except for those new towns in remote areas which are free from temptation. Yet virtually all our national territory, with the exception of some of our great deserts, is within commuting range of some existing urban center.

Health, Justice, Opportunity

One of the most persistently advanced purposes of the new towns might be classified under mental health. According to this view, big cities impose role-segmented contacts on people and keep them from knowing each other as whole persons. Due to the scale and impersonality of the city, people cannot understand the forces that affect their destinies and consequently experience alienation and *anomie.* New towns, by contrast, will be smaller and simpler; they will provide a single locus for home, school, job, shops, recreation, and civic activities; and thus they will afford deep and enduring relationships as well as a comprehensible environment in which the individual may participate and which he may, to a degree, control.

Millions of words by thousands of writers dispute this dismal picture of life in the big city and the correlative idealization of the small town. Jane Jacobs' picture of ethnic life in the big city makes even the most glowing description of new towns reminiscent of the atmosphere among strangers in an English train compartment. Studies by Gans, Young and Willmott, Fried, White, and others differ considerably from the traditional equation of the big city with alienation. On the other side, a far less flattering picture of life in the small city is drawn by Sinclair Lewis, Thomas Wolfe, John O'Hara, Warner, Kornhauser, the Lynds, and others. In sum, the traditional dichotomy between the alienating metropolis and the cohesive small city is a gross oversimplification, and it would appear that people can lead alienated or full lives in either place.

New towns present a particular difficulty to those who stress the importance of participation in their planning. The great problem with such participation is that several years of planning and development must take place before a new town has any residents. Except in rare cases where a specific group of families is to be transplanted to a new town, there appears to be no feasible mode of participation that would amount to more than a consumer survey. In this respect, new towns are rather like space ships. There must be a detailed plan for the vehicle and its course before the launching; and once under way, travelers can make only small choices of their own. This accounts for some of the tensions that commonly occur between residents and developers in some of the new towns now under way. The developers struggle to keep control of the nature and timing of the development according to their physical and financial plans, while the residents struggle to achieve the measure of local autonomy which is normal for a city or town.

Some writers associate physical and mental health directly with physical density of population rather than with life style. This argument is based on concepts of territoriality and personal space and derives from studies of the unfortunate effects of high density on rats, fish, lemmings, and large ungulates. But there has been no finding of comparable effects in the case of human beings. Further, this concern about the noxious effects of high densities is inconsistent with the concern about low densities created by sprawl.

It is sometimes suggested that new towns will be healthier in other ways. Walking or bicycling to work is salutary, the more so since there would be less automobile exhaust in the air. (One enthusiastic author includes the reduction of cancer among his new towns objectives.) Further, the small scale of new towns and their relative isolation would ease the dispersion of pollution and wastes. However, a new town policy would affect pollution levels for the vast majority only by the marginal amount accounted for by the population diverted from metropolitan areas, where any solution would continue to require some form of control over pollution sources. It is far simpler to take pollution from the people than to take the people away from pollution.

"Social balance" is a traditional objective of new town theorists, who argue that new towns should contain substantial social, economic, and ethnic diversity.

In many cases it is proposed that such integration take place within districts of the town as well as in the town as a whole. The prospects for such a policy are not encouraging. Indeed, many early new towns made quite purposeful exclusions on economic and ethnic grounds. And some recent studies suggest that many people are attracted to new towns in part precisely by promises of "planned growth" and high levels of amenity which they interpret as code words for social exclusion. At the extreme, some of the "new communities" in major cities are advertising guards, fences, gate check points, and other security measures. Recent studies of the British new towns, which were supposed to mix social classes, indicate that wealthier classes have tended to leave the towns and that residential areas are now differentiating by class.

There is also an economic barrier to such social balance. At present we cannot produce new housing for people below middle class income levels without heavy subsidies. In existing cities, the less affluent live in housing made cheap by age and the filtering process of the market. If new towns lack a stock of older housing, "social balance" would require enormous subsidies. They are not likely to be forthcoming because the urban majority will see no reason why new towns, as against old cities, should get them.

One argument for new ones which is now in great favor is that they will increase the range of choice of living environments. It is far from clear, however, in what ways new towns would differ from existing cities of equivalent size. Architectural and other physical features seem to be the principal probable differences, but there are also suggestions for such diverse sorts of new towns as a black town (Soul City, proposed by Floyd McKissick), a technological utopia (the Minnesota Experimental City), hippie communes, maximum security developments, and resort towns. Although those who want to live in such special settlements should be able to do so, the provision of such exotic residential opportunities for various minorities does not appear to constitute an adequate basis for a large scale national new towns program. It makes no economic sense, and it is a political absurdity.

Considerations of land use are often adduced in behalf of new towns. One of these is the difficulty of assembling large tracts of land on the edge of metropolitan areas because of their fractioned ownership and the game-like complexities of speculation. Large tracts may permit economies of scale in construction and allow certain interesting design features. Hence, urbanization should be easier where large pieces of land can be put together, presumably at some distance from existing settlements. But if there are such great advantages to large development tracts, much could be done to make land available at the margin of existing cities through institutional instruments such as land banks, property and capital gains taxes, and public intervention through policy powers and eminent domain. Choosing distant locations for the sake of land assembly, is a rather roundabout way of getting the job done. True, it isn't easy to assemble large tracts. But it isn't easy to build new towns, either.

The companion argument is based on land prices. Suburban land prices have risen sharply for many years, and it is suggested that development on cheap, distant land would both provide land at less cost to new town residents and discourage speculators at the edges of existing cities. The lower price for new town residents would certainly facilitate the development of new towns. But would it justify? The price of urban land is based primarily on the value of its location by reason of its accessibility. Cheap land will probably be inconvenient land, and might prove to be very expensive land by the time you get through providing transportation, utilities, etc.

Finding alternative environments

Perhaps the most deep-seated reason for wanting new towns lies in images of their physical form. The new towns literature usually offers photographs of European new towns where the sun always shines. Nevertheless, the specifics of the alternative environments provided by new towns are elusive. There is no dominant school of thought: some plans feature cluster housing and grade separation of different types of traffic; others are based on mixing various types of buildings and land uses which are usually separated; still others emphasize outdoor facilities; and a few plans envision towns of medieval densities, or domes covering the entire town for climate control

Yet the technological alternatives foreseen for new towns are generally minor or undeveloped. What is persuasive is the notion that new towns would be more beautiful and sensually satisfying than most of our cities and suburbs. No one can avoid being struck by the aesthetic poverty of most of our urban environments. Other places and other times, with only a fraction of our resources, have produced districts and whole cities whose extraordinary beauty and efficiency contribute greatly to the pleasure of their inhabitants.

Two causes for the ugliness of urban America suggest themselves. The first is that we lack feasible models of superior physical environments. Most of the physical design ideas proposed for new towns *could* apply to residential and commercial land uses and *could* be incorporated into the extension and rebuilding of existing urban areas. Here and there, this is actually occurring. But there is little doubt that new towns might have a powerful demonstration effect and assist greatly in the diffusion of design innovation.

The second reason for environmental drabness is that urban beauty is a public good and, as such, is difficult to produce through a market economy. Production of beauty may conflict with other uses of the urban plant. Moreover, beauty is not only not measurable but also highly problematic: what is beautiful to some is ugly to others. To a large extent, new towns would substitute developers' control for the market, and permit expert opinion to determine what is beautiful and how much to pay for it. In this respect, alas, they would not be likely to help existing cities frame institutional mechanisms to produce urban beauty. Our cities are not governed by appointed experts but by elected politicians and the forces of the market.

One of the most traditional arguments for new towns is that, being small, they would give residents ready access to open land. By contrast, a resident of a large metropolitan area may have a long ride to get out of the urbanized area if he has a car, and he may find it hard to do that if he is poor and without a car. Yet this distance from open land can also be psychological rather than geographical. A small square within the city can be as powerful an antidote to claustrophobia as farmland on the city's edge. Although the restoring powers of contact with nature are an important motif in our culture, a question must be raised of the meaning and functions of different types of open land. An urban park, a regional park, agricultural fields, and untrammeled nature may all be colored green on a land-use map, but they are quite different from one another as potential places for recreation and contact with nature. One would have to attach an extraordinary importance to immediate access to *agricultural* land to advocate a new towns policy on this basis, which seems to point instead toward expanding urban parks and facilitating access to them.

Conclusion

On the whole, a national policy of settling millions of people in new towns is not likely to succeed and would not significantly advance the national welfare if it could be done. The principal flaw in new town proposals is their underestimation of the integration of modern society, which is expressed in the complex reticulation of functional areas and the counterpoint of centers and subcenters which constitute a metropolis. This complexity allows specialization and complementarity; its fluidity makes it capable of producing innovations and accepting innovations and accepting change; and its ambiguities permit it to encompass the strains and inconsistencies which inevitably accompany change. We may be vexed at our slow response to problems like pollution, segregation, and ugliness; but new towns, with their stress on diverse "balances," seem to fall into a deterministic fallacy which, under the guise of increasing choice, would actually reduce it in nearly-closed subsystems of too small a scale. It is curious that an idea rooted in humanism should assume such materialistic and deterministic dimensions, and end up slighting the importance of freedom, communication, and interaction.

One notable kind of myopia in new town proposals is to regard the system of existing metropolises as one that grows only by proportional expansion while ignoring the continuous processes which create urban novae. Washington, Dallas, Los Angeles, Chicago, and others have risen in the last century to join the constellation of large urban areas, absorbing in their growth larger shares of our population than those proposed for new towns and cities. This crucial aspect of national urbanization differs from the new towns proposals in that *the growth occurred because it wanted to be there and not because it wanted to get away from something.*

A new towns policy that aims at housing a substantial portion of the population makes little sense. But there is much to be said for a new towns policy that would create new towns to test or exhibit innovations which might be adaptable by existing cities. Such experiments in new towns should, of course, be carefully designed to fulfill certain requirements. The first is that the findings be transferable to other areas. The second is that the experiment must be a reliable indicator of the probable success or failure of further applications of the innovation. The third is that the findings be available fairly promptly. The value of the expected findings must be discounted with respect to the time of their availability. In addition, there must be provision for objective reportage and evaluation, and only those experiments should be undertaken where there is the political will and means to learn from the findings. Most of the value of today's experiments is vitiated by the hyperbole and puffery of most new town advocacy, which effectively conceals what we might learn from our experience thus far.

There is much to be done to improve our cities, and perhaps some experiments with new towns would help. I say only that, even if new towns turned out to be wonderful places, they would still be almost powerless to affect our present urban problems; and I fear that, as sirens of utopia, they might distract us from our proper work.

WILLIAM H. WHYTE

THE NEW TOWNS

The next step, many people believe, should be the building of whole new towns. Better big subdivisions are not enough, they say; what we should do is carry the cluster concept to the ultimate; group not only homes, but industrial plants, hospitals, cultural centers, and create entirely new communities. These would not only be excellent places in their own right; together, they would be the last best chance of the metropolis.

It is a hope that at last seems nearer the threshold of reality. Developers have been moving in this direction and across the country a dozen large-scale communities have been started, each of which is meant to have an eventual population of 75,000 or more. In addition, there are some two hundred "planned communities" being built which, if smaller, claim the same basic approach. Big corporations have been getting into the business. Gulf Oil financed the start of Reston, outside of Washington, and has now taken over the whole operation; the Connecticut General Life Insurance Company is financing Columbia, outside of Baltimore. General Electric has set up a special division to assist the builders of new towns and a Rand-type of think center for the planning of them.

Some of these new communities have been having their troubles. Almost all builders have been hurt lately by tight money, but those who have launched the large scale developments have been particularly vulnerable. They have to borrow huge sums of money to get such operations going, and if house sales falter, they can quickly find themselves hard put to meet the interest payments. For want of enough cash flow, a number of developers have had to stop at phase one of their communities and several have gone bankrupt.

But this is the way things often go in the industry and new town advocates remain optimistic. The credit bind, they point out, does not prove that the new town idea is faulty; what it proves is that better financing arrangements are in order, and that the federal government should lend more of a hand. The administration has declared strongly in favor of new towns but the support it has been enabled to give so far has been largely moral. Through mortgage insurance and loans for land assembly, the Department of Housing and Urban Development has been offering some incentive for communities and developers to work together on new town projects. The enabling legislation is full of bugs, however.

The administration is now proposing as an aid the "federally guaranteed cash-flow debenture." This would provide developers of new towns the wherewithal to pay the interest charges on their borrowed capital until sales were rolling sufficiently to generate some real cash for them. In return for such underwriting, the developers would have to include in their plans some housing for low- and and middle-income people. The administration is also proposing additional incentives for state and local government cooperation in new town projects. Congress has not been keen on subsidies for new towns—big city mayors don't want any at all—but as time goes on it will probably authorize more aid.

But this does not mean we will get a lot of new towns. Let me define terms. I am not taking up the pros and cons of better-planned suburban developments; and this essentially is what most of the new communities that appropriate the title of new town really are. What I want to explore is the validity of the ideal new town model, as planners see it. It is far more than a matter of degree. Philosophically as well as physically, the true new town is to be a *complete* community—so complete that it can exist independent of the old city, and, quite literally, help cut it down to size.

The specifications are remarkably similar to those laid down some half century ago in England by Ebenezer Howard. Like many generations of planners after him, Howard sought an antidote to the city. "There are in reality," he said, "not only, as is so constantly assumed, two alternatives—town life and country life—but a third alternative in which all the advantages of the most energetic and active town life, with all the beauty and delight of the country, may be secured in perfect combination."

He proposed a garden city in the countryside—a community of about a thousand acres set in a green belt of five thousand acres. The community would own the land and lease it to people who would build according to the plan. It would be a balanced community; in addition to residential development, there would be local industry, thriving agriculture, and in total there would be enough jobs for everyone in the town.

Howard saw this not only as good in itself but as a solution to the problems of the city. London, he thought, was monstrously big and unhealthy, and its land values inflated out of reason. If garden cities were built, they would prove so attractive that they would draw people from the city; this would depress the land values in London, thus making it possible to redevelop the city at a much lower density. The new towns, he prophesied, would "be the magnet which will produce the effect for which we are all striving—the spontaneous movement of the people from our crowded cities to the bosom of our kindly mother earth."

The language of this kindly utopian is not that of today's new town planners, but in their own more scientific way they are saying the same thing. They, too, are repelled by the city. New town proposals are generally prefaced with a sweeping indictment of the city as pretty much of a lost cause. We tried, the charge goes, but the city is a hopeless tangle. Medical analogies abound. The city is diseased, cancerous, and beyond palliatives. The future is not to be sought in it, but out beyond, where we can start afresh.

The possibility of working with a clean slate is what most excites planners and architects about new towns. Freed from the constraints of previous plans and buildings and people, the planners and architects can apply the whole range of new tools. With systems analysis, electronic data processing, game theory, and the like, it is hoped, a science of environmental design will be evolved and this will produce a far better kind of community than ever was possible before.

On the main specifications, however, there is already considerable agreement. First, the new town must be balanced. It must have people of all income groups and houses to match. Second, it must be self-contained; it will have its own industry and commerce and jobs enough for all who wish to work within the boundaries of the community. No one need commute to the city.

No one will need visit the city for culture either. The new town will be self-contained in this respect as well, with its own symphony orchestras, little theaters, junior colleges, and colleges, and the town center will have all the urbanity and services of the center city. Recreation will be built in, and close to every home will be green space, tennis courts, golf courses, hiking and riding trails.

To offer all this, a new town would really have to be a city, and lately proponents have been using the term "new city" in describing their communities. But these are not to be like cities as we have known them. There is not to be any dirty work in them. There are not to be any slums. There are not to be any ethnic concentrations, or concentrations of any kind. Housing densities will be quite low. There will be no crowded streets. Yet, it will be a city—"a whole city," one developer puts it, "with all the texture and fabric of the city." It will have everything the city has, in short, except its faults.

This is an impossible vision. Certainly there are going to be more and bigger new communities built and it is good there will be. Architecturally and otherwise, some of the ones that have been going up are excellent, and as I will take up in the next chapter, they are providing many important lessons in large-scale land assembly and development.

But this is not the same thing as building self-contained new cities, and it is the validity of this concept that I am questioning: the pure, uncompromised vision—the community we would get if all the necessary legislation were passed, all the funds needed were provided, and all of the key specifications were followed.

It would not work. The reason it would not work does not lie in the usual obstacles that are decried—fragmentation of local government, lack of trained design terms, and so on. The substance of this critique is that the trouble is in the idea itself.

As elements of the metropolis, new towns could not take care of more than a fraction of our future population growth, even under the best of circumstances; nor could they significantly change the structure of the metropolis. The English new towns have not; the Scandinavian new towns were never meant to.

As a community, the self-contained new town is a contradiction in terms. You cannot isolate the successful elements of the city and package them in tidy communities somewhere else. And if you could do it, would you be able to have only the good and none of the bad? The goal is so silly it seems profound.

I would further argue that the idea of getting people to stay put and work and live together in the same healthy place is somewhat retrogressive. Americans move too much to be thus beneficently contained. Their mobility does breed problems, but it is also a dynamic and in the oversight of this the self-contained community is irrelevant if not contradictory to the main sweep of American life.

American planners tend to overplan, even where the constraints of reality are great, and when they are given a clean slate to work with, the temptation to overplan can be irresistible. There are exceptions, but physically the most striking thing about plans for ideal new towns is their finality. Everything is in its place: There are no loose ends, no question marks, and it is this completeness of the vision, more than the particulars of it, that stirs recalcitrance. It is one thing to be beckoned down the road to a distant utopia, quite another to be shown utopia itself in metes and bounds and all of it at once.

This, the plans seem to say, is the way it jolly well is going to be. There is to be no zigging and zagging to adapt the plans to people. It is the people who are to do the adapting and if there is anything they cannot adapt to, it will be just too bad because there is no provision for changing the plans as time goes on. These designs are so ordered in their intricacy that if you changed just one element, the whole thing would be rendered inoperable.

As planners of more pragmatic learnings have noted, this fixation on the "end state" plan runs directly counter to the profession's favorite axioms about interaction, feedback, and planning as an ongoing process. "The planning is neat, rational, logical, and fixed," says one critic, Marshall Kaplan. "The range of alternatives given is quite limited. . . . That the community will change, will develop after 1980 is acknowledged by the planners but often denied by the plan. Every area is planned, with little flexibility provided in the design for unforeseen want. Obsolescence—either planned or unplanned—is not a considered input."

There is really only one plan. The kind of geometrics favored may differ, but whether linear or concentric or molecular, the plans end up looking so alike it is a wonder such large staffs are deemed necessary to draft them. Several graduate students steeped in current planning dogma could work up almost identical plans in a few weeks—they do it regularly as class projects, and how they do it is pretty close to the way the most elaborate plans are drafted. The plans come into being almost full-blown. They start with a visual concept. The approach is graphic, and for all the to-do about sociological and economic research, this is supporting documentation. The design comes first.

The designs all look the same because they spring from the same design philosophy. It is the design philosophy embedded in the standard redevelopment project, with its high-rise slabs and aseptic open space. Just at a time when it is finally being conceded that the design doesn't fit people too well ("I certainly don't agree with Jane Jacobs, but . . ."), the whole thing is about to be reincarnated in suburbia, only called something else and stretched even further.

The center of the new city is a vast expanse of mall surrounded by office and apartment towers and beyond these the various neighborhoods, or "villages," stretch off in the distance, each encircled by its own spaces. The sweep is awesome. The planners will have a great deal to say about human scale, and to make up for its absence in the plan, they supply it in the brochures with ground-level sketches of what life will be like. The sketches are now standard: people sitting at outdoor cafés, mothers with baby carriages looking at Paris-style kiosks or waiting for the monorail.*

* Planning brochures and promotional literature for new towns have become so standardized in their themes and illustrations that much effort could be spared if one all-purpose brochure were worked up. It would include the following: (a) aerial picture of farmland taken in 1945; (b) aerial picture of same area ten years later, covered with subdivisions; (c) photo of massed rooftops and TV aerials; (d) photo of neon signs, gas stations, and pizza stands on commercial highway; (e) photo of cars in traffic jam; (f) sign at entrance to state park saying "filled"; (g) bull-

But it is the same old redevelopment project, magnified. There is the same compartmentation of activities, the same insistence on order and symmetry, the same distaste for the street and its function, the same lack of interest in the surroundings.

There are no surroundings. In birds-eye renderings of urban redevelopment projects, the grubby details of neighboring streets and buildings are customarily airbrushed away. People who sketch new towns have no such impedimenta to contend with, but even so, they give little indication of what, if anything, might lie beyond the project. They don't seem particularly interested. The background is shown as a boundless tract of undifferentiated space. It is almost as if the planners had come upon a habitable planet unmarred by previous habitation. You see no palimpsests of previous towns, factories, trailer villages, or railroad tracks. Even the greenery is indeterminate; you cannot tell whether it is farmland, forest, upland or lowland, or some algaelike growth.

The treatment of space within the boundaries is similarly grandiloquent. New towns do not squander space the way conventional large-lot subdivisions do, but this is not saying very much. New towns have especial reason to waste no space at all; the whole rationale of the accompanying wedges and green belts rests on this point; if planners are to justify setting aside such vast acreages the better to contain development, the development should be very contained indeed.

But it is not. The densest part, the core, seems extraordinarily expansive. The essence of a downtown is concentration and mixture, but the malls that are sketched in the plans are quite vast, even for a big city. Beyond the core, the densities decrease further, with the houses on the periphery set in half-acre and acre lots. This, too, begs the question of the green belts beyond. For whom are they

---

dozer hacking at hillside. Next come the good things: (a) photo of new town center at Stevenage or Vallingby or Tapiola; (b) the Tivoli gardens in Copenhagen; (c) impressionistic drawing of U.S. new town center, with a group of children holding balloons; (d) picture of intelligent-looking people around a table looking at a planner pointing to a map; (e) flow chart of proper planning steps. Either at the front or at the back there will be one or two mood pictures. A special favorite is a photo of two children walking hand in hand through a woods.

functional? The people who live next to the green belts have already been provided with the most open space of their own. The majority of the people are put in the middle, in high-rise towers and garden apartments. These are the people who need the open space the most and yet they are the farthest away from it—in some plans, up to two miles away.

True, the people up high can always look out their windows at the green belt, and the distances are not so great that they couldn't walk there if they are of a mind to. However, if the pedestrian habits of present suburbanites are any index, even relatively short distances are a deterrent, and as these are increased, the use of open space falls off drastically.

In this best of both worlds there is to be bustle without noise, concentration without confusion, people without traffic, excitement without danger. What the planners mean to do, in short, is to isolate each of the good qualities of the city from its context and reconstitute it in suburbia without its companion disadvantages. In a word, urbanity without cities.

The good elements of the city and the bad elements, alas, are often different aspects of the same function. We should try to make the most of the good and the least of the bad, but separating them out is extraordinarily difficult. Where does the bad leave off and the good begin? One of the charms of the city, most people agree, is the cosmopolitanism of its small shops—the Irish bar, the German *Konditorei*, the Italian grocery which makes its own line of pasta, the street festivals on the saints' days. But this kind of cosmopolitanism goes hand in hand with ethnic concentrations and it is certainly not the kind of thing new town planners wish to perpetuate.

Conversely, among the obvious bad things about cities are the old, dilapidated loft buildings and the once-grand neighborhoods gone to seed. But the loft buildings are a haven for marginal enterprises and an incubator of new ones because they are dilapidated and inexpensive to rent. Similarly, slightly seedy neighborhoods are the makings of new bohemias, and eventually, as the advance guard moves on to another seedy neighborhood, high-rent areas.

It would be wonderful indeed if one could isolate the desirable qualities and export them without their context. Architects and planners have a gallery of urbane places they would like to borrow from: the hill towns of Italy and Provence, for example, are great favorites for exemplifying compact development; Venice, for the pedestrian's city. In citing the desiderata, however, the tendency is to slough over the not-so-good elements that make the good elements possible, and this is even more pronounced when planners consider what is worth copying from American cities.

Let us take the matter of urbanity. Almost all new town prospectuses make a big point of it. No typical suburban shopping center for them. Their centers are going to be highly urbane, with a full range of cultural activities, specialty shops, second-hand bookstores, craft shops, off-beat restaurants, sidewalk cafés, and a host of touches evoking the flavor of Greenwich Village and Georgetown, for which latter place a considerable number of new developments have been named.

But it never seems to work out that way. What middle-class suburbia gets are shopping centers for middle-class suburbia. The institutions that flourish here are those which do an excellent job of catering to the middle range—such as Sears Roebuck and Howard Johnson—and where there is a branch of a large downtown department store, the top and the bottom of the line are left out. The supermarket provides the same kind of choice; acres of goods lie before you but they are the same goods, and they will be the same in the other big supermarket. You can find every known brand of corn flakes, or tomato catsup, or processed cheese, but if it is something slightly special you want, like a good head of lettuce, you will roam the aisles in vain. Only small stores have this kind of variety.

Restaurants seem to be an especially vexing problem for developers. In most of the new postwar communities, the restaurants are rather bland, and residents will frequently complain quite strenuously about them. Developers never planned it that way; many of them have made special efforts to bring in a good specialty restaurant or at least a first rate operation. In one case, the developer offered generous lease terms in an unsuccessful effort to get an Italian family to set up a Greenwich Village-type restaurant in his new town center.

But the environment is not right. In the first place, the kind of restaurateur that is sought does not have the capital to wait out the lean years while the population builds up sufficiently to provide a reasonable market. Only chain operations usually have the capital for that. Secondly, well-capitalized or not, the operation must inevitably become an all-purpose one. It will be a service element—the place, for example, where the local groups will hold their meetings. The lunchtime clientele will be the people who work in the center and they are the blue-plate-special or club-sandwich crowd and not the two-martini people who provide the midday support for a city's French and Italian restaurants. The weekend business will be mainly prospective homebuyers with children in tow, and the restaurateur will have to put in a supply of high chairs. And whom does he get at nights? A few regulars in the bar, a smattering of residents, and a few visitors.

To survive, the operation will have to adapt to the median. From community to community you will find that even the best of the operations generally feature the all-American menu—shrimp cocktail, baked potato with sour cream and chives, steak, salad with roquefort dressing, and selections from the dessert wagon. As staples go, these can be pretty good fare; nevertheless, the residents will complain that there is no decent place for eating out, and even if the food were really good, they still might complain.

The image has been fixed. At nighttime the restaurateur can put checkered cloths over the formica tables, dim the lights, put out candles in fishnet containers and add a pianist. But it just won't wash. To the residents, it is still a community-service center and in their mind irrevocably coupled with daytime shopping, children, and luncheon meetings of women's groups.

In another respect, the new towns lack self-sufficiency. There's to be no sin in them. Despite the claim that the new towns are to have all of the attractions of the city, there are no provisions for night clubs, bookie joints, or any but the mildest of vices. The new towns are to cater to the widest possible range of tastes, but there is not to be any bad taste. There will be no raffishness, no garish "strip," no honky-tonks. Some suggestions have been made about filling the void with a "fun palace," an idea bruited in England for a large factorylike structure in which, as in a free play period, people could improvise all sorts of activities. But the fun would be wholesome, and as with a similar suggestion for a permanent carnival for the town centers, one senses a monitoring and somewhat condescending presence.

The bars are to be genteel, too: In the new towns of England some of the pubs are so prim they look as though they should be called alcohol dispensaries, and the ones over here are not real bars but the cocktail lounges of adjoining restaurants, the kind with Muzak. All this is understandable enough, and new towns are not to be scorned for such wholesomeness: It's one of the reasons they would be nice places to live in. But would you want to visit them?

The affinity of such communities for the middle range is a universal phenomenon. When they planned the new town of Vallingby, the Swedish planners, who are quite city-minded, were especially anxious to have a highly urbane town center, and they went to considerable lengths to provide attractive plazas, fountains, and well-designed street furniture. But the urbane shops did not take root. To the disappointment of the planners, the shops that flourished were good average, but not much more.

The same thing is true of the English new towns. The planners have lavished fine statuary on the centers, elaborate water fountains, and so forth. Enterprises that have leased the shops, however, are of a more mundane style, some rather plebeian, and the effect of the whole is somewhat tacky. (The food in the restaurants is beyond description. It is so awful that even new town planners blanch; they much prefer to eat in old towns nearby, and will be sure to take a visitor there.)

There is not very much planners could do to change things. These centers lack the essential quality of the city—its location. Urbanity is not something that can be lacquered on; it is the quality produced by the great concentration of diverse functions and a huge market to support the diversity. The center needs a large hinterland to draw upon, but it cannot be in the hinterland; it must be in the center. This is the fundamental contradiction in the new town concept of self-containment.

The kind of self-containment that most excites new town proponents is the idea of everybody's working and living in the same place. It is not to be just another suburb. In the ideal new town the planners mean to provide as many jobs as there will be workers, and the jobs will cover the whole range of skills and occupations.

Some kinds of jobs, of course, won't be included. Plans do not call for dirty work and the kind of smoky, noisy plants that would pollute the environment. But the planners don't think there will be any imbalance, for they are sanguine that the industrial trends are going in their direction. What with automation, atomic power, computerization, they hold, industry is transforming itself into the kind of clean, white-collar, smokeless facilities for which new towns would be the ideal setting. Because of this affinity, they further argue, the new town will be a powerful vehicle for the decentralization of employment. The present pattern of industrial clusters close to the city will be loosened up, the components dispersed all over the region, and each encapsulated with its own resident work force.

The planners are misreading the trends. Suburbia is going to get more plants, just as it's going to get more people, but the two are not to be so neatly packaged together. As far as employment is concerned, I hope to demonstrate, the self-contained community is impossible to achieve and it is a very good thing that it is impossible to achieve.

To have any claim to self-containment, the new towns must provide something for export. Taking in each others laundry can keep a lot of people busy, and almost any new community provides a considerable number of local jobs—store clerks, deliverymen, service-station attendants, doctors, lawyers, bankers. But there is a limit to the number of service jobs a community can provide, and vital as these are, they give the community no dynamic. The new town must have primary industry. It cannot have just one kind, either, for it would be simply a new version of the company town.

Significantly, the most notable communities built from scratch have been built around the industry of government—Washington, D.C., Canberra, Brasilia, Chandigarh, and Islambad. These capitals may have many admirable features but they are essentially one-function towns and they are anything but models of the complete community.

New town planners are very keen on having a "balanced" population, with a pretty complete spectrum of income, education, and skills. This is all very fine, but to match all these people with jobs would require that the planners create not only a miniature city but a miniature metropolis.

No new town comes close to these specifications. The English new towns, some of which are factory-worker communities, do provide a good number of jobs, but the range is not a broad one, and a sizable number of people journey into the towns or out of them to earn their living.

In practice, it is virtually impossible to tie jobs to homes. Even when a lot of jobs are provided in a community, the people who fill them will not necessarily be the people who live there. As a matter of fact, the chances are strong that a great many won't be. In a number of places where a large supply of close-to-home jobs has been provided, there has been a large amount of commutation and reverse commutation. Vallingby is a case in point. There are 9000 jobs there, but most of the people who work at them do not live in Vallingby. They commute to them, some 7000 people, and as they do, the bulk of the wage earners who do live in Vallingby—25,000 of 27,000—commute outward, mostly to the center of Stockholm. In varying degrees, this mixed commutation pattern is true of most new towns in any modern industrial society and it is hard to see how it could be otherwise.

The oneness concept of work and residence is at odds with our dominant growth trends. It is true enough that factories are moving outward and that certain expanding industries find outlying locations excellent for new facilities. To deduce from this that a massive decentralization of employment is taking place is quite wrong. As factories have been vacating their cramped, high-cost city locations, there has been a corresponding increase in managerial, professional, and service jobs in the center city. More, not less than before, the city is headquarters. The people who service it are basic to any balanced population; any new town that is to have its share of them is going to have a lot of people who must commute, just like any other suburb.

And what, it might be asked, is so therapeutic about working close to home? There is much to say for it, and it is a beguiling thought that one could take a five-minute walk along a footpath, or a short ride on a minibus, to a campuslike office in the woods, and even perhaps return home for lunch, like French businessmen used to do. But all this propinquity is not without price. The fact is that a lot of people rather like the separation of work and home. They enjoy having as neighbors people who are not the same people they have been working with all day; they even enjoy the geographic buffer between the work place and their wives, and many of the wives do too. The commute, furthermore, is not always the ordeal it is often pictured; for many people it is the only time they ever get to do any reading, and the ride back can serve as a decompression period.

But let us suppose, for the sake of argument, that in one case the new town planners achieve their dream. They do reproduce the metropolis in miniature; they attract a broad range of people—low income, high income, blue collar, white collar—and on a one-to-one ratio, for every kind of person they provide jobs to match.

Self-containment still wouldn't work. There would be no real choice. In the aggregate there might be a lot of jobs, but for any one person there would be only a few that were suitable, and the more educated and more skilled the person, the fewer. If you were, say, a certain kind of electrical engineer, there might likely be only one job slot in the whole area for you—the one you have. You are, in effect, in a company town. If you came to dislike the job, you would have no practical alternative within the community. If you did like it, you would be in a poor bargaining position with your employer. In the tacit negotiations for raises or advancement, or, simply, having your opinions prevail, your ability to get as good or better a job, and the employer's awareness of this, is crucial. Pleasant surroundings cannot compensate for a lack of choice.

Self-containment would hurt employers as well. When residence in a certain place is packaged with a job, the employer may have some good talking points about the good life and the non-job benefits. But for all this, he is under severe disadvantage in competing for people with specialized skills. Just as the worker needs access to a wide range of jobs, the employer needs access to a wide range of people, and the further he is out on the periphery, the tougher his position. In a more central location he can compete much more effectively for prospective employees, for he does not have to persuade them to pick up stakes and move to the new town as part of the deal.

Theoretically, the accessibility problem could be solved if the new towns were linked directly with each other with a circumferential rapid transit system. Then a man might live in New Town A and journey around the circle to work in New Town B, or C, or D. Ebenezer Howard suggested something like this in his original prospectus. He proposed a circular arrangement of municipal railways that would link the new towns in a system. Much the same idea has been advanced for tying together future new towns, with the inevitable monorail sketched as a possible means. Another suggestion is creation of an additional set of belt freeways around the outer ring.

This circumlocution would be very bad transportation planning. To be economic, mass-transportation routes must tap great concentrations of high-density traffic. We are having enough trouble in getting good mass-transit systems even when they go with the region's traffic flow, which is essentially radial, with the lines converging toward the center. The capital cost of another mass-transit system cutting across the grain would be prodigious.

Highways, of course, can go where mass transit cannot. The new beltways have created a great deal of suburb-to-suburb traffic and in some areas more commercial development is being built to tap these circumferential routes than the old city to suburb axes. But only so many circles can be built. Additional freeways across suburbia would consume inordinate amounts of expensive land, and would further aggrandize the role of the car, a prospect that should be anathema to planners. In the long run, such freeway systems would be economically unfeasible for the same reasons that a similar rapid-transit system would be; high-cost facilities to serve low-density traffic.

Theoretically, the only way you could generate enough traffic to justify these systems would be to force new town people *not* to work in their own new town or in the city but in another town along the ring. But this would be a refutation of the new town ideal, and the worst of both possible worlds—suburbias without a city, a vision truly peripheral.

As the major answer to the growth problems of the metropolis, the new town concept is not practical. For the New York metropolitan area the Regional Plan Association has figured that to take care of the expected population growth over the next two decades via the new town route, one hundred new towns of 100,000 each would have to be built. This would take some doing and even if it were possible, the Association does not think it would be desirable. The result would be an extremely inefficient pattern, for the dispersal would rule out any effective mass-transportation system.

The Regional Plan Association believes that the heart of the growth problem is employment. The RPA is trying to encourage a concentration of industry and business in a relatively small number of centers; some would be new, some would be built on existing centers. There would be residential development around these centers, to be sure, but job and residence would not be tied together.

Access to jobs, not propinquity, is what is important. "For the same reason that people prefer to live and work in large metropolitan areas," says Stanley Tankel, RPA's planning director, "they are willing to trade a walk to work in a self-contained new town with its limited choice of jobs for a somewhat longer trip to work to a center where job choices abound. A region with deep and well-greased channels of transportation provides security of choice whether you are seeking work or workers."

In the new town scheme of things, people not only won't have to leave the town to go to work; they won't have to leave ever. The new towns are to provide total environments so encompassing, so beneficent that they will to a large extent eliminate the rootlessness and mobility of urban life.

The ultimate aim is the "life-cycle community" with a full range of accommodations, activities, and culture for every stage of life's journey. It is conceded that there would be some transients—the plans for the culture centers virtually require some staff bohemians on the premises—and undoubtedly there would be constant leakage as some people broke out of the cycle. For the bulk of the population, however, there would be no point in leaving. From cradle to grave they could progress through all phases—kindergarten, school, college, child rearing, retirement—moving within the community to the kind of housing units and neighborhoods appropriate to the particular stage of the cycle. (The planners do not pursue the logic of the progression to the conclusion, however. In no new town plan I have seen is there space allotted to a cemetery.)

The idea is a very old-fashioned one. From the time of utopian communities of the early 1800s there have been many attempts to encompass the good life within the physical boundaries of an ideal community. They have all foundered. Even in the more agrarian days of the early eighteenth century, such communities were at odds with the main currents of American life. Today they would be utterly inconsistent.

Planners are behind on their sociology. Several decades ago there was a tendency to look on mobility as a bad thing, and there was much concern over the *anomie* of rootless people and an exaggerated veneration of the psychic benefits of the structured society and the belongingness of small-town life. But this was nostalgia even then. Americans move; they always have, and though they have paid in many ways for this mobility, they move because of opportunity, and the people who move most are the managerial and professional people the new towns would like to have—such as planners, who are among the most mobile of professionals.

Characteristically, new middle-class suburbs have a relatively high rate of turnover, even the best of them. A case in point is Park Forest, south of Chicago. When developer Philip Klutznick built it shortly after the war, it was the most advanced new town in the country. In some respects it still is. Unlike most new towns, it was set up at the beginning as a self-governing political unit.

Developers are usually fearful of such an arrangement. They prefer to be benevolent on their own terms, with democracy expressed through unofficial civic organizations. They fear that if the residents had political control, they would raise all sorts of mischief over zoning and taxes. But a real government also means a real community. Park Foresters did give Klutznick some rough times, but their involvement in the community was thorough and deep and the community was much the better for it. People are more attached to a place they run than one they do not.

Compared to older communities, however, Park Forest has had a fairly high turnover. Residents tend to be touchy about this, as I found when I published a study on Park Forest. I had noted that the greatest number of transients were in the rental units and that as the proportion of single family homes increased more people would be staying on. But many people bristled just the same, especially those who were staying on. Like developers and new town planners, residents want to see the stabilities emphasized and they regard talk about turnover as a reflection on the quality of the community.

But the turnover is normal. It is not a defect of new communities that they harbor transients; it is one of their great functions. No matter how "balanced" the community, it is the college-educated, middle-income people who usually provide its leadership, whatever their numbers. When they leave a community, they are not necessarily rejecting it. Many leave because they have to. Their organization may be transferring them to another post or they may be moving because they are switching to another company. It is the game.

There are some people who do not have to leave but do so because the community has no housing suitable to the next rung up. As they sometimes put it, it's time they "graduated." The new town approach, by providing a broader selection of housing, would tend to cut down this kind of turnover. (This certainly was the case at Park Forest. When it was first built, the developer concentrated on rental units and houses in the $14,000–$18,000 range, and all the young people spoke warmly of the benefits of living in a "classless" community. But then time went on and incomes went up, and some people left for more expensive houses in nearby communities. The developer wisely began adding new units in higher price ranges and this allowed a considerable number of people to "trade up" within the community.)

A broad range of housing is certainly a worthy goal for new towns. Any new community which provides a range will be more adhesive than one that does not and probably a better place for people to live in. But not forever. The community is bound to have a lot of turnover and it would be a failure otherwise. The only way to have a very low turnover is to have a one-class static community. If the community is to be truly balanced, turnover is going to be a built-in feature.

Whether or not the new town ideal is impossible to achieve, as I have been arguing, the sheer effort to achieve it can have important consequences. Some of them will be good; a number of the communities that are going up under the new town banners will probably end up as excellent places to live in—even though they do not really measure up to the true new town ideal, or, rather, because of the fact that they do not.

But an equally important question is what is not going to be built. The new town movement is essentially decentralist. The physical specifications virtually dictate that the planners look away from the city to the periphery and beyond, for the large virgin sites that are called for are not to be found within the present metropolitan area.

If the new town movement could be stripped of its anticity utopianism, there would not have to be this decentralist effect. Many goals of the new town approach are excellent—the range of housing types; the mixture of industry, commerce, and homes; the weaving in of recreation and open space. They are quite applicable to the more built-up areas; indeed, as some have suggested, there is a case to be made that new towns should be in the city, or very close to it. A new town that would make a lot of sense, for example, is the one recently proposed by the State of New Jersey; it would like to create an authority to build an urban complex on the Hackensack Meadows, a boggy expanse five miles from mid-Manhattan.

Within the metropolitan areas, of course, there are tremendous problems to be surmounted. For one thing, there is apt to be a difficult tangle of governmental jurisdictions—in the case of the Hackensack Meadows proposal, some eighteen local governments would be involved. Good sites are hard to come by, they are usually irregular and they are expensive. The land would have to be much more efficiently used; the development more compact. But the communities would not necessarily be the worse for the discipline of these realities. And they would be where the need is.

But then, it can be argued, they would not be true new towns. The whole idea of new towns, advocates maintain, is not to try and rework a hopeless tangle but to get away from it and start fresh. That blank slate is crucial. Listening to some new town discussions, one gets the feeling that the end object is not a workable community so much as the untrammeled exercise of expertise in planning it. The approach must be experimental, new, uncompromised by the present. At one recent meeting, a new-town advocate was asked why there couldn't be new towns close to the city. He said: "If you try one of these ambitious and innovative projects in a situation where you are going to be forced by circumstances that are far beyond your control into all sorts of compromises, then I think you are likely to be forced to erode the vision with which you began." The city of today, then, will not do. It is a tangle of situations with circumstances.

But this fractured, messy, tangled place is where the main problems are, and to talk of seeking its redemption somewhere else is sheer escapism. Building new towns can greatly improve suburbia but as a means of saving the city the movement is somewhat off-center—rather like taking a mistress, Robert Herman has observed, to improve relations with your wife.

And is the tangle so hopeless? It is hopeless if the measuring stick is perfection; it is hopeless if we demand a solution. There is no solution to the city. It is full of circumstances; some of them are good, some of them are bad, and as soon as one bad one seems about licked, others will crop up. That is the way of cities, and of people.

EDWARD P. EICHLER

WHY NEW COMMUNITIES?

The modern New Town or New Community movement in America began in 1958 with the announcement of Eldorado Hills, a ten-thousand-acre private development north of Sacramento, California. Since then, almost every trade journal and popular magazine has painted a glowing picture of the promise of this new concept. Underlying this great interest, and, as a matter of fact, a cause of the New Towns movement itself, has been what I call the urban development critique. This critique has developed, partially, from the ambivalence Americans have always felt toward their cities and toward big cities in particular. At its inception, and throughout its great period of western settlement, this country was regarded by its citizens as the garden of the world. Even though the onset of industrialism and the growth of the cities transformed the garden of the world into a land of machine-produced plenty, mechanical agents of luxury and change have always remained somehow alien presences.[1]

Although the nation has been flooded with diatribes about

[1] See Leo Marx, *The Machine in the Garden* (New York and Oxford: Oxford University Press, 1964), for a penetrating discussion of the pastoral ideal in America, both in the general consciousness and American literature and how this ideal responded to the coming of the machine.

Shaping an Urban Future. B. J. Frieden and W. W. Nash, Jr., Editors. (Cambridge, Massachusetts: The M.I.T. Press, 1969) 95-113. Copyright ©1969 by the Massachusetts Institute of Technology. Reprinted by permission of the author, editors, and publisher.

urbanization since World War II, perhaps one can date the resurgence in contemporary American thought about the defects of urban life from the time of Ebenezer Howard. Certainly, his proposal for satellites to London remains the central thesis in the plans of both British and American New Towns devotees.

THE REGIONAL MESS AND THE URBAN DEVELOPMENT CRITIQUE

The contributors to the urban development critique recoil in horror and outrage at what they assume are the effects of urbanization run wild. Each has his crusade, and where one leaves off, another begins in a bewildering bombardment which seems to leave no region of America unsinged. In their descriptions, language often abounds in science fiction images of devastation and monstrous growths. Lewis Mumford attacks the city itself and says that by failing "to divide its [the metropolis'] social chromosomes and split up into new cells, each bearing some portion of the original inheritance, the city continues to grow inorganically, indeed cancerously, by a continuous breaking down of old tissues, and an overgrowth of formless tissue."[2] Then the California architect Richard Neutra takes over, turning attention from the cities to the blighted countryside. In the analysis to which he gives the dark title *Survival Through Design,* he asks:

Must we remain victims, strangled and suffocated by our own design which has surrounded us with man-devouring metropolises, drab small towns manifesting a lack of order devastating to the soul, blighted countrysides along railroad tracks and highways, studded with petty 'mere-utility' structures, shaded by telephone poles and scented by gasoline fumes?[3]

Peter Blake, the editor of the *Architectural Forum,* summarizes these two attitudes in one of the most direct and concrete formulations of the basic response to the contemporary situation by the proponents of the development critique. In his book *God's Own Junkyard* he says,

. . . we are about to turn this beautiful inheritance [the American landscape] into the biggest slum on the face of the earth. "The mess that is man-made America," as a British magazine has called it, is a disgrace

[2] Lewis Mumford, *The City in History* (New York: Harcourt, Brace and World, 1961), p. 543.
[3] Richard Neutra, *Survival Through Design* (New York and Oxford: Oxford University Press, 1954), pp. 5–6.

of such vast proportions that only a concerted national effort can hope to return physical America to the community of civilized nations.[4]

According to the critique, neither city nor suburb nor countryside escapes the brutal marks of urbanization. In the established large cities, decentralization of mid-town business areas has begun. "Business wilts in the traffic congestion, property values sink, tax revenue declines, slums multiply and the need for a larger urban renewal program intensifies."[5]

While losing its economic function and viability, the city also loses its social function.

Suburban sprawl negates and frustrates the purpose of cities, which is to let more people live and work close together and so utilize and enjoy the maximum efficiency of community facilities and community enterprises, with easy access and cheap distribution.[6]

One might ask, then, if the suburbs are shouldering the social and economic functions that the city can no longer handle. William Whyte, in *The Exploding Metropolis*, says "no." He believes that waste and economic inefficiency are high even in new developments.

Where the new developments are scattered at random in the outlying areas, the costs of providing services become excruciating. There is not only the cost of running sewers and water mains and storm drains out to Happy Acres but much more road, per family served, has to be paved and maintained. . . . Sprawl also means low volume utility operation for the amount of installation involved.[7]

Aesthetic damage occurs. One learns from a brochure describing the situation in California in 1962, "California, Going, Going . . ." issued by California Tomorrow, a nonprofit educational institution, that

The character and quality of such urban sprawl is readily recognized: neon-bright strip cities along main traveled roads; housing tracts in profusion; clogged roads and billboard alleys; a chaotic mixture of supermarkets, used car lots, and pizza parlors; the asphalt plain of parking spaces; instead of parks, gray-looking fields forlornly waiting

[4] Peter Blake, *God's Own Junkyard* (New York: Holt, Rinehart and Winston, 1964), p. 8.
[5] Senator Harrison Williams, U.S. Congress, Senate Committee on Banking and Currency, 87th Congress, 1st Session, *Hearings*, S858, Housing Legislation of 1961, p. 998.
[6] "Land," *House and Home*, Vol. XVIII, No. 2 (1960), p. 114.
[7] William Whyte, *The Exploding Metropolis* (Garden City, N.Y.: Doubleday, Anchor Books, 1958), p. 122.

to be subdivided. These are the qualities of most of our new urban areas—
of our *slurbs*—our sloppy, sleazy, slovenly, slipshod semi-cities.[8]

A new kind of emotional pressure is involved:

There is a certain psychic relief in open space that cannot be underestimated.
It gives us visual relief from the tangled, jarring, and often monotonous
sight of urban development, and a sense of orientation and
community identity.[9]

What of the developments themselves? What are they like? How do
their residents fare? The authors of the critique see no relief here either.
John Keats describes the life offered in his best-selling book on
conditions in the new suburbia, *The Crack in the Picture Window:*

. . . a housing development cannot be called a community, for that
word implies a balanced society of men, women and children wherein
work and pleasure are found and the needs of all the society's
members are several. Housing developments offer no employment and
as a general rule lack recreational areas, churches, schools or other
cohesive influences.[10]

E. A. Gutkind, discussing suburbia in his book, *The Expanding
Environment,* sums up all the apocalyptic horror of the urban
development critique in the following statement:

The last vestiges of a community have disappeared. They are hardly
anything else than an agglomeration of innumerable and isolated
details, of human atoms, and rows of boxes, called houses, interspersed
between the industries. It is a total victory of a laissez-faire insensibility and
recklessness over organic growth and even over organized development.[11]

HOW DID IT HAPPEN?

The urban development critique lists many factors that have contributed
to the present crisis of our cities. Prominent among them are rising
levels of income, population growth, and the increased mobility
provided by the automobile. The most fundamental factor, however,
has been speculation by developers and misguided, piecemeal federal
policies. The writings of those who espouse the urban critique say this

[8] Samuel E. Wood and Alfred E. Heller, *California, Going, Going . . . ,* (Sacramento:
California Tomorrow, 1962), p. 10.
[9] Williams, *Hearings,* p. 997.
[10] John Keats, *The Crack in the Picture Window* (Boston: Houghton Mifflin, 1957),
p. XVI.
[11] E. A. Gutkind, *The Expanding Environment* (London: Freedom Press, 1953),
quoted in *ibid.,* p. 176.

again and again, but, once more, the most concise formulation of the argument appears in Peter Blake's *God's Own Junkyard*:

> Suburbia got that way for two simple reasons: first, because the developers who built it are, fundamentally, no different from manufacturers of any other mass produced product: they standardize the product, package it, arrange for rapid distribution and easy financing and sell it off the shelf as fast as they can. And, second, because the Federal government, through FHA and other agencies set up to cope with the serious housing shortages that arose after World War II, has imposed a bureaucratic straight jacket on the design of most new houses, on the placement of houses on individual lots, on landscaping, on street planning, and on just about everything else that gives suburbia its "waste-land" appearance.[12]

In short, the disastrous sprawl of the past twenty years is the product, together, of the merchant builder and the government bureaucrat, each in his own way responding only to the immediate needs of the moment.

The past twenty years have been a period of pernicious individualism and destructive chaos in urban development. Against these forces, the critique opposes the rational mind and its ability to plan. To supporters of the critique, it is planning, executed from a sufficiently high level of comprehensiveness, that will build "Jerusalem in England's green and pleasant land."

This relentless and seemingly thoroughgoing critique was bound to influence men whose general interest in civic affairs was already high. For owners of large parcels of land, like Janss and Irvine (developers of Janss/Conejo and Irvine Ranch, respectively), for inheritors of wealth accumulated through real estate ventures, like Robert Simon (the developer of Reston), and for some who had earned their own fortunes in a field related to real estate, like James Rouse (the developer of Columbia), the chance to shape a new life style in suburbia was irresistible. At the same time, men such as these were products of a culture which grants esteem to those who make a profit. Thus, they wished not only to "create better communities" but desired to earn money doing it. The great aim of the community builders is to prove that the profit motive can be coupled with an interest in civic affairs to meet head on the deficiencies exposed by the critique of urban development.

[12] Blake, *God's Own Junkyard*, p. 17.

AMERICA'S NEW COMMUNITIES

The Community Development Project was one of the results of this critique. In addition, since the announcement of Eldorado Hills, a great many individuals, companies, and landholders stated their intentions to build New Towns. Therefore, during February and March 1964, under the auspices of the Community Development Project and assisted by Richard Raymond, Bay Area planning consultant, I spoke with over forty large landholders, land developers, and land seekers. Of these forty, nine later agreed to participate in the program for its entire life by engaging in periodic meetings and by permitting certain forms of investigation to be done. Initially, however, the interviews aimed neither at detailed review of company finances and structure nor at an examination of the site each had chosen but rather at general answers to the following questions:

1. Why were these companies thinking about undertaking a venture like community building (or why had they decided to do it)?
2. How large was their site and what section of it was under intensive planning?
3. Who was doing the planning, what were the planning goals, and who had set them?
4. How far did the company expect to go in actually carrying out and managing their development?
5. How did the owner see the relation between the metropolitan market and the location of his site?
6. How was the project being financed?
7. Under what sort of jurisdiction was the site being developed?
8. When would physical work start or what had already been done?
9. What other business activities were conducted by the company?

From the answers to these questions came a working definition of a community builder: an owner of a large, contiguous parcel of land (2,500 acres or more) who aims at applying the "best" known techniques of planning to develop industrial, commercial, residential, and public facilities, as well as amenities not normally found in new suburban developments. Scale, amenities, planning, control of all uses; these were the basic criteria.

It became clear to me as a result of these interviews that the community builder's project is, or will be, quite different from a New Town, if we use the term in the sense which was incorporated into law in Great Britain in 1947. There, it has meant the creation by the national government of a public corporation with the power of condemnation and with public funds not only to purchase land but to finance the town's infrastructure and even to build residences. The government can and usually does, subsidize the housing.

Even more important than the financial and legal powers given to the public corporations are the measures taken by the British government to ensure that a New Town will have industry and that the land surrounding the New Town will not be developed. In most cases, new industrial plants cannot be located without the permission of the government. By refusing this permission in metropolitan London and in other urban areas and by exerting other forms of subtle and not so subtle persuasion, the government has considerable power to direct industrial settlement to a New Town. It may also offer direct subsidies to industry in the form of low land prices, although American experience suggests that these low prices, in and of themselves, are at best marginal considerations in industrial location decisions.

By refusing to give permission to develop the intervening land between New Towns or between a New Town and a nearby metropolis, the British government can control the size of the town and prevent competing development at its fringe. No such governmental power exists in the United States, and there is serious doubt that our Constitution would permit it. Thus, a community builder must compete with owners of surrounding land, and only the inherent attributes of his location and/or his business skill give him any special advantage.

The result, then, is that while a British New Town is a separate physical entity where people are intended to, and to a great extent do, spend most of their daily lives in the community itself, an American New Community is merely a different way of organizing private development at the urban fringe of a metropolis. Neighborhood and regional shopping centers, industrial parks, detached housing, and garden apartments are the principal facilities in areas developed around American cities since World War II. They are also the principal facilities in a New Community, although in the latter case the land is held by a single owner who intends to provide such facilities or, at least, to have a major influence over their planning and character.

Compared to the suburban development of the past twenty years,

New Communities will offer a greater variety and probably a higher quality of recreational facilities, such as lakes, parks, and golf courses, and they will set aside more open space. Otherwise, there has not been and, in my judgment, will not be much about New Communities to differentiate them from suburbia as we know it.

Some New Town devotees believe a town of 200,000 or less, whose surrounding area is protected from development, is large enough to support a reasonable variety of life style and small enough to promote civic concern, which many believe to be impossible in the metropolis or the megalopolis. Although I do not agree with either contention, the point remains moot in the United States because we are not building any towns or communities so separated from an existing metropolis. If we were to adopt policies similar to those of Great Britain, we too could build New Towns, but I see little reason to believe that the massive expenditures and the legal changes required to do this would be warranted. As I turn now to the discussion of American New Communities and their relation to the problems they were created to solve, I hope that my reasons for these statements will become apparent.

RESEARCH FINDINGS

Some of the urban problems to which the character of suburban development presumably contributes and the responses of incipient community builders to these problems were examined in the Community Development Project.

The most persistent criticism of suburbia was its homogeneity. Suburbanites, it was claimed, are predominantly young middle- and upper-income, white familes with children. New Communities or New Towns were to change this situation. Yet, almost without exception, community builders told us that they would not offer any housing at prices less than $20,000 at least in the early stages of development. (Purchase at this price would necessitate an income of about $8,000 per year.) The reason they gave was the standard real estate argument that the introduction of any large number of low-priced houses, and thereby, low-income families, at the early stage of the project would seriously damage its whole image. Community builders added their belief that, given their location at the metropolitan fringe and their hope to sell "planning," the demand by lower-income families was automatically limited. In business terms, they were saying that their product was being geared essentially to a middle- and upper-middle-income market and that, by offering houses to lower-income families whose demand was limited, they would be seriously reducing the product's essential appeal.

In the light of the criticism about the one-class nature of suburbia, a condition that was thought would be fostered by community building, we commissioned two specific research projects. One was conducted by Dr. Wallace Smith of the School of Business Administration at the University of California, Berkeley, and the other by Carl Werthman, a sociologist at the same university. Smith was asked to analyze housing in the Los Angeles metropolitan area with special emphasis on the needs of families earning less than $8,000 per year. Specifically, we sought to ascertain whether Los Angeles contained a significant unfulfilled demand by families in this income range for houses selling for less than $20,000, and whether Janss-Conejo (a New Community at the fringe of metropolitan Los Angeles) had failed to tap this demand. Los Angeles was chosen because it was the location of so many New Communities, and Janss-Conejo, because it had already been offering houses for several years.

Smith confirmed the findings of several previous reports claiming that new housing is primarily built for families earning more than the median income, but he did not draw the standard conclusion from this information: that there is a great shortage of, or unmet demand for, housing for low- and moderate-income families. Rather, he presented the following argument: "It is often suggested that low income groups are not served by the home building industry while high income households have a wide choice among new dwellings. This is a misleading impression. Correctly defined, the situation is more nearly the opposite of this commonly held view."

Smith maintained that one cannot analyze the housing market merely by asking what percentage of the new housing serves families of a given income. The housing situation should be viewed as one in which people move through a given stock of units, made up, in any short time period, primarily of the existing supply of houses plus a small number of new additions. Thus, the situation has been as follows: As income has risen, most new housing has served the needs of higher-income groups. Families with lower incomes (which also have risen) have gotten some new housing, but most have improved their condition by occupying the used housing abandoned by the more affluent. Given the logic of these trends, it follows that if income continues to rise and if, as has been the case in Los Angeles, the construction of new housing units continues to exceed the combined total of family formations and in-migration, the worst housing ultimately will be abandoned. (It is clear that not *all* lower-income families have participated in this "filtering" process.)

Smith forecasted the Los Angeles housing demand for the 1960–1970 decade on the assumption that income would increase at the same ratio as it did in the previous decade and concluded that the "great bulk" of demand for new housing would come from families earning more than $10,000.

This assumption was corroborated by men who possessed direct business experience in the area. In 1964 we interviewed six California merchant builders who historically had devoted all or most of their energies to building the least expensive housing possible under existing legal and cost conditions. Their comments were almost identical. Since 1959 or 1960, the prices of their cheapest house had risen, each year, $500 to $1,000 above previous prices. Further, the low-price models represented a decreasing portion of their total sales. A representative example came from one builder who had sold most of his houses in 1959 in the $13,000 to $15,000 range. By 1964, his least expensive house was $18,000.

Part of this general price increase, the builders explained, was attributable to rising costs, principally the cost of land and site improvements. The balance was owing to improvements in the housing itself and to space and quality changes that had been necessitated by shifts in buyer preferences. "We cannot sell a minimum house," said one builder, "because people demand more features like shake roofs and built-in appliances."

All the builders agreed that the families who could not afford new houses were buying used houses or renting houses or apartments. An increasing percentage of the new house buyers were moving within a radius of five to fifteen miles of their former homes, thus leaving them empty for lower-income families.

These assertions suggest that builders no longer can compete with the used house market by offering a minimum new house but must provide more space and quality. Most families see a used house to be a better buy than a new minimum house. This situation is no doubt influenced by the way jobs are distributed. Most employment opportunities in

California for blue-collar and clerical workers are near the supply of used housing. A sizable percentage of employment in the fringe areas where there is land for new housing, is in the higher-paying job categories.

None of this should be taken to mean that there is *no* demand in a New Community for houses selling for less than $20,000. Thus, we still wanted to make some judgment on the validity of the community builders' fear that trying to tap such a market would have serious adverse repercussions upon higher-income buyers. We therefore began our second research project. We asked Carl Werthman, a University of California sociologist, to conduct a series of "depth interviews" of residents in two California New Communities, Foster City and Janss-Conejo. Werthman and his associates addressed themselves essentially to two questions:

1. Do buyers in new communities interpret "planning," especially the amenities, in the same way the planners and community builders do?
2. What effect would the inclusion of lower-priced homes have on the demand for houses selling for more than $20,000?

Werthman concluded that, to a great extent, the answer to both these questions was the same. "Planning" to these residents was a guarantee against the introduction of "undesirable" elements close to one's house and immediate surroundings. Not surprisingly, the most undesirable of these elements was the lower-priced home sold to the lower-income person. Sixty-nine per cent of the residents in Foster City, where the least expensive homes sold from $23,000 to $26,000 said they would oppose including a neighborhood of $20,000 homes even if they were separated from other neighborhoods by a lagoon and a row of apartments. We concluded from the interviews that people feared the introduction of low-income families partly because they thought this was synonymous with the introduction of Negroes. When pushed, respondents indicated that middle-class Negroes were more acceptable than lower-class residents of any race. However, it was also clear that these residents in general found it difficult to accept the idea that Negro and lower-income are not synonymous.

Most residents of both communities emphasized declining community appearance as one adverse result of nearby lower-priced homes. As one Foster City owner put it:

I think the people in this community are going to take pride in their homes because they are middle class. If this were in the class of say $9,000 or below, it would be different. In your $9,000 income or lower, the poor guy is worked to death and he ain't got time to get out in the yard. It's not that they care less, it's simply that the next door neighbor doesn't give a damn and pretty soon he's convinced he don't give a damn either. Yet you'll get a few out of the bunch that will take care, but in the long run it will all go down.

Thus, to the buyers in these New Communities, "planning" means protection from "negative knowns and unknowns." The most important known is the introduction of lower-income families, but other knowns might include industrial plants, offices, and stores too close to the homes themselves. Obviously, all the unknowns cannot be enumerated, but the residents indicated their belief that "planning" would ensure that they, too, did not encroach on nearby vacant land.

The assurances against these negative knowns and unknowns come in two ways: The first is by the existence of a detailed plan, approved by a governing authority, which represents a commitment on the part of the developer who is seen as having not only the will but the ability to carry out the plan. The other relies simply on the reputation of a developer himself. The Janss Corporation never presented a very detailed plan to its prospective buyers, but the Janss family is highly respected and well known. T. Jack Foster & Co., on the other hand, is not particularly well known in the Bay Area but presented a very detailed plan and engaged in an extensive public relations campaign to assure people that the plan would be carried out.

In both Foster City and Janss-Conejo, the sales literature put heavy emphasis on recreation and community facilities. Werthman found, however, that few residents expected to make great use of the major recreational facilities. This did not mean that these facilities played no role in the purchase decision, but that the role was not so much anticipation of use but, as one respondent put it, "To add to the general atmosphere."

The findings of Smith and Werthman suggest that the marketing strategy of community builders has considerable merit insofar as price range is concerned. However, the rather minimal interest that buyers display in the community facilities and their rather narrow definition of the benefits of "planning" suggest that when a developer owns a large parcel of land at the metropolitan fringe and uses "the best known planning techniques," he may not necessarily be establishing much of an advantage in the market place. This conclusion led us to question the validity of community building as an investment and a business enterprise.

Throughout the early interviews and subsequent meetings with community builders, we tried to ascertain what techniques were used for projecting the market and for calculating a rate of return on invested capital. Most community builders spend considerable sums of money employing consultants to analyze the market. It is my judgment, however, that it is difficult, if not impossible, to make long run projections of housing demand either by estimating total demand or by breaking that total into categories of price range, size, and housing type. In addition, community building requires especially high commitments of capital (in the case of Columbia, more than $30 million) long before any revenues can be obtained by sales or leases. An unpredictable market and high initial capital outlays are the classic characteristics of a high-risk investment. By all reasonable business standards, a high-risk investment should offer the possibility of a high rate of return. Yet, we did not find a single community builder who had developed a technique for calculating this rate based on a single set of assumptions as to sales rates, sales prices, interest rates, or other costs. As a result, none could try to measure the impact of any changes in such assumptions on rate of return.

For these reasons, we commissioned Dr. Sherman Maisel, then of the School of Business Administration at the University of California, Berkeley (now a Governor of the Federal Reserve Board), and Ted Dienstfrey to develop a computer model, based on the standard system of discounting cash flows, which could be used to calculate the rate of return.

Because community building is such a new type of enterprise, we could not get very reliable estimates of the dimension of costs, sales rates, or sales prices. However, using what information we did have, we calculated that a prototype New Community would achieve an annual rate of return of 7.4 per cent on invested capital. To arrive at this figure, we assumed that 75 per cent of the total capital cost would be financed at 6 per cent interest. These terms would correspond to the figure suggested in proposed federal legislation to provide FHA insured loans for the land and the site improvements in a New Community. If, however, we had been able to drop the interest rate to 4 per cent to correspond to the approximate cost of government borrowing rather than the cost of issuing insurance, the rate of return would have risen from 7.4 per cent to 11.2 per cent.

We may, of course, have overestimated costs or underestimated sales prices, which would project a lower rate of return than that which would actually occur. However, to balance this we did use an optimistic annual sales rate of over 2,000 units starting with the fourth year after land purchase. To date, no New Community has achieved an annual sale rate of 1,000 units.

It is obvious that rates of return between 7 and 11 per cent on invested capital are hardly what one would expect from high-risk ventures.

THE PROBLEMS AND GOVERNMENT AID

As mentioned earlier, the urban critique cited a long list of problems which were to be solved or alleviated by New Communities. Our findings about the market suggest that New Communities will not alleviate separation by class, race, and income and, in fact, may exacerbate this trend.

Other problems with which New Communities were expected to deal were fiscal inequity, high costs resulting from low density, the loss of a sense of community, the dominance of the automobile as a means of transportation, and air and water pollution. Yet, we found no reason to believe that New Communities would bring about change in these areas. If class and income separation continues, and if local services continue to be financed by property taxes or any other locally based revenue system, naturally, fiscal inequity will continue. The density in New Communities, about 3.2 families per acre, is lower than that of many suburban areas developed under fragmented ownership. There is no evidence that a sense of community is created by these projects except when the community builder fails to fulfill his commitments and therefore arouses the ire of his residents. To assume that the installation of a regional shopping center, a lake, a golf course, a bridle path, some open space, and perhaps, a general purpose building will suddenly give middle-class Americans a new sense of civic pride, seems to me romantic in the extreme. With the exception of Columbia, which now plans to install a separate bus system with its own right of way, no New Community proposes to provide any transportation system other than the automobile. I cannot think of any reason why a

New Community would decrease air and water pollution in the metropolis as a whole. Of course, by keeping out any heavy industry, even where there might be a demand, it might prevent pollution in its particular area, but this would only reroute the polluting industry to some other part of the region.

For three successive years, the administration has requested Congress to pass a two-part New Communities program. The first part would provide FHA insurance and FNMA funds for up to 75 per cent of the cost of land and site development. The presumption here has been that while New Communities are considered virtuous, financial aid is required to stimulate their initiation and to make it difficult for developers to abandon virtue under later financial pressures. The second part proposed direct federal loans to state or metropolitan governments for the purchase of land and the installation of basic improvements. Presumably, the land would then be sold to private enterprise for actual construction, much as is the case with urban renewal.

Neither part of the program has ever gained any great support either from private industry or state governments. Yet, because of the administration's persistence and the absence of any organized opposition (although big-city mayors have been dubious about the whole affair), a modified version of the insurance scheme was passed by the 1966 Congress. I can find little justification for this legislation because, as I have tried to illustrate, New Communities, aided or unaided by government, will not materially affect our major problems. If anyone gains, it will be either the landowner, the developer, or the middle- and upper-middle-income residents who are likely to become the principal residents of a New Community. In addition, the program would be extremely difficult to administer and financially very risky. It seems to me that government aid for New Communities has all the wrong characteristics for a public venture. It requires a great deal of money, it involves high financial risk, it is fraught with administrative difficulties, and, worst of all, its potential benefits are minimal, and those that do occur will accrue to people in our society who are least in need of help.

There is one type of governmental involvement in New Communities which might have some merit, but it bears no relation to the problems which current proponents of legislation are trying to solve. It is conceivable that significant technological advances could be made in the study and development of community infrastructure. It is difficult to experiment with such technology without sufficient scale and a guaranteed market. The federal government, however, could provide funds to a publicly chartered corporation whose avowed purpose would be the construction of a New Community with innovations in sewer and water systems, transportation, power, and communication. Governmental funding would be necessary to such a program, even assuming the active cooperation of industry, since experimentation necessarily means risk with the likelihood of financial loss greater than the likelihood of profit.

SOME REFLECTIONS

As I arrived at these conclusions, I began to wonder why so many people have made such a great fuss about New Towns and New Communities. Almost every national publication has done one or more major articles about the glowing prospects this new phenomenon offered. I am sure this editorial proliferation has been caused, partially, by the nature of communications in America, but I would suggest that much of its nonsensical nature has been inspired by the characteristics of most people who call themselves city planners or urban critics.

Until very recently, education in architecture and city planning schools and the writings of most observers of the urban scene were both simplistic and anti-intellectual. One manifestation of this is the lack of precision in the use of words and phrases employed to criticize urban life and urban development in America. Critics use terms like "inefficient land use," "sprawl," "balance," "human scale," "community," and "explosion." But when one asks for definitions, one usually receives either a blank stare or the comment that "everyone knows what this means, and everyone knows that these are problems." I wonder, however, if "inefficient land use" refers to the total amount of land used for development, the type of land developed, or the density of development? At what scale are we to judge "balance": the municipality, the neighborhood, the block, the metropolis, the state, or the nation? "Sense of community" can be defined as shared interests. In many cases this means common fear. Many small towns in the United States, particularly in the South, are characterized by great distrust of outsiders and of ethnic or racial minorities. Is it this sense of community which urban critics cherish and hope for in New Towns or New Communities? I suggest that we need a number of master's or doctoral theses on almost all phrases and words which find their way into city planning literature.

Obviously, I am asserting that, all too often, urban commentary is fraught with oversimplification. We need much more hard thought about why and how people and institutions function. This should not be taken as a belief that urban analyses or urban problem solving can be made easily into a science. Recently there has arisen considerable interest in the incorporation of computers and mathematics into what is called "systems analysis" or "regional science." These new techniques have potential value, as they may increase our ability to understand the complexities of urban life, but such techniques are in their infancy and the data upon which they must depend are extremely unreliable. The claim that the space age industries and the computer technologists now possess the ability to produce nirvana is simply another manifestation of our addiction to proclaiming solutions to problems we have as yet been unable to define.

Another way of characterizing the style of city planners and urban critics is to say that they are Messianic. Their feeling seems to be that they know what the problems are and know how to solve them but Philistine politicians and entrepreneurs will not give them the power. An example of this can be found in Victor Gruen's book *The Heart of Our Cities*. Like a great many architects and city planners, he thinks urban ills can and should be solved by a new type of professional man, "the environmental architect." As Gruen puts it:

The shaping of the human environment cannot be achieved by the assembly line technique. There is an urgent need for the training of a new type of professional man. Lacking a better term, I will call him the environmental architect. He won't need a special title, a special license, or membership in one or another of the professional organizations. But he will have to possess, through a combination of aptitude and training, and as a result of restless seeking for deeper insight into the nature of man, the kind of understanding and convictions that will allow him to view problems and to find their solutions from a high vantage point (not to be confused, however, with an ivory tower).[13]

To me, this is a deeply offensive notion. I do not believe that any amount of professional training somehow equips a small group of men to make decisions about something as complex as urban development, which might affect so many millions of people. This is not to say that

[13] Victor Gruen, *The Heart of Our Cities* (New York: Simon and Schuster, 1964), p. 342.

there is not a role for the profession of city planning, but we should realize that the definition of that role is still evolving. In determining the relationship of the city planner to the populace, we might consider the more deeply established relationship of lawyer to client. Here, a body of knowledge and a set of techniques have been developed which permit the lawyer to give valuable advice to his client. He can suggest goals and illustrate the effect of alternate forms of behavior upon these goals. The practicing lawyer is not afraid to acknowledge his uncertainty, and, in the last analysis, he respects the principle that the client sets his own final goal.

For the city planner the client may be a businessman, a government agency, or an elected official. If the city planner, knowing the limitations of his skill and knowledge, sees his role as improving the ability of his client to define his goals and to discriminate among tactics and strategies to reach these goals, he can play a responsible and meaningful role.

As an individual, he can be a crusader, but then he is no longer acting in his professional capacity but simply as a citizen who wishes to urge his fellow citizens and elected officials to adopt what he believes to be appropriate courses of action. Even if he understands this, the city planner should be aware of how often predictions, particularly those of demographers, have turned out to be false.

It is very common for city planners to seek ways "to preserve the integrity of the plan." I think we should not seek adoption of precise plans which will constrain future behavior. In fact, our goals should be the opposite: to adopt policies and install physical facilities which will keep open the maximum number of options for future actors, whether they be architects, developers, consumers, or politicians. We might accept the view expressed by George Kennan, who concluded his book *Russia and the West Under Lenin and Stalin* as follows:

One of our purposes should be to stress the necessity of an American outlook which accepts the obligations of maturity and consents to operate in a world of relative and unstable values.

The picture, then, which I hope I have presented is that of an international life in which not only is there nothing final in point of time, nothing not vulnerable to the law of change, but also nothing absolute in life itself: a life in which there is no friendship without some element of antagonism; no enmity without some rudimentary community of interest; no benevolent intervention, which is not also in part an injury; no act of recalcitrance,

226 / EDWARD P. EICHLER

no seeming evil from which—as Shakespeare put it—some "soul of goodness" may not be distilled.

A world in which these things are true is, of course, not the best of all conceivable worlds; but it is a tolerable one, and it is worth living in. . . . I am content to dismiss you, as Bismarck once did some of the more curious and impatient of his former associates, with the words: "Let us leave a few problems for our children to solve, otherwise they might get so bored."[14]

In a century of economic uncertainty and war, I am not worried that we shall solve so many problems that our children will be bored. Much progress has been made, but much remains to be done. The horrors of war did not end in 1946, nor were racial problems solved in 1865. Observing this, some of our brightest college students rail at the hypocrisy and complacency of their parents and their substitute parents, college teachers. We may not share their style, but what justification do we have to tell them to accept ours?

New Towns, New Communities, or whatever you want to call them, stem from the outworn notions and ideologies of Ebenezer Howard and nineteenth-century England. They are not evil, but they are not really very interesting. As an intellectual or social concept, they commit what is to America's activist youth the worst sin of all: They are irrelevant. I know very little about what "urban form" is more desirable than another. Like Kennan, I limit my goal: to pass on to succeeding generations a world, and an urban society, more or less intact, and free of most constraints. To seek to do much more would be evidence of both arrogance and shortsightedness, qualities which we Americans have already displayed far too often.

[14] George Kennan, *Russia and the West Under Lenin and Stalin* (Boston: Atlantic-Little Brown, 1960), pp. 397–398.

PART FIVE
PLANNED PLURALISM IN
NEW TOWNS AS AN
ALTERNATIVE TO SUBURBIA

BENNETT M. BERGER

SUBURBIA AND THE AMERICAN DREAM

AMERICANS HAVE NEVER BEEN
other than ambivalent in their commitment to cultural variety, as
against their longing for cultural uniformity. Today, this ambivalence
is becoming a central concern of public policy. For, as urban planning becomes an increasingly visible and legitimate part of the activity
of the public sector, its power will grow to support or to undermine
cultural diversity in the traditional seat of that diversity — the cities.
Like the myth of a homogeneous "suburbia," which for a long time
obscured, and to some extent still obscures, the actual variety of suburban life, complacence about the cultural diversity of cities may
blind us to the conditions which sustain it. My aim in this essay is to
take what I and others have learned about the variety of suburban
styles of life, and to relate this knowledge, first to some of the more
pervasive pluralisms of American culture, and then to a few of the
problems of planning for urban diversity.

The persistence of the myth of suburbia

Some years back, I undertook a study (reported in *Working-Class
Suburb,* Univ. of Calif. Press, 1960) in order to observe the transformation of a group of automobile assembly line workers into the "suburbanites" who had become stock figures in American popular culture
in the 1950's through the satirical and other efforts of a variety of pop-

The Public Interest, No. 2 (Winter, 1966) 80–91. Copyright © 1966 by National
Affairs, Inc. Reprinted by permission of the author and publisher.

ular magazines. It seemed to me that, having found a working class population more than two years settled in a new suburb, I was provided with an almost natural experimental setting in which to document the processes through which "suburbia" exercised its profound and diffuse influence in transforming a group of poorly educated factory workers into those model middle-class Americans obsessed with the problems of crab-grass and "conformity."

Well, it is now a matter of public record that my basic assumption was wrong. As the interview evidence piled up, it became clearer and clearer that the lives of the suburbanites I was studying had not been profoundly affected in any statistically identifiable or sociologically interesting way. They were still overwhelmingly Democrats; they attended church as infrequently as they ever did; like most working class people, their informal contacts were limited largely to kin; they neither gave nor went to parties; on the whole they had no great hopes of getting ahead in their jobs; and instead of a transient psychology, most of them harbored a view of their new suburban homes as paradise permanently gained.

But (appropriately enough for a Ph.D. candidate) I was cautious in the general inferences I drew from that study. It was, after all, based only on a small sample, of one suburb, of one metropolitan area, in one region, and it suffered from all of the methodological limitations inherent in small case studies. None of my findings gave me any reason to doubt the truth of what William H. Whyte, for example, had said of his organization men; but it also seemed to me that there was little reason *not* to believe that my findings in San Jose would be repeatedly confirmed in many of the less expensive suburbs around the country whose houses were priced well within the means of unionized workers in heavy industry, and of lower white collar employees as well. I did, in short, question the right of others to generalize freely about suburbia on the basis of very few studies of selected suburbs which happened to be homogeneously middle or upper middle class in character — especially when it seemed apparent that suburban housing was increasingly available to all but the lowest income levels and status groups.

The considerable bulk of research that has been done on suburbs in the years since I did my work has given me no reason to alter the conclusions I drew then. Indeed, none of this research can be expected to give much comfort to those who find it convenient to believe that a suburb exercises some mysterious power over its residents, transforming them into replicas of Whyte's practitioners of "The Outgoing Life." There seems to be increasing consensus among students of suburbia that suburban development is simply the latest phase of a process of urban growth that has been going on for a long time, that the cultural character of suburbs varies widely in terms of the social make-up of its residents, and of the personal and group dispositions that led them to move to suburbs in the first place; that the variety of physical and demographic differences between cities and suburbs (and there *are* some) bears little significance for the way of life of their inhabitants, and that some of these differences, although statistically accurate, are sociologically spurious, since the appropriate comparisons are not between residential suburbs and cities as wholes, but between suburbs and urban residential neighborhoods. In general, the reported changes in the lives of suburbanites were not *caused* by the move to suburbia, but were reasons for moving there in the first place. In suburbs, as in city apartments, social class, the age-composition of residents, the age of the neighborhood, etc., are much more profound predictors of the style of life than is residential location with respect to the city limits. Analysis of national samples has provided confirmation neither of a trend to Republicanism in politics nor a return to religion. Suburbs, in short, seem — as Reissman and Ktsanes have characterized them — to be "new homes for old values."

It appears, then, that there are no grounds for believing that suburbia has created a distinctive style of life or a new social character for Americans. Yet the myth of suburbia persists, as is evident from the fact that it is still eminently discussable over the whole range of our cultural media, from comic books to learned journals. One should not be surprised at this, for myths are seldom dispelled by research; they have going for them something considerably more powerful than mere evidence. And though nothing I say here can change this fact, it may give us some comfort to understand the sources of the myth, the functions it performs for the groups by whom it is sustained, and the nature of its appeal to America's image of itself.

In my book, and then, again, later in an article, I undertook a functional explanation of the myth of suburbia. I pointed first to the fact that suburbs were rich with ready made visible symbols: patios and barbecues, lawnmowers and tricycles, shopping centers, station wagons, and so on, and that such symbols were readily organizable into an image of a way of life that could be marketed to the non-suburban public. I also pointed out that this marketing was facilitated by the odd fact that the myth of suburbia conveniently suited the ideological purposes of several influential groups who market social and political opinion — odd because these groups could usually be found disagreeing with each other, not only about matters of opinion, but about matters of fact as well. Realtor-chamber-of-commerce interests and the range of opinion represented by the Luce magazines could use the myth of suburbia to affirm the American Way of Life; city planners, architects, urban design people and so on could use the myth of suburbia to warn that those agglomerations of standardized, vulgarized, mass-produced cheerfulness which masqueraded as homes would be the slums of tomorrow. Liberal and left-wing culture-critics could (and did) use the myth of suburbia to launch an attack on complacency, conformity, and mass culture, and found in this myth an up-to-date polemical vocabulary with which to rebuke the whole slick tenor of American life: what used to be disdained as "bourgeois" was now simply designated as "suburban." In short, the *descriptive* accuracy of the myth of suburbia went largely unchallenged because it suited the *prescriptive* desires of such a wide variety of opinion, from the yea-sayers of the right to the agonizers of the center to the nay-sayers of the left.

But though I still think this analysis of the myth makes good sense, I think too that there is something more — something, if I may be permitted to say so, deeper, profounder, and which I was only dimly aware of then. I think now that the myth can be understood also as our society's most recent attempt to come to terms with the melting pot problem, a problem that goes straight to the heart of American ambivalence about cultural pluralism.

Cultural pluralism and the melting pot

America has never really come to terms with the legend of the melting pot. That legend, if I may quote the windy text of its original source, saw America as the place where "Celt and Latin, Slav and Teuton, Greek and Syrian, Black and Yellow, Jew and Gentile, the palm and the pine, the pole and the equator, the crescent and the cross" would together build "the Republic of Man and the Kingdom of God." Despite the hope that a unified American culture might emerge from the seething cauldron, it didn't happen; instead, the formation of ethnically homogeneous communities — ghettoes — helped the immigrants preserve large segments of their cultures, and the tendency to endogamy helped them preserve it beyond the first generation. But in spite of the evident facts of our cultural pluralism (by which I mean the persisting correlation of significant differences in values and behavior with ethnic, regional, and social class differences), attempts are continually made to create an image of *the* typical or representative or genuine American and his community. These attempts have usually succeeded only in creating stereotypes — most familiarly, perhaps, a caricature of one or another variety of Our Town: white, anglo-saxon, Protestant, and middle class. *Saturday Evening Post* covers, white picket fences, colonial houses, maple hutches and the like have historically played an important role in such attempts. *The myth of suburbia is the latest attempt to render America in this homogeneous manner,* to see in the highly visible and proliferating suburban developments a new melting pot which would receive the diverse elements of a new generation from a society fragmented by class, region, religion, and ethnicity, and from them create *the* American style of life. Suburbia as America is no more false a picture, probably, than Babbitt or Our Town as America; but it fails as a melting pot for the same reason that the original melting pot idea failed: like many other urban neighborhoods, specific suburbs developed a tendency to homogeneity, almost always in terms of social class and very often in terms of ethnicity.

The myth of American cultural homogeneity and the stubborn fact of heterogeneity reflect a persistent ambivalence in American society regarding cultural unity and diversity, between the melting pot idea and the pluralist idea. During and after the period of rapid immigration into the "teeming cities," for example, free public education expressed the need for some minimum "Americanization," whereas the ghetto expressed the impulse to cultural self-preservation (both by the natives who excluded and the immigrants who segregated themselves). In the rest of the country, 4th of July style patriotic rhetoric expressed the gropings toward an elementary national identity, whereas provincial arrogance — and hostility to "the government" and to centers of cosmopolitan influence — expressed the affirmation of narrow local autonomies. The ambivalence was really a double ambivalence; each polar position was itself unstable: to be truly tenable, a pluralist ideology must accord intrinsic honor and value to a diversity of life styles, and this it has never completely done. The salient features of minority subcultural styles have more often than not been regarded as stigmata by dominant groups, tolerable so long as they were temporary, that is, *transitional* to something approaching the dominant cultural style. On the other hand, the attempts of provincial, nativist, ("WASP") groups to secure their own style as *the* American style stopped short of supporting the emergence of broadly inclusive *national* institutions which would have facilitated that transition. The most enthusiastic celebrators of "Americanism" were precisely the groups who were most wary of integrating the varieties of the national life into a unified culture.

Indeed, a unified national culture has until quite recently been a most improbable prospect, since the United States has traditionally been a society without very powerful national institutions with which to promote that unity and pass it on down the generations. Without an established church or a powerful federal government, without national political parties or a standardized educational system, enormous distances and poor communications enabled local economies to breed a highly differentiated system of *native* subcultures — in addition to those created by the immigrants. Even today, there are probably dozens of distinctive American types, to some extent stereotypes, perhaps, but which nevertheless call attention to the wide variety of *native* styles: Vermont farmers and Boston Brahmins, Southern Bourbons and Tennessee hillbillies, Beatniks and organization men, Plainvillers, Middletowners, and cosmopolitan intellectuals, to say nothing of teenagers, the jet set, and many, many more, all American, all different, and none probably very eager to be integrated into an idea of "*the* American" at a level of complexity suitable for a *Time* cover story or a patriotic war movie.

It is not surprising, then, that when one tries to abstract from American life a system of values which can be called distinctively or representatively American, the task is immensely difficult. The most systematic attempt by a sociologist, that of Robin Williams in his book *American Society,* is foiled by the fact that important groups in American society do not share the 15 or 16 values which he offers as basically American. There is no question that values such as "achievement," "work," "efficiency," "equality," and the rest have played a significant role in creating the quality of American life, but important parts of the lower and working classes (important because of their numbers) do not share them, and important parts of the upper class (important because of their influence) do not share them — although they may affirm them when a journalist is nearby.

Myths and styles of life

The persistent attempts to find some transcendent principles or values which define the unity of American culture have been defeated by the persistence of important class and ethnic differences. Even under natural or "organic" conditions, then, "American" patterns of culture are enormously difficult to describe with any accuracy. This difficulty is exacerbated when a society becomes sophisticated enough to be self conscious about its culture and rich enough to do something about it. The maturity and the luxury of our civilization constrain its elites to define an "American" style, and the miracle of our technology arms us to manufacture it. Our society is wealthy enough to support a substantial class of intellectuals devoted to staying on top of contemporary events to "spot the trend," "see the pattern," "find the meaning," "discover the style." And our media are such that these spottings and seeings are more or less instantaneously communicated to audiences of millions, whose demand upon the marketers of opinions and interpretations for sensible and coherent syntheses is greater than the available supply.

Under such conditions, we do not get serious historical interpretation of contemporary events; we do not even get responsible journalism; we get myths, which themselves become part of the forces shaping what is happening, and which hence function ideologically. The myth of suburbia fosters an image of a homogeneous and classless America without a trace of ethnicity but fully equipped for happiness by the marvelous productivity of American industry: the ranch house with the occupied two-car garage, the refrigerator and freezer, the washer and dryer, the garbage disposal and the built-in range and dishwasher, the color TV and the hi-fi stereo. Suburbia: its lawns trim, its driveways clean, its children happy on its curving streets and in its pastel schools. Suburbia, California style, is America.

Most American intellectuals have sustained this myth in order to hate it; but the bases of their antipathy have never really been made clear. Somehow associated with these physical symbols of suburbia in the minds of most intellectuals are complacency, smugness, conformity, status anxiety, and all the rest of the by now familiar and dreary catalogue of suburban culture. But the causal connection between the physical character and the alleged cultural style of suburbia has never been clearly established. It is almost as if American intellectuals felt, like some severe old Calvinist prophet, that physical comfort necessarily meant intellectual sloth. Perhaps it is because we have been too well trained to believe that there is somehow a direct relationship between the physical structure or the esthetic shape of a residential environment and the sort of values and culture it can possibly engender — so that the esthetic monotony of suburbia could house nothing but a generation of dull, monotonous people, and its cheerful poverty of architectural design could breed nothing but a race of happy robots. The only trouble with this view is that there is little evidence and less logic to support it. Most of the adult suburbanites were *urban* bred, and hence presumably already shaped by the time they became suburbanites. And although it is still a little too early to tell what kind of culture will be produced by the generation bred in the manufactured environment of suburbia, we might remember that the generation bred in the endless and prison-like New York tenements did not do badly.

But becoming aware of the myth of suburbia, and pointing to the disparities between it and what we actually know of suburbs we have closely studied, should not be confused with a *defense* of suburbia. Nor should anything I have said about the critics of suburbia be interpreted as an expression of my personal bias in favor of suburbia. As I suggested earlier, myths are potent enough to survive evidence; they are not disarmed by understanding. Quite the contrary. Once myths gain currency, once they go, as we say, "into the cultural air", they *become real*, and function frequently as self-fulfilling prophecies. Life copies literature; fact is affected by fiction; history is constrained by myth. "If a situation is defined as real," said William I. Thomas, "it is real in its consequences," and I have no doubt (though I have no data) that family decisions regarding whether to move to the suburbs have been affected (both pro and con) by the myth of suburbia. And despite everything reasonable I have said about suburbs, I *know* that the fact that I unreasonably dislike them has been conditioned, *beyond the possibility of redemption by mere research*, by the very myth of suburbia I have helped explode.

In the sense in which I have been speaking of them, myths are more or less noble fictions; fictions in that they are *made*, and noble depending on the art with which they are made, the extent to which one is in favor of the consequences they foster, and, most particularly, the forms of solidarity they promote. In the context of the debate over "suburbia," what is usually at stake is whose version of America shall become "American."

Pluralism and planning

Whose shall? I want to suggest that the question is relevant to the way in which the future quality of urban life is planned. Like Emile Durkheim, who suggested that the punishment of crime was signifi- cant less as a deterrent or as simple revenge than as a collective reaffir- mation of cultural values, I want to suggest that we look more closely at the images of solidarity which inform the proposals for dealing with social problems in general, and with urban problems in par- ticular. For social problems, of course, have no objective existence — although the facts to which they refer may. It is objectively true that some people have always lived in dilapidated, unsafe, unheated, vermin-infested residences, but "slums" have not always been a social problem. Slums become a social problem when a large enough group of important people decide that poor people ought not to live in such places.

Americans have a propensity to find social problems. By defining them as real and hence setting ameliorative forces into action, we affirm our liberal heritage. To find problems, to mobilize opinion about them, to shake our social structure by its metaphorical shoulders and force it to *pay attention* to these matters, nourishes our beliefs in progress and perfectibility. America is a country dedicated to the propositions that no evils are ineradicable, no problems insoluble, no recalcitrance beyond conciliation, no ending need be unhappy; we are a most un-Greek democracy. Finding and dealing with prob- lems, then, are necessary conditions for the verification of these prop- ositions; the very existence of social problems to ameliorate, reaffirms our principles more than any imaginable utopia could. But not just any problems at any time. Because at any given moment there is an indefinitely large number of social problems which are theoretically identifiable, public concern with some (to the exclusion of others) can be understood not only in terms of the salience of the difficulties of those who *have* the problems but also in terms of the relevance of proposed solutions to the dominant forms and rhetoric of solidarity.

When we set out to improve the quality of urban life, what we are most likely to be doing is altering the conditions under which weak and vulnerable sections of the population live. The wealthy, who also have problems, are protected from the welfare impulses of others. The strong and the autonomous grant no one the right to alter the conditions of their lives — that is what strength and autonomy are about. Public concern over, and desire to plan for, "the problem of" the increasing proportions of aged persons in our society, for example, do not extend to Dwight Eisenhower, Harry Truman, or H. L. Hunt, all of whom qualify for the statistical category "aged," but not for our image of those who need help — although, if consulted, I might have several suggestions as to how they might spend their declining years more wholesomely. The people who have the problems which are defined as "real" are those who are vulnerable to public action, and thus to the implicit images of solidarity which underlie that action. I think it is essential that we be very clear about these images, for to plan for the *quality* of urban life is to be concerned with the *culture* of urban life, and hence with the forms of human solidarity which planning is likely both to foster and discourage.

I see three broad alternatives for those who are confronted with the problem of planning the quality of urban life. First of all, planners can simply abdicate from any concern for the cultural consequences of what they do, and instead interpret their mandate narrowly — for example, the improvement of the physical environment for the poorly housed. To the extent that they have been planned at all, most new, inexpensive suburbs have been developed in this way — with occasional exceptions, as in the gestures by the Levittowns toward the provision of some institutional facilities. More centrally located urban residential development for the poor and the less-than-affluent has also been dominated by considerations such as square footage, hygiene, and domestic technology. Now to provide room, cleanliness, comfort, and convenience to people who have previously been without them is an important achievement; but it is not planning for the quality of urban life. Quite the contrary; the *quality* of urban life is precisely what is usually left out of consideration — perhaps as a luxury rendered expendable by the need to bring large numbers of people up to some minimum physical standard. Under these conditions of planning, images of human solidarity seem limited exclusively to *households* within which *family* solidarity may be symbolized by culinary and recreational technology (refrigerators, freezers, barbecues, TVs, etc.), whereas solidarities beyond that of the family and household seem irrelevant, alien, or distant. There is a sense in which this alternative is evasive because such planning *does* engender a quality in urban life, but it is the quality that most cultivated foreign observers complain about in most American cities.

Planning's second alternative, it seems to me, is to make a conscious effort to alter the environments of certain groups, with the overt intention of bringing their culture closer to some monolithic or homogeneous ideal. Presumably, this would be some more advanced version of the melting pot idea, in which either a bureaucratic or entrepreneurial version of a middle class life-style would be given as an ideal toward which the poor should be encouraged to reach. Here the aim would be to make the society more monolithically what it already dominantly is. This alternative founders on its utopianism, on its assumption that a cultural consensus can be engineered or induced in a society in which conflict is endemic and which will remain so as long as the interests of groups and classes remain opposed. In the absence of any ability by planners to wipe out class differences, we must expect, in any multi-class community, controversy not only over the appropriate means to reach agreed-upon goals but over the goals themselves and the priorities to be assigned to them. This is the stuff of politics and culture, and where interests and norms are rooted in a class-based style of life, the attempt by one group to elicit the commitment of the entire community to a specific goal will very likely threaten another group and elicit its opposition. Moreover, these political and cultural diversities have a right to exist and persist. We can be reasonably sure that the vulnerable and dependent groups most readily affected by planning would gladly be rid of their slums, their poverty, and the discrimination against them. Beyond this it is difficult to assume anything with great assurance except, perhaps, that groups develop an attachment to those aspects of their culture which have not been imposed by necessity, an attachment made evident by their tendency to take the culture with them when they move from one environment to another, and to preserve whatever of it that circumstances permit. On the other hand, utopian planning dominated by visions of profound cultural changes is always interesting, and such planners might well devote more energy to making these visionary ideals manifest and rhetorically vivid, if only in order to help others to know whether to be for or against the form of solidarity they envision.

The pluralist alternative

Finally, there is the pluralist alternative, an alternative perhaps best expressed in the recent work of Herbert Gans, and, to a lesser extent, of Jane Jacobs. Whatever reservations one may have about the work of either, each of them projects an unambiguous image of the kind of human solidarity they would like to see fostered by urban planning. This solidarity is loose and heterogeneous, composed of more or less autonomous groups and neighborhoods formed on the basis of ethnicity and social class; communities attached, perhaps, to the notion that good fences make good neighbors, but necessarily related to one another through those political and economic accommodations long characteristic of urban life. If they are open to criticism as "romanticists" (although it is not clear to me why a preference for dense street life, or an insistence that an ethnic working-class neighborhood is not necessarily a slum, renders one vulnerable to such criticism), it should at least be said in their defense that they obviously care enough about the *quality* of urban life to evoke a strong and clear image of it (something their critics do not always do)—strong enough in Mrs. Jacobs' case and clear enough in Professor Gans' case to make it easy for a reader to be for or against them.

I am mostly for them, since planning for pluralism seems to me not only the most sensible way of responding to the fact of persisting cultural diversities but the most honorable way as well. In making their assumptions, planners might first of all assume (it is the most reasonable assumption) that most groups which are displaced by planning *will take their culture with them* if they can. Planners would do well to anticipate this, and to modify their plans accordingly, to facilitate the preservation of those parts of their culture that the groups want preserved. This means that planning would have to be done *for specific types of people with distinctive cultural styles*, that is, for a variety of specific, known tastes rather than for faceless densities with a given amount of disposable income for housing. A working class group with a durable pattern of sexual segregation (husbands and wives living largely separate extra-familial lives) requires for its sustenance residential and community facilities different from those required by a middle class group with a culture pattern emphasizing companionable family togetherness.

If the strain put upon the middle class biases of professional planners by such considerations seems excessive, I ask only that you think of the problem of the Negro ghetto and the potential controversy about whether *its* subculture ought to be preserved. People as different as a sociologist like Lee Rainwater and a Negro leader like James Baldwin have remarked (without clearly deploring it) upon the Dyonisianism prevalent in the Negro ghetto. Now, this is a culture pattern which clearly is both at once an adaptation to the trapped character of ghetto life, and a means of providing compensatory satisfactions for that blocked access to middle class life. If the satisfactions are not only compensatory but real, planners might think about providing facilities for the nourishment of this psycho-cultural pattern — even as they think about eliminating the enforced segregation and demoralization which make it more attractive.

Even after discrimination on the basis of race disappears, however, we have no evidence to suggest that segregation will ever disappear. If the experience of other ethnic groups is any guide (and I know of no better guide), many Negroes will choose to live among their own "kind" even after they have formally free choice of housing. However "kind" may be defined in the future, there is no reason *not* to expect social class and ethnicity to continue to play an important role — although it is quite conceivable that color may eventually not have much to do with ethnicity. We know little enough about the nature of ethnicity — and even less, perhaps, about which members of an ethnic group *prefer* to live in ghettoes, or why, even after they can live almost wherever they please. But the *fact* that many of them do is beyond question. We have no reason *not* to expect this to be true of Negroes also, particularly of those whose views are represented by the most militant Negro leaders, insistent upon the acceptance of Negroes into American society *as Negroes* — with all that this historically implies.

I hope it is clear that these remarks are not the elaborate rationalizations of a conservative searching for an acceptable rhetoric to defend the *status quo*. Quite the contrary; they are the remarks of a sociologist who, being for the extension of the widest possible range of choice to all segments of the population, nevertheless knows that choices are hardly ever random, and that no man is so free that he is not constrained by the norms of the groups to which he belongs or would like to belong. This is as it should be; but the sense of choice rests on the existence of real alternatives. Cultural diversity has somehow been maintained in the suburbs without much help from planners. We may not be so lucky in the cities unless planners begin to understand the conditions of cultural distinctiveness and to design for it.

MARGARET MEAD

NEW TOWNS TO SET NEW LIFE STYLES

An examination of the mass of experience on new towns points to many purposes—new towns to develop new areas, to house special populations, or simply (it is to be hoped) to serve as experimental models for new planning. In analyzing the literature I was struck by two things: (1) the socioeconomic emphasis in which people are thought of in large groups or categories of race, class, age, and income level, with the possible assumption that individuals are interchangeable within such categories; and (2) the relative absence of any explicit tracing of the connections between actual physical design—size and shape of a house, design of the streets, kind of amenities and how they are housed and located—and the quality of life. Partly in response to the need for this emphasis, and also in response to the importance of dealing with the human factor, I want to emphasize these two points, which seem to me to have been severely scanted. I also want to discuss the way in which the pressures to modify our way of life that come from the recognition of the environmental crisis may provide the necessary frame within which needed changes may be undertaken.

To date, public plans for the design of cities or towns, or private plans for the design of mansion houses, or rows of tenants or workers' cottages, have been responsive to a series of constraints, including the amount of resources available, and the social doctrines of the period—the way in which it was appropriate to lay out a city in honor of a monarch or a newly created state, or suitable to provide housing for the necessary poor (those who tilled the fields, worked the mines, unloaded the docks, or lived in slave quarters on plantations). Architects and planners worked, on the one hand, to enhance the prestige and glory of noble or wealthy patrons, and on the other to economize and still house the poor.

New Towns—Why and For Whom? H. S. Perloff and N. C. Sandberg Editors (New York: Praeger Publishers, Inc., 1973) 117-129. Copyright © 1973 by Praeger Publishers, Inc. Reprinted by permission of the author, editors, and publisher.

It has been in rare instances that whole towns have been laid out for all those who were to live in them, providing shelter and security, dignity and participation for all. Even in the egalitarian and town-conscious days of our colonial forefathers, there was a grading of residences closer to the center for the more prosperous who might be the least likely to move on. Cities and towns around the world have been marred by the disregard, the contempt, or the downright hostility of those who planned for some of the people who lived just within or just without the gates. Now, as much as any time in the militaristic and imperialistic pasts, the same tendencies prevail; whole towns are built to someone's glory, need is rated low, and there is very little participation by those who will live there.

Yet I think it is very clear that unless a town is planned by and with, as well as for, those who will live there, we will continue to be plagued by the evils of which we have such an abundance at the present time. It is true that our own condition is exacerbated by the long history of immigration and the contemptuous relegation of the new immigrants to the worst housing, by the virulence of our racial prejudices, and by a class system in which the status of members of each class is endangered by the close presence of members of a lower class. It is also undoubtedly true that these factors, combined with the influx of unskilled and unwanted labor into the cities, and the exodus of both affluent families and the newer, cleaner and more affluent industries from the cities, have contributed to the present crisis. But in the course of our preoccupation with the desperate social, political, and moral evils that have accompanied our present urban arrangements (all of them derivative of and worsened by the automobile), we have become so preoccupied with one set of consequences—the condition of rural and urban slums—that we end up forgetting that the terrible conditions of any part of a population reflect directly upon all the rest.

I believe that the present growth of suburbs—residential units homogeneous by age, class, and race primarily designed as bedrooms—is itself a reflection, cause, and condition of our planning priorities, in which no one, except the occasional wealthy man who can employ an individual architect, has any real choice in how a couple and their children will live. Hunting for a house in a strange city where one has found a new job is as unrelated to genuine human values as trying to find half a room in a slum or half a kitchen in an Eastern European country with a housing shortage. For all the appearance of affluence in many of our upper-middle-class suburbs, and for all the appearance of adequacy in the gadget-filled house with garage available to many members of the working class, we are nevertheless all trapped in a no-choice residential world as far as fundamental human values are concerned.

In a situation as desperate as the urban crisis in the United States, with the kind of tie-in between government and private industry in which radical change is very difficult to bring about, there is a tendency to overestimate one set of factors. So, in the UN Ad Hoc Expert Group Meeting on the Role of Housing in Promoting Social Integration, held in Stockholm, May 8-13, 1972, integration was seen as the proper aim for every society, and the right of people to associate closely with their own kind—with those who shared the same manners and aspirations—was only grudgingly accorded as something that might be permitted, but certainly should never be assisted in any way by public funds. Yet integration, while emphasizing the need to permit disallowed minorities the choice now permitted majority or affluent groups, also carries within it an implicit endorsement of the values that are presently being denied to the poor and the racially disallowed. It carries the same kind of self-regarding ethnocentrism that any other doctrine of integration carries; the extension, to those who are not like them, of a better chance to be like the majority group. If the children of the minority group can play on the same street and attend the same school, if in fact the neighborhood is integrated, or microintegrated (as Herbert Gans uses the term), they will, it is assumed, be better off.

It is also assumed that segregation automatically carries with it poverty, disease, educational disability, and crime, which in turn make those who emerge from segregated areas unable to compete in the larger world. The argument then proceeds that, because new towns seem to offer very little in the way of mitigating racial and class segregation and little for the very poor, they are automatically not worth building and can contribute nothing that is needed in our harassed society.

I would maintain, however, that if we abandon our class-centric attitudes, which presume that whatever the most affluent of us have is good, and say instead that there are virtues in diversity and virtues in similarity, that both need protection, and that our cities are bad cities because neither value is adequately recognized, we may approach closer to the ideal of designing towns for all the people who are going to live there. If people are not given some device through which those with common social and cultural backgrounds can live close together, share each others cooking smells and lullabys and jokes, there is no hope of their children growing up with a relationship to their pasts that they will be able to transmit to their children. Single households of Germans or Irish or Eastern European Jews or Southern blacks cannot transmit their version of their ancestral culture to their children. To do this takes a neighborhood where the children must come in at the same time to supper, or are allowed to play all night in the street. Under the guise of attempting to remedy the terrible conditions to which we have steadily reduced the poorest and most helpless among us, we are still insisting, in the old patronizing strain, that they should be forced to accept the majority values, along with jobs, security, and decent homes.

Actually, though, our policy of segregating the newly arriving poor—in the past those who had another version of European culture and, today those who have another version of American culture and are distinguished by physical differences—has deprived all Americans of choice and of their rights to shared diversity, and has resulted in segregating the whole country. Only in the small towns that are rapidly vanishing do we have anything like a society where there is a place for everyone. All go to school together and each has an opportunity, even in the acrimoniously prejudiced present, to find that others are human because they are like themselves, and interesting because they are different.

Those who lack interest in new towns because they seem unlikely to solve our massive problems fail to emphasize the large number of inhumanities that now characterize our present-day residential arrangements. If new towns would give us an opportunity to develop social forms and architectural styles that would make life more human again, then they could make a great contribution—one that is wholly disproportionate to the amount of capital or effort that goes into them, or the number of people they house.

I am speaking here of a new town as being any newly built community in which comprehensive planning for all aspects of life can be included, whether it is a new town staked out in a meadow, a new area of city where the old buildings have been mainly or partly demolished (a new-town-intown), or a well-designed new town erected on top of an old one. None of the contributions I wish to emphasize are restricted to any one of these. What is needed is a new conception of what a community is and how it can be designed and built with and for its residents. Any one of these three kinds of new towns can be used for experiments in meeting human needs.

A community is a group of people with ties to each other, ties of kinship and friendship, ties of shared work and shared responsibility and shared pleasure. The nucleus of any community is people who know and value each other. Therefore the first requirement for constructing a new community is to devise a way in which people who already know each other can form the nucleus. It has been argued that in a completely new town the inhabitants are not there yet and so cannot take part. But the residents of new towns, even of some single-industry town in a remote wilderness, are not recruited from the moon. And in most cases the people who will move into a new town already live and work somewhere nearby under somewhat less satisfactory circumstances. They could be recruited early, to come as friends and neighbors and kin, to plan how they would like to live, how close or far away from each other they would like to be, how they would like to provide for privacy, one from another, and for shared pleasures within the generations. Yet little consideration is given to the fact that friends may just possibly like to live near each other; that although a family does not want grandmother in the house they would enjoy having her down the street, comfortably on her own; or that the best friends a boy has may turn out to be the children he played with in a sandpile years before.

Paying some attention to creating the conditions in which people who enjoy taking vacations together or working together could also enjoy living within easy visiting distance of each other would accomplish several objectives: provide a planning nucleus of participating residents, provide a base for citizen responsibility, and create a very different life style.

It was this life style, where people lived around the corner and married daughters saw their mothers several times a day, that was wrecked in England when the first new housing was built. This is the destruction of life style that is lamented by inhabitants who remember an earlier Harlem, and which third-generation Czech and Polish and Italian communities are complaining about all over the United States. Poverty and crime and misery in the inner city, and planned one-class, one-age, one-occupational style suburbs, have robbed people of the right of living close together. Neither the block where the poor, living on welfare, move in and out, nor the suburb where the newcomer knows no one (and thinks he wants to know no one), meet this need. Moving among strangers, such people are wary of strangers. In some of the new developments outside Sydney, Australia, residents said they kept themselves to themselves so that a collection agent who came snooping about after a time-payment could not get any information.

In these noncommunities, where everyone is a stranger and equally lost, there is no basis ever to become friends, except when there are children who play together. The idea that this is the way to plan for living is as stupid as the notion that it is good for college students to be assigned roommates as freshmen, and only allowed to choose roommates as upper classmen. What happens more and more is that, coming from a nuclear family without close kin or neighbors, the boy or girl is so unprepared for sharing anything with anyone that a year of living with a stranger prepares them only for a desire to live alone, or with one mate replicating their parents' home. Forced propinquity does not make people into community members.

A second defect of our present system of residential non-choice is that suburbs and apartment houses in so-called developments are constructed in such a way that young people have no expectation of living anywhere near where they now live. Part of the furious repudiation by young people of their parents' way of life—the more affluent, the more furious—comes from growing up in segregated suburbs in which they themselves will not be able to live, and from which their wealthy parents will have to move when they retire. Equally, the widow who has lived for twenty years in a modern suburban zoned community will have to move because the town does not have any apartment where she can live. Here we see a clear case of the way in which the kind of zoning designed to keep "undesirable people" out of a town—because they are poor or black, have a lot of children to burden the school system or would rent and contribute less to the school tax—ends up with depriving the very people who have participated in the exclusionary zoning and contributing to a segregated, fragmented way of life.

For community we need three generations. We need a place that the young can grow into, where the adults move about, leave and return to, and where the old can live out their days close to children, in a familiar landscape. We need adequate provision for young people to have haunts of their own, where the noise they have invented to encapulsate themselves does not deafen the ears of their elders. We need places where those in need can find work because they are close to those who need them—to clear snow, baby-sit, or provide daily household or garden assistance. We need places where young beginning professionals, teachers, and white-collar workers can live close by the places where they work, near the schools and banks and public offices that serve members of other income groups and other occupations.

A second human need, as important as the need for community, is the need for continuity, which is strongest in infancy and early childhood, essential for the sanity of the old, and essential too for the humanity of all ages. Where infants and children just learning to talk are concerned, this means that no professionally manned day-care center can substitute for the continuing care that can be provided by an individual who knows what that child saw and heard yesterday. Where mothers work, only communities where there are older people, free to spend time with children, can provide such continuity. And only in communities where the housing and neighborhood plans are designed to accommodate diversity can such needs be met.

So the intimate relationships between town planning and meeting human needs for community and continuity become immediately clear. If members of different generations are to live near each other, certain kinds of housing needs must be met. There must be provision for older people to walk to shopping centers, to visit each other, and to visit the playground or the nursery; there must be housing which they can afford and manage without undo strain, and where they will be safe. The special needs of older people, both men and women,

can be determined only by careful observation combined with a chance
for them to participate in the planning process. If our old people were
properly provided for, we would no longer have to shunt them off into
retirement ghettos where they have to smile and pretend they are
content when their children come long distances to visit them.

So community is something that demands that there be diversity
of housing types—housing for the young, the old, the middle-aged and
the single—and services that permit people to live in these different
ways close together. It requires meeting places where a meal can
be shared, places where casual meetings with people one knows are
always possible—as there were and still are on the streets of a small
European town. It means that a young couple should not have to buy
a large house, rattle around in it until their children are born, and
cling on to it after the children have left home. It ought to be possible
to move just a few blocks or miles away, as life situations change, or
find a home again after having been abroad or in another part of the
country for a decade. We need to invent much lighter ties to the
ownership of a particular dwelling and much stronger ties to a community, so the ownership of a particular house would constitute a
sort of residential charter, rather than just a material asset to be
narrowly guarded, or a liability that limits freedom and association.

A further human need is the one for women to have a place in
the world that is comparable in dignity and importance to that of men.
This was provided for historically by the expectation that every woman
would devote her entire life to the tasks of homemaking and child-
bearing, being busy and troubled over the needs of the next generation,
and supporting the efforts of a husband to devote his talents and
strength to that next generation also. When people lived at a subsistence level, neither men nor women had time or energy to spare
for anything other than mere subsistence. When agriculture was
invented, society could support a few men who did other things besides
seeking for tomorrow's food but women remained dedicated to child-
bearing and childrearing.

The population explosion has changed all this; society now needs
a stabilized population, not an ever-increasing one, and this in turn
means that only a small portion of the working life of either men or
women will be devoted to rearing children. Many people will have
none children, others only one or two. Our present residential
style—the single house with its expensive use of energy and space,
and its isolation from others—is designed for the single family with
several children. We now need entirely new designs, ones that make
new provision for privacy for parents away from children, for care
of children in groups, for houses that do not demand the continuous
attention of a woman, and for services that can be obtained centrally.
We need designs that permit families with children to find appropriate

housing, but do not force everyone to live as if they had four young children throughout the whole fifty years of an active adult life.

But most of the modern world is covered with attempts to provide each family with a self-contained house, and new housing everywhere treats the family unit of parents and children as if it could move anywhere, unencumbered by other ties, not even intimately related to the place where the husband works, and with no provision at all for the place where the wife might work or for a home that can be maintained without her continuous presence. It is a human need today to provide for modern changes in the career line, to make it possible for women to contribute to public life as individuals, to construct the physical relationships between residence and work so that both men and women may be able to combine work, avocation, and residence in ways that are much more economical and humane.

Human beings, especially children, need closeness and familiarity with all of life, with their own bodies and the bodies of adults, with birds and beasts and blades of grass, with changes in the seasons and movements of the stars, and with the quiet that is invaded by no mechanical sound, where they can listen to their own heartbeats. Yet we have built in such a way that much of this is denied to them. Instead we are providing for a kind of vacation in which people, moving in hoards, descend upon and destroy our few remaining large pieces of natural wilderness, rather than building parks, pools and small wildernesses, and farms and gardens within the limits of the city.

These are demonstrated human needs—the people's need for community and continuity, their need for participation in constructing their own communities, their need for choice in where and with whom they will live, their need to remain or leave or return to places they have lived before, and their need to provide their children with closeness to the natural world.

But all of these needs appear in far more diverse forms than the needs for nutriment that are so easy to demonstrate, with physiological tests of the body and chemical tests of the food. It is difficult to draw blueprints for mass production that can fit human needs; it has been much easier to mass produce dwellings that are straightjackets within which human beings fitted willy-nilly, to put people into the mold that is now continually described as middle-class, selfish, narrow, prejudiced, xenophobic and egocentric—all characteristics that have been nourished by the residential life that has grown up in the last hundred years and become intensified in the last twenty-five.

It is clear that new towns would give an opportunity to experiment in change. Earlier participation in planning, delaying the completion of some parts or sections of a town, postponing the exact location of a path until footsteps have worn it, designing units that are convertible into different sizes, designing neighborhoods in ways that produce clusters of ethnic or life-style seclusion within larger areas that provide contact with many other kinds of people, allowing for choice of neighbors and friends instead of for atomization—all this could be done, and done more easily in a new town than in an old one. Nothing is harder to convert into a community than a well-zoned modern suburb where there are not even sidewalks on which people can walk, if there were anywhere to walk to.

But several questions remain. Where does the demand for such ways of life come from, and has it enough strength to meet the intention of planners if that intention were in fact there? Will people indeed simply echo what they see pictured on the ads today, stating, for example, that they are willing to give up a dining room for a family room—(which simply reflects the disappearance of servants in the upper-middle class and the revolt of the middle-class wife against playing the role of a servant)? Will they demand replicas of what they see on television, the homes which the poor rightly despair of ever attaining, so that many of them turn to crime instead? Will all the resources of the market, not only of available funds but of manufacturing and employment styles, foil any attempts even to experiment architecturally and in town-planning with such innovations in making our residential arrangements more human?

These are basic objections and they are advanced in terms of several kinds of rationale. One objection is the intractability of human nature; tastes are deeply engrained, and those people who have been reared within the lack of neighborhood in our segregated world will want just that and be unable to change; they will reconvert whatever is built into a replica of the old.

Our belief that this does not have to be so, is based on many kinds of observed change, where change in social expectations has established a new style, as when the wealthy deserted their great houses that required an army of servants, and moved into small apartments that could be run without servants—a change that was completed very rapidly during the 1940s in the United States. We have seen Puerto Rican immigrants, highly resistant to changes in nutritional style at home, become amenable to suggestion when their entire physical circumstances were changed by living in high-rise flats in mainland cities. We have seen experiments showing that people are much more willing to accept a new food in a new container than either an old food in a new container or a new food in an old container.

As a field anthropologist I have followed in detail a Melanesian people—the Manus—who took their entire cultural style into their own hands, redesigned every bit of it—village plan, house, furniture, social organization, village responsibility—and with this across-the-board change were able to skip centuries into the modern world. But there were several essential ingredients in their success: they overhauled everything; no slight detail escaped scrutiny; they did it themselves under their own power; and they brought all three generations with them, leaving no old-fashioned people to pull them back. The implications of this historical experiment for new towns is obvious: the town would be new, everything could be rearranged, the residents could participate in the planning, three generations could be welcomed in.

But the case of the Manus contained one other element—a remarkably intelligent and charismatic leader. In the contemporary world, such single leadership is being replaced by teams that are able to diffuse a knowledge of what they have done. A new town that met these needs sufficiently dramatically, but in ways that are not as strikingly different and as unacceptable as Buckminster Fuller's original dymaxion house, would catalyze building and planning throughout the country and the world. It is particularly important to realize that every innovation in town-planning and styles of housing, good or bad, reverberates around the world; new towns designed for new countries are built by international firms, using models from their own countries. Experiments must be conducted and popularized with all the reservations that will protect those who would wish to copy them whole. What is needed is not to popularize a particular kind of housing or housing mix or town plan, but to popularize the idea that there can be kinds of housing and housing mixes and participant planning that will suit other situations.

Ideas like these can be spread; the whole notion of "do-it-yourself" during the 1960s was a case in point. Ideas such as slow completion with resident participation, house designs that can be altered easily, access to different kinds of housing for different life periods, the need to include homemaking styles and accessibility to a labor market for women as well as for men—all these could be experimented with and then diffused.

There are also other changes coming that should make such experiments more viable. One of these is the demand for the rationalization of power lines, communication lines, and highways so that properly planned utility corridors will make it possible to lay out space that is no longer controlled by small recalcitrant local governments, and guarantee the possibilities of building and locating industry within such a matrix. This should make it possible to translate the inventions made in planned new towns into the planning of less controlled and more market-directed housing.

A second change is the demand of young people—the style-setting, upper-middle-class young people, who had such an influence on the life styles of the 1960s—for a more humane, more diversified kind of society, where people live closer together and depend upon each other more, where there is more joy and less competition. These are the young people who are looking for more human places to live and who may become early participants and creative style-setters in planned new towns.

A third change is the whole ecological movement, which demands a more economical use of energy and use of biodegradable materials. These demands reinforce attempts to design more human, less artificial, more interdependent ways of life, where power and machinery can be centralized, energy conserved, space allotted to protected open areas, transportation rationalized, and dependence upon the automobile minimized. All of these demands, dramatized in an enormous number of activities, are favorable to the kind of experimentation and diffusion I have been discussing.

The time seems to be ripe for experiment; those who could participate are clamoring for new life styles and recognizing that, without a well-designed structural basis in town-planning, regional planning, and new architectural forms, the kind of life style they would like to see will be impossible. If each experimental component is examined in the light of criteria for providing community and continuity, choice of association of friends and relatives and colleagues, ability for people to move within a community and not merely into and out of it, conservation of resources and protection of the environment, then the chances of diffusion of innovations will be enormously enhanced.

REFERENCES

Doxiadis, C. A. City for Human Development. Athens: Athens Center of Ekistics, 1972.

_____. "Networks: Movement of People and Public Services: 1967," Ekistics, XXXIII, 197 (April 1972).

Garvan, Anthony N. B. Architecture and Town Planning in Colonial Connecticut. New Haven: Yale University Press, 1951.

Gordon, R. E., and others. The Split-Level Trap. New York: Geis; Toronto: Random House, 1961.

Hall, Edward T. The Hidden Dimension. Garden City, N.Y.: Doubleday, 1966.

Keniston, Kenneth. The Uncommitted: Alienated Youth in American Society. New York: Harcourt Brace, 1965.

Keniston, Kenneth. Young Radicals. New York: Holt, Rinehart and Winston, 1968.

Mead, Margaret. "Broken Homes," Nation, CXXVIII, 3321 (February 1929), 253-55.

_____. "Cross-Cultural Significance of Space," Ekistics, XXXII, 191 (October 1971), 271-72.

_____. "Cultural Discontinuities and Personality Transformation," Journal of Social Issues, Supplemental Series No. 8 (1954), pp. 3-16.

_____. "Cultural Factors in the Housing Patterns of the United States," Ad Hoc Expert Group Meeting on the Role of Housing in Promoting Social Integration, May 8-13, 1972. Stockholm, Sweden: in press.

_____. Culture and Commitment: A study of the Generation Gap. Garden City, N.Y.: Natural History Press/Doubleday, 1970.

_____. "Energy Changes Under Conditions of Cultural Change," Sociometry and the Science of Man, XVIII, 4 (December 1955), 201-11.

_____. "Ethnological Aspects of Aging," Psychosomatics, VIII, Section 2 (July 1967), 33-37.

_____. "Megalopolis: Is It Inevitable?" Transactions of the Bartlett Society, III (1965c), pp. 23-41.

_____. New Lives for Old: Cultural Transformation—Manus 1928-1953. New York: Morrow, 1956; reprinted 1966.

_____. "Outdoor Recreation in the Context of Emerging American Cultural Values," in Trends in American Living and Outdoor Recreation, pp. 2-25. Washington, D.C.: Government Printing Office, 1962.

_____. "Problems of the Late Adolescent and Young Adult," in Children and Youth in the 1960's: Survey Papers Prepared for the 1960 White House Conference on Children and Youth, pp. 3-12. Washington, D.C.: Golden Anniversary White House Conference on Children and Youth, 1960.

_____. "The Crucial Role of the Small City in Meeting the Urban Crisis," in Richard Eels and Clarence Walton, eds., Man in the City of the Future, pp. 29-57. New York: Macmillan, 1968.

_____. "The Pattern of Leisure in Contemporary American Culture," Annals of the American Academy of Political and Social Science, CCCXIII (September 1957), 11-15.

_____. "Towards More Vivid Utopias," Science CXXVI, 3280 (November 1957), 957-61.

_____. "Values for Urban Living," Annals of the American Academy of Political and Social Science, CCCIV (November 1957), 10-14.

_____. "Working Mothers and Their Children," Manpower, II, 6 (June 1970), 3-6.

Mead, Margaret, and Muriel Brown. The Wagon and the Star: A Study of American Community Initiative. Chicago: Rand McNally, 1966.

Myers, Dowell. "Forest Hills: The Function of Scattersite Housing in the Integration Process." Unpublished manuscript, 1972.

Pettigrew, Thomas F. Attitudes on Race and Housing: A Social Psychological View. Washington, D.C.: National Academy of Science, Division of Behavioral Sciences, 1971.

Schwartz, Theodore, and Margaret Mead. "Micro- and Macro-Cultural Models for Cultural Evolution," Anthropological Linguistics, Vol. III (1961) pp. 1-7.

Waddington, C. H. "Space for Development," Ekistics, XXXII, 191 (October 1971), 268-69.

Waddington, C. H., and others. Biology and the History of the Future, IUBS/UNESCO Symposium. Edinburgh: Edinburgh University Press, 1972.

BARRIE B. GREENBIE

SOCIAL TERRITORY, COMMUNITY HEALTH AND URBAN PLANNING

Sociological research has established the harmful effects of disrupting ethnic and other social structures in the central city. Proposals to redistribute urban poor in middle class suburbs may repeat these errors. Cassel and others have correlated various diseases with disordered social relationships that often accompany migration. Physical and social stress are show to be least harmful to all classes when familiar group support is present; also the effects are most severe on individuals with lowest social status. Where a strange population is introduced into the territory of an indigenous one, social health and stability require protection of the cultural integrity of both groups. Legal and institutional changes of this sort should be accompanied by careful application of what might be called current anthropology or human ethology.

The effects of human population growth, in one way or another, have become the central problem of our time. In this country a number of widely acknowledged warnings have appeared, beginning with Ehrlich's "Population Bomb" (1968), and most recently followed by Meadows (1972) and the report of the Commission on Population Growth and the American Future (1972). The continued deterioration of both our urban and our natural environment has lent increasing urgency to the need to control, restrict, or reorganize the impact of people on resources.

This has, of course, always been the primary concern of planners. But, ironically, relatively little consideration has been given to the question of the effect of the *impact of people on other people.* The magnitude of the problems and their relative universality lead planners to think of human beings as aggregations of essentially similar entities, divided at best into certain crude—very crude—categories, such as income level, age, occupation, or race. Despite the current fashion for "social," as opposed to "physical," planning, social considerations continue to be framed

Journal of the American Institute of Planners, Vol. 40, No. 2 (March, 1974) 74–82. Copyright © 1974 by American Institute of Planners. Reprinted by permission of the author and publisher.

in terms of very material economic needs, and a traditionally physicalist view of health. A century after Sigmund Freud and Charles Darwin, much of what has been learned about the nature of man as a unique being and man as another animal is still largely ignored in the framing of public policy.

Migration and Disruption

One aspect of population growth in particular that is insufficiently considered is the effect of *migration* on people, as individuals and as groups. Toffler (1971) has observed that changes of all sorts now take place much more rapidly than the human mind can cope with them, bringing about what he has called "future shock." One of the most disturbing forms of change for many people is a constant change in social milieu, the familiar "cultural shock" which Toffler has paraphrased. In such situations *cultural shock* and *future shock* combine, and we have ample evidence that the shock can be great indeed.

For many years thoughtful observers have warned that the mass relocations of poor people, as a result of urban renewal and relocation in high-rise public housing projects, have been disrupting intricate social relationships which contribute to the stability of the various ethnic, racial, and cultural groups affected (Jacobs, 1961; Anderson, 1964). The degree to which such policies have contributed to the unrest, crime, violence, dope addiction, and general social breakdown in large American cities can only be guessed at, but the social cost of failure to understand the relationships involved must be staggering. The dollar cost to taxpayers has recently been illustrated by the partial demolition and final abandonment of the notorious (and former prize-winning) Pruitt-Igoe housing project in St. Louis.

More than ten years ago, Herbert Gans (1962) examined the social relationships among working class Italians in what was then an "Urban Village" in Boston's West End, later to be destroyed in the name of "renewal." Marc Fried (1963) followed up Gans' study with a most sensitive investigation of the effect of dislocation on the lives of these people, eloquently entitled "Grieving for a Lost Home." Fried noted that the emotional effects were very similar to grief for a lost person. Rainwater (1966) examined the destructive impact on the lives of low-income people of relocation in the St. Louis high-rise Pruitt-Igoe project. The last two studies and a number of others, showing intricate connections between physical space and established social relationships, have been brought together by Gutman (1972) in his *People and Buildings*. But perhaps the most convincing examination of this whole problem has been Newman's (1972) brilliantly quantified empirical study of the relationship of residential design to crime and what he calls "Defensible Space."

Homogeneity or Diversity

These questions have special urgency in regard to two alternatives which are increasingly being considered by social and physical planners. One of these is the legal assault on so-called exclusionary zoning to permit increased construction of low income development in middle-class suburbs (Davidoff et al., 1970; Downs, 1973). This policy is also generally recommended by the Commission of Population Growth and the American Future. The other is revival of the heterogeneous *new town*, to which Congress has given impetus by Title 7 of the Housing Act of 1970. Implicit in any program to increase the social heterogeneity of a community, whether by introducing new populations into old ones, or by planning new cities from scratch, is the democratic axiom that the breaking down of social barriers between subcultural segments of the population is in and of itself a public good.

There is obvious justification for such a viewpoint. Clearly the complex social interactions and intricate webs of cooperation required by modern technological societies also require a high degree of communication across socioeconomic lines, and the elimination, in so far as possible, of prejudice, hostility, and fear, based on ignorance of other lifestyles. In particular, the social wastefulness and cruelty of racial barriers hardly need reiteration. But the incontestable social value of reducing barriers to human communication, understanding, and cooperation does not necessarily suggest that indiscriminate mixing of populations will achieve such a result. There is much evidence that the opposite is true, that protection of ethnic and other social constellations, and repect for the self-defined boundaries or spatial arrangements which identify them, are an indispensable condition for human cooperation and wellbeing (Glazer and Moynihan, 1963, 1970; Gans, 1961; Hall, 1966; Sommer, 1969; Greenbie, 1971, 1973; Goffman, 1971; Novak, 1972; Levine and Campbell, 1972; Suttles 1968, 1972).

One may expect this to be particularly true in countries, such as the United States, which, because of immigration, have emerged without the unifying influence of a long-established, preindustrial culture. There is also reason to believe that opposition to the homogeneity of the suburbs, which has been so much deplored in current popular and academic literature, is based on an unrealistic stereotype of suburbia (Berger, 1960; Dobriner, 1963; Wood, 1959; Clark 1966; Gans, 1967; Donaldson, 1969; Greenbie, 1969). It is quite probable that this homogeneity, for all its limitations, may contribute to the stability which makes such communities a focal point for new low-income housing policies on the one hand, and an implicit, if not overt, model for new towns on the other. Whether or not this is so, it is clearly of the utmost urgency that current policy and planning be based on as accurate an understanding as possible of how human beings mix well and safely and in what ways mixing produces negative consequences.

High Densities and Disease

I will examine some theories that the social dislocations that result from forced mixing under the wrong conditions, as well as from overcrowding under certain circumstances, may not only contribute to social problems, but also to physical disease. For more than a century, reformers and city planning theorists have looked upon high densities as the chief evil of modern cities. Ebenezer Howard's classic formula for new town planning was subtitled "Nothing Gained from Overcrowding." From nineteenth century utopian reformers to the present day, most writers on the subject of slums have attributed their worst effects to conditons imposed by high densities. A conspicuous exception has been Jane Jacobs (1961), who took the opposite position, ascribing the chief virtues of cities to high densities. Her insights into modern city life have made a most important contribution to urban knowledge, but this aspect of her theory has been severely challenged by most urbanists. In the field of public health, the prevalence of disease has been associated with crowding, on the general theory that disease-bearing germs and pollutants have a greater opportunity to build up under such conditions.

The grim statistics of poverty have long showed a correlation between certain kinds of disease and low socioeconomic status. In this country these statistics show up conspicuously among the black population. It is generally assumed that poor physical conditions, such as sanitation and exposure, as well as poor nutrition due to limited food budgets, are the primary cause. The evidence correlating crowding with certain types of poverty, and poverty with social and physical pathologies of all sorts is immense, but the nature of the processes involved has been far from clear.

For instance, McHarg and his students mapped a number of physical, mental, and social disease variables for the city of Philadelphia. They found that all of these increased toward the city center and correlated highly with each other. The incidence of disease did not, however, correlate directly with poverty per se, although both poverty and disease of sorts were concentrated toward the city center, but disease did correlate with high densities (McHarg, 1969). On the other hand, Dubos (1968a) notes that some areas like Holland and Hong Kong which have the highest densities in the world also have the highest levels of physical and social health. He feels that the greatest danger to human life, and particularly to human culture, may lie in the fact that man can adapt to conditions which among societies of other animals would normally limit population growth (1968b).

From a wide range of animal studies we have corroborating evidence that crowding does correlate with physical, psychological, and social breakdown, and that this is a primary means of population control, particularly where the consequences of such breakdowns are reflected in inability to mate and rear young (Calhoun, 1952, 1968, 1971; Wynne-Edwards, 1962). One of the generalities often used in connection with the negative effects of high densities is the concept of "stress," and stress is often assumed to be the result of interactions between individuals and each other or individuals and their environment per se.

Stress and Cultural Dislocation

Studies of John Cassel and his associates at the University of North Carolina School of Public Health have used behavioral references from other species in examining disease patterns in our own, and he has concluded that the destructive consequences of crowding do not derive from either *densities* or *stress* per se, but rather from the particular *kind of stress* that arises from the disordered social relationships which normally accompany extreme densities. These are particularly acute in human beings when familiar customs, status hierarchies, and emotional group support systems based on specific cultures are disorganized through enforced migration (Cassel, 1961, 1970, 1971; Nuckolls and Cassel, in press).

Animal ethologists have shown that when an intruder approaches a conspecific's home territory, a ritualized set of behaviors will be initiated on both sides (Lorenz, 1966, 1967; Wynne-Edwards, 1962; Tinbergen, 1953, 1961, 1967). Under normal conditions, behaviors will go on until the intruder retreats or the proprietary animal yields up his territory. In either case, the behavior of one animal is dependent on a predictable response from the other one; in other words, the behavior is reciprocal and may be called a form of communication. This has led Tinbergen (1951) to describe aggression among animals as a form of social behavior. However, if for some reason one animal doesn't respond predictably to the other, the confused animal will tend to indulge in behavior which is quite bizarre; he will do inappropriate things like pulling up grass, attempting to copulate, or even lying down and going to sleep. Lorenz describes this as *displacement* behavior, which in his theory performs the function of diverting aggressive energy into harmless forms. Cassel notes that a more common consequence of failure to get a proper response is that the animal will continue to repeat the behavior, and that this is accompanied by very marked changes in powerful neuro-endocrine processes and the distribution of crucial hormones in the animal's body. It is these physiological concomitants of failure to get a proper social response to conventional behavior signals which, in this theory, lead to making the body vulnerable to various insults, such as a disease-bearing virus, or a functional breakdown, like stomach ulcers.

Human beings communicate not only by spoken words and written symbols, but by very subtle changes in gesture and inflection, facial expression, or bodily movements, most of which will vary considerably from one culture to another (Hall, 1959). Cassel believes that althought the disorganization of the social cues which individuals depend on to relate properly to others will almost always result from crowding in animals, among humans it may show up in both crowded and uncrowded situations. He notes, however, that even among animals, crowding will be tolerated much better among litter mates than among strangers. For lower class humans, migration is most likely to result in movement from lower to higher density areas, but in Cassel's view it will be the changed social situation, and not the density, that is most critical.

Disease Cycles and Implications

Cassel (1971) examined the history of disease patterns which accompanied the industrial revolution. Tuberculosis has been a prime example of a disease which is associated with crowding, poverty, and unhealthful living conditions. He notes that this disease rose sharply for seventy-five to one hundred years after the beginning of industrialization in Britain and the United States, and then started to fall spontaneously between 1850 and 1900, fifty to one hundred years before effective means of treating it became available. Furthermore the rate of decline in this disease has not changed significantly following new drugs for its treatment. As tuberculosis began to decline, it was replaced by malnutrition syndromes, such as rickets and pellagra, which also peaked, and, for reasons only partially understood, also began to decline. These in turn were replaced by childhood diseases, which waxed and waned, "largely but not entirely" due to immunization and improved sanitary conditions. A new cycle introduced an increase in duodenal ulcers, particularly in young men, to be replaced in the present time by epidemics of heart disease, cancer, arthritis, diabetes, and mental disorders, some of which have already peaked and declined. Cassel believes these cycles cannot be attributed entirely to developments in medical practice. Apparently they do not correspond to equivalent fluctuations in crowding, either, which as a general phenomenon has continued to increase more or less constantly.

He has looked at data from military camps, for instance, where upper respiratory disease is common. The agent responsible is Adenovirus 4, and the orthodox explanation is that crowding in barracks and elsewhere facilitates the spread of the virus, but he notes that the virus is equally present in schools and colleges, where it is rarely implicated in similar infections. Examination of military camps revealed that the permanent staffs were not involved in the outbreaks under study, but *only the recruits*. When the latter were immunized against Adenovirus 4, they continued to experience the same amount of respiratory illness, now associated with a *different* virus. Even more importantly, studies at a Marine base found that there was a definite cycle of the disease during the eight week basic training period, in which the number of respiratory infections increased from the first to the fourth week, decreased during the fifth and sixth, and rose again during the last two (Cassel, 1971).

Data from epidemiology shows furthermore that increases in diseases do not always take place in the crowded cities, but that often the reverse is true, and that this cannot always be explained by improved health services in the city. An example is the greater preponderance in rural areas of streptococcal infections, for which there is no known preventative. Urban data for tuberculosis show that it is not more prevalent among people who are most crowded, but rather among people who are socially isolated in what must be considered relatively low densities, on a person per room basis. A study in Britain found the tuberculosis rate among lodgers living alone was three to four times as high as among families living in otherwise similar conditions (Cassel, 1971).

Cassel's Four Principles

Cassel believes that data from both human and animal studies of crowding can best be examined in terms of four principles: The first is the hypothesis that "the social process linking high population density to enhanced susceptibility to disease is not crowding per se but *the disordered relationships that in animals are inevitable consequences of such crowding."* (My italics.) The clear implication of this hypothesis is that for human beings crowding may facilitate *social disorganization,* but will not necessarily produce it. Cassel's second general principle is that not all members of a population will be equally *susceptible* to these processes, and that the most *dominant individuals* will show the *least effects,* while the subordinate ones will show the most extreme responses. His third principle is that two types of buffers will cushion the individual against the consequences of social disorganization, one *biological,* the other *social.* The biological buffer is the capacity of all living organisms *over time* to adjust psychologically and physiologically to new circumstances. The social cushion is the strength of *group support* given by familiar conspecifics. The fourth principle he advances is that the consequences of social disorganization in these terms do not directly cause a specific illness, but rather they enhance susceptibility to disease in general, and that it will be a matter of which agents, independent of social factors, happen to strike at any particular place at any particular time (1970a).

These principles are supported with considerable evidence from his own and others' research. Supporting the first hypothesis is a great deal of information linking various indicators of social or family breakdown, such as divorce or sudden unemployment, to various diseases. It is supported conversely by the examples already given of very crowded societies which do not have a high incidence of disease but which are also very stable socially. The second principle is supported by similar data which shows a high correlation of illness to low social status and to job positions which occupy a subordinate role in society. The biological adaptability in the third principle is confirmed by experience with animals raised in crowded conditions, as compared with those moved into them after maturing in less crowded ones. In humans the incidence of lung cancer (when controlled for cigarette smoking) is actually higher among farm-born people who move to air-polluted cities than for lifetime urban residents, despite greater exposure of the latter to cancer-producing agents. The group-support hypothesis is reinforced by studies of rats, for instance, where peptic ulcers caused by electric shocks are much less likely in animals who are shocked in the presence of litter mates than those who are stressed that way alone. In humans, stress induced by being given unsolvable problems to solve was much greater in a group of strangers than in a group of friends. There is much evidence that diseases such as tuberculosis are more common among marginal people who, for one reason or another, are deprived of meaningful and stable social contacts. The final principle, that disturbances in group relationships will not lead to specific illnesses (such as job frustration causing ulcers), but rather to a susceptibility to disease in general, is supported by data which show that those regions having highest death rates, for instance from cardiovascular disease, also have higher than expected death rates from all causes.

It is apparent that all such phenomena are interrelated. Studies in Scotland, for instance, show that male red grouse who failed to obtain territory were also unable to make a pair bond with females, generally were prone to various illnesses, failed to protect themselves from predators, and did not survive the winter (Watson and Moss, 1971).

Status, Crowding and Change

If Cassel's theories are correct, we may conclude that the mechanism which enables man to remain healthy at densities higher than most animals could tolerate, also enables man to structure his environment and his social relationships conceptually, as suggested by Calhoun (1971) and Esser (1971, 1972). In a very real sense, it is probably not densities that cause a person to feel more or less crowded, but *what he thinks being crowded is,* and the effect this has on his social interactions. Crowding does not only affect the amount of interaction, but also changes the nature of the interaction. At the same time, a person's concept of status and of family or other in-group relations will be very critical in determining how he adjusts both to crowding and to change. A study by Christenson and Hinkle (1961) showed a much lower incidence of disease among a group of managers who had completed college, as compared with those doing the same job for the same pay who had only completed high school. The college graduates were generally sons of high status managers and white collar workers from middle class neighborhoods; the non-college managers were children of working class immigrants. One may assume that not only did social class status play a role in this phenomenon, but also the symbols of middle class life, which would normally be part of the managerial world. Cassel and an associate made a series of studies of two groups of rural mountaineers who had moved to urban areas and taken industrial jobs in factories. The groups were similar in age and other factors, but one had recently migrated from the mountains, while the others were the children of factory workers who had previously come from the same mountain coves. It was hypothesized that the second generation workers would be better prepared than the first group for the expectations and demands of industrial living, and would, therefore, exhibit fewer signs of ill health. Health was measured according to the Cornell Medical Index and various indices of sick absenteeism. As predicted, the highest health scores and lowest absenteeism was from the group whose parents had been employed in industry before them (Cassel and Tyroler, 1961).

The second principle of Cassel, that social disruption hits hardest on the least dominant, will also be compounded because the shift will often be accompanied by a loss of status, if only because the person becomes a newcomer and, even when potentially a leader, will have to establish that fact in a new group. In any case, it is the least dominant who are most likely to be forced to migrate. The third principle, that time and group unities provide buffers, is a function of migration under such circumstances; the group is left behind, and the instability resulting from the first situation may force continued migrations which will not permit the healing adaptations in one situation long enough for new codes to be established. In any case, these may often require more than one generation, especially in people with limited educational, and therefore limited conceptual, resources. So the three principles become negatively reinforcing, and lead inevitably to the fourth, a propensity for disease.

To test the proposition that health is correlated negatively with changes in life situation and positively with group support, Cassel and his colleagues did a study of young women having their first pregnancy (Nuckolls and Cassel, in press). They developed a score system which incorporated such changes as moves to a new community, and family breakups, which in other studies have shown a high correlation with illness. These were combined with what the researchers called a "social asset" score, which included whether or not the woman wanted the pregnancy and how much support she felt she had from husband, family, and community. They found that ninety percent of the women who had high life-change scores and low social-asset scores developed pregnancy or postpartum complications, whereas of those with equally high life-change scores, but high assets, only thirty percent had difficulties. Significantly, the *adequacy of social assets was irrelevant where life-change scores were low.* Cassel also notes a study of immigrants to Israel, which found that those who migrated as families had much better health records than those who did so as individuals.

In view of the fact that our core cities are more and more populated not only by poor, low status, minority people crowded into slums, but also by people who have recently migrated from rural areas, this is pretty crucial information for planners to chew on. It is particularly crucial in terms of the dissolution of family life that so often accompanies rural to urban migration, aggravated by lack of housing and the inability of male heads-of-households to find work. It may help to explain why our present welfare program fails to offer even a palliative for this kind of poverty.

Moving the Poor to the Suburbs

Now that the arrogance of well intentioned ignorance has helped many of our large cities to become virtually uninhabitable, we are faced with propositions that may, if what I will call "Cassel's Syndrome" is not carefully considered, extend the same disastrous policies to the suburbs. Whatever else they may or may not be, these have, at least until recently, tended to be stable communities. That, of course, is why they are being looked to by reformers who have given up on the central city. Many of the campaigns to relocate core city poor are based on a legal assault on what is called "exclusionary" zoning. As the Davidoffs (1970), and more recently Downs (1973) have noted, present residential patterns in most metropolitan areas represent an unworkable and unbalanced distribution of populations in relation to resources, both economic and natural. But if we look at the problem closely, it is not the "exclusionary" nature of zoning that is causing the trouble, but exclusion in the *wrong places.* What *is* needed, of course, is a restructuring of the way residential communities are organized around centers of employment, transportation, commerce, and available space, with due regard to the eco-system. But the rhetoric of these projects, with terms such as "snob zoning" and an "open society," seems to me not only to be wide of the real mark, but self-righteous, troublemaking, and likely to make a difficult problem harder to solve.

Zoning originated in an attempt to bring form to an otherwise formless urban environment. It did so precisely because the forces which shaped earlier communities were no longer operative. In general it has proved to be a crude and blunt instrument, mangling the physical environment and permitting no subtleties, either in human or nonhuman relationships. But the fact that it has proved to be a poor solution on the one hand, and that it has lead to a new problem of community structure on the other, does not mean that it can be breached like a castle wall without recognizing and respecting the more constructive purposes it was designed to accomplish in the first place.

Social Mixing

Jane Jacobs and others have made an excellent case for social diversity of all kinds, and there is no question that under proper conditions social heterogeneity is a prerequisite for cross-cultural cooperation and for civilization in any real sense. The achievement of such conditions may certainly be regarded as a primary object of planning. But rarely are plans for social mixing accompanied by consideration in careful detail of who is to be mixed with whom, how, where, and under what conditions. If a chemist advanced the proposition that a "mix" per se is good, we would call him mad! If a cook advanced such a notion, we would go elsewhere to eat. Yet the evidence we have looked at suggests that some people mix well and some do not, that the same people can mix safely and happily under some conditions but not under others, and above all that he who would intrude one group into another's territory had better be prepared to guarantee the safety of both if his egalitarian predictions prove false.

Established presuburban old towns contain a real measure of social diversity precisely because that diversity holds at least some common features. Everyone, or almost everyone, knows everybody else, and shares not only a common geographical space, but a common conceptual territory as well. The modern zoned subdivision attempts to cope with the fact that in our socially, economically, and physically mobile world, diversity is accompanied by widely disparate conceptual territories carried by continually shifting groups to new places, and that therefore the only way that a common set of references can be established is through considerable social stratification based on externalities.

If particular land use and building laws are an expression of a conventional culture, and are relied on to preserve a predictable and intelligible environment, and if, in the name of social justice, these are to be radically altered, we may well ask what is to take their place? What sort of cultural institutions will immigrate with those for whom geographical doors have been opened? Is the middle class, in being forced to yield many of its own conventions, expected to welcome alien ones? Is this, with the best of intentions, possible? If so, what sort of cultural trade-offs or compromises can be negotiated, and how? To what extent when social systems mix are they mutually reinforcing or mutually destructive?

New Laws and Institutions Needed

In the general pattern of United States history, whatever equality of opportunity there has been for succeeding generations of immigrants has resulted in acceptance of middle-class conventions, including housing patterns, by those who moved up the socioeconomic ladder. Now the immigration of city poor to the middle-class countryside is being proposed as a conscious and deliberate assault on the status quo. It is being proposed in some cases on the ideological grounds that the status quo is immoral. This is predictably perceived by the middle-class territory holders exactly as what it is claimed to be, an invasion. Under such circumstances, laws and institutions to resolve contests must be imposed. There is a very real question as to whether the abrupt and forceful dislocation of community norms in the case of the middle class will prove to be any more salutary for society as a whole than such dislocations have proved to be in the case of the urban poor. But can the *imposition* of new norms, via changed laws and institutions, be limited to the middle classes on the site? Will not something have to be imposed on the new *immigrants?* And if so, will *what* is imposed on them be any more likely to provide satisfactory environments than the impositions of public housing authorities and relocation agencies back in the city core? Who is to determine the nature of the imposed institutions, and how will the determination be made, if the collective opinion of the existing community is made invalid?

Let us suppose the culture of the new residents is one which involves a lively street life, and some care has been taken in the physical design of the new residences to provide opportunity for it. How will the attendant noise and general commotion fit in with the internalized lifestyle of many middle-class nuclear families? What of differences in manners and general deportment, especially as regards the behavior of children (which can cause a problem even in socially homogeneous communities)? To what extent will the inevitable conflicts result in voluntary withdrawal on all sides into culturally segregated enclaves, replacing big city ghettos with small city ghettos? To what extent will this raise the question Newman addresses regarding abdication of responsibility for the affairs of the community, and consequent opportunity for criminal behavior? In short, what sorts of socially organizing principles can or cannot be written into the new laws and institutions which will preserve the stabilizing functions of the older, indigenous ones.

These questions are answerable in principle, but it is unlikely that the answers will be available prior to assaults on the laws and institutions that bring about the changes that make them necessary. Certainly much more careful, systematic, perceptive, and *empathetic* research will be needed than now appears to be going on, and what is going on should find its way more readily into public policy making. If the official rhetoric regarding the "public welfare" and an "open society" continues to provide the conceptual framework for research, it seems likely that the right questions will not be asked.

Conceptual Territories

Elsewhere (Greebie, 1973) I have suggested that the fewer conceptual resources people have, the more, rather than less, dependent they will be on relationships which are defined by geographical space. For sophisticated urban man, conceptual territories may be provided by professions, hobbies, and religious or political organizations, which can substitute for physical territory. Such people may be relatively indifferent to physical design and location. The poor and cultural minorities will be most likely to need secure physical-cultural boundaries. To intrude them heedlessly, in the name of improving their lot, into territories where residents have more conceptual, as well as physical, resources, can be expected to benefit only the most able and conceptually agile among them. On the other hand, they will be well received only by those whose conceptual territories, or self-images, are, in one way or another, secure from invasion.

In a most interesting, ongoing study of migration in an Argentine village, R. W. Wilkie (1972) has found that the portion of the population most able to cope with change through migration was a part—and only a part—of what he defined as its *middle class*. (The entire village, a peasant community, would be called by most sociologists lower class.) Wilkie observed that the upper and lower class in this village were conservative for different reasons, the upper because it was oriented to peer group expectations, and the lower because it lacked confidence in its ability to cope with new environments. In addition, a portion of the middle class also resembled these groups.

Conclusions

We who propose, devise, and administer laws and institutions are very likely to come out of the professional middle class. We may in some cases be people of little formal education, but who nevertheless have had tremendous conceptual resources of some sort. We will be most likely to organize space and events in abstract, conceptual, intellectual terms. We will continually model environments on our own needs for intellectual complexity, projecting as a universal good what is in fact a minority point of view, even if a most important one. We can afford to be relatively indifferent to other people's needs for secure physical-cultural territory, because we have other resources. We can moralize about the "greed" of affluent groups whose security depends on material welfare, because we have other symbolic ways of maintaining status and power. Yet our problem is, like that of everybody else, how to bring about environments which will enable all of us at least to survive, let alone live happily together.

Wherever mass migrations occur, the interests of two opposing parties must be considered, and constructively provided for; the cultural integrity of the incoming people and the territorial integrity of the proprietary group. The law and its institutions can provide a structure for appropriate compromise, but the negotiation and arbitration will have to be personal and particular in each case. Because modern society requires cross-cultural communication and cooperation on an *intellectual* basis, spaces and social mechanisms for this must be created. On the other hand, studies by ethologists have shown that nonhuman animals gain a psychological advantage on their own territory (Wynne-Edwards, 1962; Leyhausen, 1965, 1971; Lorenz, 1966), which enables them to defend themselves against larger, stronger, and more dominant creatures who would prevail on neutral ground. For human beings also, on the most primitive level of experience, this appears to hold true (Ardrey, 1966, 1970). Physical-social buffers are therefore essential. The first requirement for a healthy change of milieu, whether physical or social, is the assurance of emotional security based on *conceptual territory*, that is, native culture. The second is opportunity for it to recombine with others and evolve safely into something new.

Since legal and institutional mechanisms cannot create these by edict, but can only discover them, changes in laws and institutions must be preceded by what might be called current *anthropology*, or better, *human ethology*. It must be applied in a creative manner that can only be described as *art*.

Author's Note: *Part of the research on which this article had been based was supported by Grant No. A 71-I-26 from the National Endowment for the Arts.*

REFERENCES

Anderson, Martin (1964) *The Federal Bulldozer.* Cambridge, Mass.: The MIT Press.

Ardrey, Robert (1970) *The Social Contract.* New York: Atheneum.

———. (1966) *The Territorial Imperative.* New York: Atheneum.

Berger, Bennett M. (1960) *Working Class Suburb.* Berkeley: University of California Press.

Calhoun, John B. (1968) "Design for Mammalian Living," *Architectural Association Quarterly* 1, no. 3: 1–12.

——— (1952) " The Social Aspect of Population Dynamics," *Journal of Mammalogy* 33, no. 2: 139–159.

——— (1971) "Space and Strategy of Life," *Behavior and Environment.* A. H. Esser, ed. New York: Plenum Press, pp. 329–387.

Cassel, John (1970a) "An Epidemiological Perspective of Psycho-Social Factors in Disease Etiology," Paper presented at the American Public Health Association Meeting, Houston, Texas, November, 1970.

——— and H. A. Tyroler (1961) "Epidemiological Studies of Culture Change, I: Health Status and Recency of Industrialization," *Archives of Environmental Health* 3, no. 25.

——— (1971) "Health Consequences of Population Density and Crowding," *Rapid Population Growth,* National Academy of Sciences, Baltimore, Md.: Johns Hopkins Press, ch. 12.

——— (1970b) "Physical Illness in Response to Stress," *Social Stress,* Sol Levine and N. A. Scotch, eds. Chicago: Aldine-Atherton Press, ch. 7.

Christenson, William N. and Lawrence E. Hinkle, Jr. (1961) "Differences in Illness and Prognostic Signs in Two Groups of Young Men," *Journal of the American Medical Association* 177: 247–253.

Clark, Samuel D. (1966) *The Suburban Society.* Toronto: University of Toronto Press.

Davidoff, Paul and Linda and Neil Newton Gold (1970) "Suburban Action: Advocate Planning for an Open Society," *Journal of the American Institute of Planners* 36, no. 1: 12–21.

Dobriner, William M. (1963) *Class in Suburbia.* Englewood Cliffs, N. Y.: Prentice-Hall.

Donaldson, Scott (1969) *The Suburban Myth.* New York: Columbia University Press.

Downs, Anthony (1973) *Opening Up the Suburbs: An Urban Strategy for America.* New Haven: Yale University Press.

Dubos, Rene (1968a) "The Human Environment in Technological Societies," The Rockefeller Review, July–August.

——— (1968b) *So Human an Animal.* New York: Scribner's.

Ehrlich, Paul R. (1968) *The Population Bomb.* New York: Ballantine Books.

Esser, Aristide H. (1972) "Environmental Design Needs Empathy to Combat Social Pollution," *Environmental Design Perspectives,* W. F. E. Preiser, ed. M-ES-FOCUS Series.

——— (1971) "Social Pollution," *Social Education,* 35: 10–18.

Fried, Marc (1963) "Grieving for a Lost Home," *The Urban Condition*, L. J. Duhl, ed. New York: Basic Books, pp. 151–171.

Gans, Herbert J. (1967) *The Levittowners*. New York: Random House.

—— (1961) "Planning and Social Life: Friendship and Neighbor Relations in Suburban Communities," *Journal of the American Institute of Planners* 27, no. 2: 134–140.

—— (1962) *The Urban Villagers*. New York: Macmillan.

Glazer, Nathan and Daniel Moynihan (1963) *Beyond the Melting Pot*. Cambridge, Mass.: The MIT Press.

—— (1970) *Introduction to Second Edition*, Cambridge, Mass.: The MIT Press.

Goffman, Erving (1971) *Relations in Public, Microstudies of the Public Order*. New York: Basic Books.

Greenbie, Barrie B. (1973) "An Ethological Approach to Community Design," *Environmental Design Research*, Vol. I, Selected Papers, 4th International EDRA Conference, W. F. E. Preiser, ed. Stroudsburg, Pa.: Dowden, Hutchinson and Ross, pp. 14–23.

—— (1969) "New House or New Neighborhood? A Survey of Priorities Among Home Owners in Madison, Wisconsin," *Land Economics* 45, no 3: 359–364.

—— (1971) "What Can We Learn from Other Animals? Behavioral Biology and the Ecology of Cities," *Journal of the American Institute of Planners* 37, no. 3: 162–168.

Gutman, Robert, ed. (1972) *People and Buildings*. New York: Basic Books.

Hall, Edward T. (1966) *The Hidden Dimension*. New York: Doubleday.

—— (1959) *The Silent Language*. New York: Doubleday.

Jacobs, Jane (1961) *The Death and Life of Great American Cities*. New York: Random House.

Levine, Robert A. and Donald T. Campbell (1972) *Ethnocentrism*. New York: John Wiley.

Leyhausen, Paul (1965) "The Communal Organization of Solitary Mammals," *Symposium*. Zoological Society, London, 14: 249–263. Reprinted in *Environmental Psychology*, Harold M. Proshansky, compiler. New York: Holt, Rinehart and Winston, 1970.

—— (1971) "Dominance and Territoriality as Completed in Mammalian Social Structure," *Behavior and Environments*, A. H. Esser, ed. New York: Plenum Press, pp. 22–33.

Lorenz, Konrad Z. (1967) "The Evolution of Behavior," *Psychobiology*, Readings from Scientific American. San Francisco: Freeman, part 1, ch. 5.

—— (1966) *On Aggression*. New York: Harcourt, Brace and World.

McHarg, Ian L. (1969) *Design with Nature*. Garden City, N. Y.: The Natural History Press.

Meadows, Donella H. (1972). *Limits to Growth: A Report to the Club of Rome's Project on the Predicament of Mankind*. New York: Universe Books.

Newman, Oscar (1972) *Defensible Space*. New York: Macmillan.

Novak, M. (1972) *The Rise of the Unmeltable Ethnics: Politics and Culture in the Seventies*. New York: Macmillan.

Nuckolls, Katherine B. and John Cassel (In press) "Psycho-Social Assets, Life Crises, and the Prognosis of Pregnancy," *American Journal of Epidemiology*.

Rainwater, Lee (1966) "Fear and the House-as-Haven in the Lower Class," *Journal of the American Institute of Planners* 32, no. 1: 23–31.

Sommer, Robert (1969) *Personal Space*. Englewood Cliffs, N. J.: Prentice-Hall.

Suttles, Gerald D. (1972) *The Social Construction of Communities*. Chicago: University of Chicago Press.

—— (1968) *The Social Order of the Slum: Ethnicity and Territory in the Inner City*. Chicago: University of Chicago Press.

Tinbergen, N. (1967) "The Curious Behavior of the Stickleback," *Psychobiology*, Readings from Scientific American. San Francisco: Freeman, part 1, ch. 1.

—— (1961) *The Herring Gull's World*. Revised edition. New York: Basic Books.

—— (1953) *Social Behaviour in Animals; with Special Reference to Vertebrates*. New York: Wiley.

—— (1951) *The Study of Instinct*. New York: Oxford University Press.

Toffler, Alvin (1970) *Future Shock*. New York: Random House.

United States President's Commission on Population Growth and the American Future (1972) *Population and the American Future*. Washington, D.C.: Government Printing Office.

Watson, Adam and R. Moss (1971) "Spacing as Affected by Territorial Behavior, Habitat and Nutrition in Red Grouse (Lagopus I. Scoticus)," *Behavior and Environment*. A. H. Esser, ed. New York: Plenum Press, pp. 92–111.

Wilkie, Richard W. (1972) "Toward a Behavioral Model of Peasant Migration: An Argentine

Case Study of Spatial Behavior by Social Class Level," *Population Dynamics of Latin America: A Review Bibliography*. Robert Thomas, ed. Muncie, Indiana: Ball State University Press.

Wood, Robert (1959) *Suburbia: Its People and Their Politics*. Boston: Houghton Mifflin.

Wynne-Edwards, V. C. (1962) *Animal Dispersion in Relation to Social Behavior*. New York: Hafner.

NEIL C. SANDBERG

THE REALITIES OF INTEGRATION IN OLD AND NEW TOWNS

Can meaningful social class and racial integration be achieved in new towns and new-towns-intown, as people regroup themselves in these new environments?

Recent trends in the United States point to increasing opposition to integration, of both the socioeconomic and racial varieties.[1] Among other indicators, this is evidenced by a substantial resistance to busing for school desegregation as well as to such programs as low-income scattersite housing. In addition, government housing policies have for many years encouraged segregation by facilitating white home ownership in the suburbs and public housing for blacks in the inner cities.

The separation of the races is further encouraged by the fear of crime and the general tendency to associate it with race.[2] This is also supported by the emergence of new social movements stemming from an ideology of separation, as disadvantaged minorities utilize new forms of social, economic, and political organization in order to gain a greater share of the goods and services of society and to influence the decisions that affect their lives.

In this context a growing climate of suspicion and fear has developed, manifested by a polarization of attitudes and a sharp increase in intergroup conflict. It seems apparent that for many people the belief in an open, integrated society based on the concept of equal opportunity for the individual is giving way to one of group interest and the utilization of power to assure group achievement.[3]

As more blacks and whites accept the notion that integration will not work and the belief grows that the social and psychological security of the individual is directly related to the support he gains from his own group, a number of important questions are being raised, including: Is integration necessary? Can we afford it? Isn't the alleviation of poverty the higher priority?

New Towns—Why and For Whom? H. S. Perloff and N. C. Sandberg, Editors. (New York: Praeger Publishers, Inc., 1973) 179-188. Copyright © 1973 by Praeger Publishers, Inc. Reprinted by permission of the author, editors, and publisher.

The questions could well be answered with still other questions in seeking to determine what kind of society this should be in the future: Can a democratic country afford to abandon integration as a major goal? Will current and projected government and private interventions lead to the institutionalization of segregation and the freezing of patterns, so that they result in an "apartheid society"?

These simple questions may lead some socially concerned individuals to simplistic answers, which often tend to express their values and points of view rather than the realities of life. And yet it seems there is an inherent truth in the recognition that policies and programs that accelerate patterns of racial separation will be bad for America, bad for both the minorities and the majority.[4]

Having said this, another belief can be stressed—and that is the view that individuals of diverse racial, ethnic, religious, and cultural groupings have a right to live apart from others if they choose to. And while integration and separatism may seem like conflicting values—and at times they are—they represent the critical ingredients of cultural pluralism, a concept that continues to be operative in American life. This notion allows for primary-group associations of friends, family, and other in-group structures, while at the same time permitting mobility in the secondary-group environment—the larger social, economic, and political milieu.[5]

Current research findings suggest that various racial and ethnic subgroups still find meaning within their own communities. In their recently revised preface to Beyond the Melting Pot, Glazer and Moynihan indicate more strongly than before that the anticipated demise of ethnicity may have been a premature judgment.[6] Other research on the assimilation of white ethnics, which points to a decrease in ethnic identification over the generations and in relation to upward class mobility, also confirms a substantial residue of ethnic vitality into the fourth generation.[7]

It appears, therefore, that integration and separatism are meaningful values, and that they are not necessarily mutually exclusive. The experience of the past, as well as present, demographic movements, points to a visible, although relatively limited, degree of integration, usually where there is social class homogeneity. At the same time one can observe the ongoing existence of racial and ethnic enclaves in the core areas of the cities and in working-class neighborhoods, many of them occupied voluntarily by those who have the capacity for outward mobility but choose not to use it.[8] This is not to suggest, of course, that the racial minorities have substantial freedom of movement, for, as a result of their generally disadvantaged condition and the prejudices imposed by the larger society, many of those who would opt for an integrated environment may not be free to do so.

Differing views have been expressed concerning the feasibility of utilizing the new town as a vehicle for racial and class integration. Some writers, such as Bernard Weissbourd, see the new town as offering opportunities for integration on a very large scale, with a consequent decrease in ghetto overcrowding and the opening-up of new educational and employment situations.[9] Others, such as Gans and Perloff, see more limited possibilities for integration in the new town and consider the new-town-intown as a more significant alternative, particularly in terms of equity for the urban poor.

In light of the burgeoning resistance to integration and the growth of separatist thinking among a number of racial and ethnic groups, it seems apparent there would be relatively little public support for the massive integration proposal of Weissbourd. Moreover a new-town policy that provided for racial integration even at such optimal current levels as in Columbia and Reston would have little significance for most black people.

Given the presently unrealistic goal of building 100 new towns of 100,000 persons each, plus an additional 10 cities of one million, and utilizing the highest current integration figure—the estimated 15-percent black population in Columbia[10]—only 3 million blacks would be provided for in new towns out of a total of 35-40 million anticipated by the year 2000. The reality of the situation is that such a policy would probably not facilitate the integration of more than the present 5 percent of blacks at Reston (down from an earlier 7 percent[11]), which, when applied in national terms, would bring only one million (or less) black persons into the proposed new towns.

New-towns-intown seem to be equally unrealistic as vehicles for significant racial integration. Millions of low-income blacks are locked into expanding urban ghettos, and the numbers of people and size of these areas are growing, as whites move to outlying places. It seems probable that differences in values and life style, combined with racial prejudice, and underscored by the fear of crime and violence, will not easily be overcome by improved physical environments, new geopolitical configurations, and even developmental processes geared to human needs.

Given the reality that present and projected integration strategies are unlikely to make much difference in light of the enormity of the problem, it may seem logical to suggest that efforts for integration be abandoned and that energies and resources be concentrated on the more pressing needs of the poor. This may be inherent in proposing the primacy of new-towns-intown, despite the suggestion that their catchment areas be enlarged to include diverse groups.

But while it is evident that the elimination of poverty must be the priority concern of all, it is also essential to find ways to improve interracial communication and contact everywhere. This applies equally to new towns, although at best they may primarily serve as models for integration, to show that the process can work given adequate support.

Some evidence concerning the integration of races and social classes is beginning to accumulate in Reston, Columbia, and other places where experiments in subsidized housing—e.g., 221(d) 3 and 236 projects—have brought together people of different backgrounds. One such place is the Copperstone project in Columbia, which is integrated both economically and racially. Some 108 families have come together voluntarily, knowing in advance they would be living with others of different races and incomes. The mix includes 40-percent blacks, families on welfare, families headed by females, the aged, the physically incapacitated, a substantial number of moderate-income people, and some families of higher incomes who are paying market-value rent.

As may be expected, the problems are very great, especially since public and private social services are not adequate to meet the need. One example is the grossly inadequate day-care facilities for working mothers whose children used to be cared for by grandmothers and extended families. Other difficulties are the limited accessibility of medical services for low-income families and the prohibitive costs of the otherwise excellent Columbia medical plan, which prices out even moderate-income families. This problem is being met in part by the new practice of accepting medical assistance cards at Columbia hospitals and clinics.

Differences in life style are also creating tensions among the Copperstone tenants. Chief among these is the problem of noise, as large families tramp across uninsulated floors and children play outdoors late at night, making it difficult for others with differing patterns to rest. Further there are some signs of racial antagonism, particularly in the schools.

One could well conclude from this that low- and moderate-income people should not be mixed. And yet the residents of Copperstone are making a valiant effort to work things out, aided by a well-motivated resident manager who acts as both landlord and social worker. A tenants' council has been formed to establish guidelines for children's play activities, residents assist each other by providing transportation, and some residents have been motivated to set up day-care facilities in their apartments for the children of working mothers.[12]

Things might have gone better if the manager and the residents had been adequately prepared for what was to take place. For those with special problems, a social worker might have been assigned to stay in touch with them before, during, and after the move—similar to what was reported in the New Haven relocation experience.[13] And, as suggested by the resident manager himself, how much more effective he could have been had he benefited from some training in social service and human relations before being exposed to such complex problems.

Under recent housing programs, similar experiments have taken place in various urban centers. Working with a consortium of religious groups, the American Jewish Committee was instrumental in creating a successful project, which is tied in with a comprehensive program of social services and is both racially and economically integrated, in the Hoover Urban Renewal Area at the University of Southern California.[14] In the Copperstone and Hoover projects, thousands of black and white low- and moderate-income applicants had to be turned away, indicating that under certain conditions (by providing amenities, services, and location, in addition to an attractive price), government-backed housing can have a great appeal for people of different classes and races.

This challenges the perception that such residents are merely captives in a seller's market, and suggests the feasibility of combining racial and class integration, given adequate economic and social help. It also supports the belief that in some areas where a hetero-geneous population exists or can be attracted, racially and economi-cally integrated new-towns-intown are possible.

While it is true that such efforts will not reduce the separation of the races on any meaningful scale, they can serve as symbolic reference points to show that intergroup living is possible and that diverse groups can relate in reasonable compatability and harmony. And despite the observation that the disadvantaged often get symbols and the advantaged get tangible benefits, these models do represent bridgeheads of integration, giving support and encouragement to those individuals and institutions, public and private, that continue to press for an open, integrated society.

As America becomes more upwardly mobile, more and more people may choose to integrate. Differences in life style and values will diminish, and class and racial integration will be more probable and acceptable. The process of preparing people to live together may be facilitated by the socializing mechanisms of society, including the media and their impact on mass culture. In time, and as a consequence of beefed-up human-resources programs provided through new-towns-intown and other urban programs, the cities may once again serve as "socialization centers" facilitating upward mobility for those who seek it, and lessening white resistance to integration.

AN INTEGRATION MODEL FOR NEW TOWNS

Notwithstanding such efforts, however, the fact is that most people, black and white, are not actively seeking integrated living. This is also true for many Mexican-Americans, Puerto Ricans, Asians, white ethnics, and others who choose to live among those like themselves.

In examining the opportunities for enclave-living in new towns, therefore, the feasibility of reserving housing entrances or blocks for individuals of different ethnic and racial backgrounds has been suggested. This concept could be expanded so that the prospective buyer or renter could be offered other choices, such as the following:

1. Reserved enclaves for particular ethnic and racial groups, or even extended families. This would be a form of macro-integration, providing both the advantages of primary-group contact on the block or neighborhood, and secondary-group contact in the service centers and town. Such areas could also be underwritten by racial, ethnic, or religious institutions, so that those who choose to relocate can do so in groups. In addition these places could be reserved by government to provide for group relocation of those such as the Urban Villagers and others displaced by urban renewal, new-towns-intown, and highways.[15] Such opportunities would in large measure help to overcome the sense of isolation and loneliness that individuals may otherwise feel as pioneers in a hostile environment.

2. Reserved areas for those who seek micro-integration. This would enable many socially motivated individuals of different backgrounds who wish to expose themselves and their children to an intercultural environment to live together on the block or in the neighborhood in appropriate proportions. Inducements of price and amenities could also be offered to stimulate others to select housing in these places.

3. Areas of random mix. These will probably be largely middle-class and white, although some middle-class blacks and others will be likely to choose this course as a means of validating their equality and mobility. These areas will also include some white ethnics who have abandoned the ecological enclaves, but who still maintain contact with fellow ethnics in psychological enclaves supported by new structures and forms of communication, and no longer constrained by the limits of neighborhood boundaries.[16]

4. New-towns-intown in white ethnic areas, which offer the prospect of helping to keep some of the younger generation more closely identified with their kinship group. It could also entail a larger catchment area, which would bring the core group into greater contact with others of diverse backgrounds. Opening up such developmental programs for working-class ethnics may well generate the

necessary political support by bringing them together with the disadvantaged in common, integrative programs.

All of the above options could allow for some socioeconomic differentiation, especially if jobs were made available for lower-income people. But if this is to be done successfully, it is essential to provide those social mechanisms that will help to deal with anticipated human-relations problems. It is here that intergroup-relations agencies and religious bodies can play a major role in ameliorating tensions and encouraging positive interpersonal contact. In addition more adequate support systems will have to be developed to facilitate access to employment, recreation, and urgently needed social services.

Various configurations could be developed in such experiments to see if they will work and to determine the best patterns. While their success would be somewhat speculative, these proposals could encourage new alternatives for integration by making available varied patterns of living. And even though they will not have a powerful quantitative impact on integration, they could be of considerable qualitative importance.

At the same time, racial and economic discrimination will have to be dealt with more effectively in all areas through the utilization of federal levers that compel cooperation. In this connection a Title VI-type program to assure equal access to all federally assisted housing could be of great significance.[17] Moreover improved enforcement efforts tied to programs of public education could sustain and nourish the notion of intergroup living as a seminal idea of a plural, democratic society.

In the unlikely conflict between the desire to maintain a separate area and the effort of someone to integrate it, the higher value will of course be freedom of mobility. Acceptance of this concept may help to overcome the resistance of those who will object to the use of group criteria in publicly assisted programs. The development of macro- and micro-integration models based on reserved areas and voluntary occupancy patterns could also be facilitated by a change in HUD guidelines, which currently stress the notion of random integration.

CONCLUSION

Despite the hope for a comprehensive approach to a more just society, it is apparent there are powerful obstacles to social progress. Current economic considerations suggest that serious constraints limit our potential for social investment, and political analysis underscores the heightened resistance to expenditures for human-resources development for the poor.

Moreover the burgeoning revolt against high taxes and government spending suggests that an approach geared largely to the core areas of the cities may not be acceptable to the majority of working-class persons, many of whom feel that they are the ones paying for progress for others. Large numbers of working-class people residing outside the central cities are themselves living a marginal existence, harried by inflation, rising taxes and technologically induced unemployment.

Faced with these seemingly insoluble difficulties, they have reacted more and more with a sense of alienation and outrage at what they perceive to be abuses perpetrated by a society that cares little about them. In this setting a strategy that commits most available resources to one area of need will probably meet with massive resistance and may be self-defeating. On the other hand the quest for low- and moderate-income housing in new towns as well as in the cities can serve the interests of both the increasingly mobile working-class whites and the disadvantaged minorities, thereby helping to bridge the gap between the competing interests and strengthening the possibility of common action.

This should be seen in the context of the present administration's efforts to shift certain aspects of decision-making from Washington to the states and local communities. The assumption behind this approach is that states and local communities are better able to determine some of their needs and priorities than is Washington. With the introduction and anticipated expansion of revenue sharing, local program direction is emerging, and this is backed by the financial and technical assistance of the federal government. (Hopefully, revenue sharing will not prove to be a euphemism for the avoidance of social responsibility.)

One consequence of this emphasis is the heightened need for a national urban policy which will serve to guide local, state, and regional programs, so that we can deal more effectively with the problems stemming from the chaotic and often destructive processes of unplanned urbanization. Despite the multiple and sometimes conflicting goals of the 1970 Housing Act and the ongoing struggle between the executive and legislative branches, many believe that such a policy, which incorporates rational developmental processes, can be created. This may lead to a conceptual framework through which new towns and new-towns-intown are viewed as important elements in a complex system for dealing with urban problems and developing optimal strategies for intervention. But, these approaches can be successful only if they are grounded in a profound respect for human and environmental values as much as a concern for market mechanisms.

Consequently it will be necessary to move beyond traditional cost-benefit analyses to include the social costs and benefits of policies that permit or encourage urban expansion. With respect to integration, this will require an examination of such matters as the alienation and loneliness stemming from living among hostile neighbors, the importance of family and friends, and the psychological and physical stresses resulting from mobility. At the same time the social costs of institutionalizing racial and class isolation will have to be considered and trade-offs will have to be made as plans are developed and programs implemented.

A basic underpinning of this effort would be the incorporation of a differential strategy that maximizes choices for individuals from diverse groups. This includes experimentation with new-town models of micro- and macro-integration, which serve to increase available options. However, it must also be related to the social, economic, and physical factors crucial to human growth and progress, such as income guarantees, universal health care, rent supplements, the restructuring of social services for improved delivery and assurance of employment for all.

But regardless of the rhetoric of social progress, little will be done, particularly with regard to low income housing and integration, unless there is some meaningful support from Washington. This will necessitate the continued and expanded pressures of individuals and institutions who seek to improve conditions for the disadvantaged and who value an open society with freedom of mobility for those desiring it.

Because of the present climate, successes will be limited and there will be many setbacks and failures. Hence, what has been proposed here represents a holding operation for a time—in the near future, one hopes—when conditions for integration may improve. It is self-evident that more comprehensive approaches are needed at all levels of government, but if we fail to take even these minimal actions, the adverse consequences may be irreversible and perhaps catastrophic to our concept of a democratic society.

NOTES

1. Robert S. Browne and Bayard Rustin, Separatism or Integration, Which Way for America? (New York: National Jewish Community Relations Advisory Council, 1968), pp. 7-15.

2. Marvin Wolfgang and Bernard Cohen, Crime and Race (New York: Institute of Human Relations Press, 1970).

3. See, for example, Stokely Carmichael and Charles V. Hamilton, Black Power: The Politics of Liberation in America (New York: Random House, 1967), Ch. II.

4. Bayard Rustin, "Black Power and Coalition Politics," Commentary XLII, #3 (September 1966), 35-40.

5. Horace M. Kallen, Culture and Democracy in the United States (New York: Boni and Liveright, 1924), p. 124; see also Milton M. Gordon, Assimilation in American Life (New York: Oxford University Press, 1964), pp. 132-59.

6. Nathan Glazer and Daniel P. Moynihan, Beyond the Melting Pot, rev. ed. (Cambridge: M.I.T. Press, 1970), Preface.

7. Neil C. Sandberg, "Design and Testing of a Group Cohesiveness Scale to Measure the Salience of Ethnic Identity Among Polish-Americans in the Los Angeles Metropolitan Area" (unpublished Ph.D. dissertation, University of Southern California, 1972).

8. Andrew M. Greeley, Why Can't They Be Like Us? (New York: Institute of Human Relations Press, 1969); see also Murray Friedman, Overcoming Middle Class Rage, (Philadelphia: The Westminster Press, 1971), pp. 15-49.

9. Bernard Weissbourd, "Satellite Communities," The Center Magazine, V, 1, (January/February 1972), 7-16.

10. Estimate of a Rouse Company executive, May 1972.

11. Estimate of a Gulf, Western Company executive, May 1972.

12. Interview with James A. Bohanon, resident manager of Copperstone, May 1972.

13. Katherine Feidelson, "A Total Approach to Family Relocation," Journal of Housing, 24, 3, (April 1967), 161-67.

14. Interview with Travis Kendall, Interfaith Housing Corporation of Southern California, May 1972

15. Herbert J. Gans, The Urban Villagers (New York: The Free Press, 1962), p. 332.

16. Amitai Etzioni, "The Ghetto—A Re-evaluation," Social Forces, 37, 3, (March 1959), 255-62; Sandberg, op. cit.

17. HEW and Title VI, A Report on the Development of the Organization, Policies and Compliance Procedures of HEW (Washington D.C., Government Printing Office, 1970).

FURTHER READINGS

PART TWO

Dyckman, John W. "The European Motherland of American Urban Romanticism." *Journal of American Institute of Planners,* Volume 28, November, 1962, pp. 277-81.

Glass, Ruth. "Urban Sociology in Great Britain" in *Readings in Urban Sociology,* edited by R. E. Pahl. Pergamon Press, 1968, pp. 47-73.

Goist, Park Dixon. "Lewis Mumford and 'Anti-Urbanism'." *Journal of American Institute of Planners,* Volume 35, September, 1969, pp. 340-47.

White, Morton and Lucia. *The Intellectual Versus the City,* Harvard University Press and The M. I. T. Press, 1962.

PART THREE

Elazar, Daniel J. "Are We a Nation of Cities?" in *A Nation of Cities,* edited by R. A. Goldwin, Rand-McNally, 1966, pp. 89-114.

Greer, Scott. "Ideology and Utopia: The Intellectual Politics of Urban Redevelopment," Chapter 15 in *The Urbane View,* Oxford University Press, 1972.

Mumford, Lewis. "Suburbia—And Beyond." Chapter 16 in *The City in History.* Harcourt, Brace & World, 1961.

Riesman, David. "The Suburban Dislocation." *The Annals,* Fall, 1957, pp. 123-45.

Wood, Robert C. "The Image of Suburbia." Chapter 1 in *Suburbia: Its People and their Politics,* Houghton-Mifflin, 1958.

PART FOUR

Brooks, Richard. "Social Planning and Columbia." *Journal of American Institute of Planners,* Volume 37, November, 1971, pp. 373-79.

Roszak, Theodore. "Life in the Instant Cities." *The Nation,* Volume 204, March 13, 1967.

Sinding, Monica. *The Philosophic Basis for New Town Development in America.* Center for Urban and Regional Studies, University of North Carolina at Chapel Hill, 1967.

PART FIVE

Fogelson, Robert M. "The Quest for Community." Chapter 15 in *The Fragmented Metropolis: Los Angeles, 1850-1930,* Harvard University Press, 1967.

Gans, Herbert J. "Levittown and America." Chapter 15 in *The Levittowners,* Random House, 1967.

Greenbie, Barrie B. "A New Look at New Towns." Chapter 12 in *Design for Diversity: Planning for Natural Man in the Neo-technic Environment; an Ethological Approach,* Elsevier Scientific Publishing Company, 1976.

Grigsby, J. Eugene. "Views of the Feasibility of Integration" in *New Towns—Why and For Whom?,* edited by H. S. Perloff and N. C. Sandberg, Praeger, 1973.

Sennett, Richard. "The Intense Family and the New Suburbs." Pp. 68-73 in *The Uses of Disorder,* Knopf, 1970.

INDEX

Note: Italicized listings represent authors of articles in this book.